THE SOURCES OF ACTS

THE SOURCES OF ACTS

The Present Position

JACQUES DUPONT

Translated by
Kathleen Pond

DARTON, LONGMAN & TODD

LONDON

DARTON, LONGMAN & TODD LTD
64 CHISWICK HIGH ROAD
LONDON W.4

Originally published in Belgium by
Editions Desclée de Brouwer S.A., Bruges,
under the title
Les Sources du Livre des Actes

Printed in Great Britain by W. & J. Mackay & Co Ltd, Chatham, Imprimi
potest Sti-Andreae, die 15ª aprilis 1960 ✠ Theodorus Ghesquière, abbas. Nihil
obstat Hubertus Richards, S.T.L., L.S.S. Censor deputatus. Imprimatur ✠ Georgius
L. Craven, Epus Sebastopolis Vic. Cap. Westmonasterii, die 12ª Sept., 1963. The
Nihil obstat and Imprimatur are a declaration that a book or pamphlet is considered
to be free from doctrinal or moral error. It is not implied that those who have
granted the Nihil obstat and Imprimatur agree with the contents, opinions or
statements expressed.

CONTENTS

FOREWORD TO THE ENGLISH LANGUAGE EDITION

THE ENGLISH translation of this work has been made from a text which in many instances differs from that published in French; it must be considered as a new edition. In particular it is marked by numerous additions, as I did not want to omit mention of the most recent studies and thought it would also be useful to add information on many studies which had not been mentioned in the French edition. Certain corrections have been made and certain passages rewritten in order to express more adequately the thought of the writers I have quoted.

My revision has had the benefit of information given by Professor E. Haenchen both in correspondence and in a then unpublished article which he allowed me to consult. I have also taken advantage of a list of *corrigenda* subsequently sent to me by Fr Joseph A. Fitzmyer. I should like to express my gratitude to them here. I also owe a debt of gratitude to those critics who have given a kind welcome to the French edition—in particular I should like to be allowed to mention Fr Fitzmyer once more (*Theological Studies*, 1961, XXII, pp. 468–70), and Professor H. J. Cadbury (*Journal of Bibl. Lit.*, 1961, LXXX, pp. 78–79). Finally, my gratitude is due to the publishers of the English edition and to the translator whose task has not been made easier by my repeated revisions. I hope that this edition will encourage and facilitate new research on the Acts of the Apostles.

J. D.

Abbey of Saint André
14th October 1961

FOREWORD TO THE FRENCH EDITION

IT IS now more than ten years since at the instance of Mgr Cerfaux I made a general survey of studies concerned with the Acts of the Apostles during the period 1940–50; the text of this survey was published in 1950 in a small volume: *Les Problèmes du Livre des Actes d'après les travaux récents*. As the edition was limited, it rapidly went out of print and has become almost unobtainable. It was scarcely possible to reprint it without bringing it up to date and extending the investigation to the period earlier than 1940 if an objective description of the present state of research was to be given. If it is realized that a work of this kind presupposes the consultation of several hundred books and articles, it will be understood that it has not been at all easy to find room for it in the midst of other occupations. It was only the pressing insistence of Père Béda Rigaux and of Canon Albert Descamps that persuaded me to interrupt other research and resume, on one point at least, this survey of the problems of the Acts of the Apostles and the hypotheses which exegetes make use of in an endeavour to solve them.

The investigation of which the result is here published takes up again on a much wider basis what was set out in pages 35 to 42 of the original survey, i.e. the first part of the chapter devoted to the sources of Acts, the one which concerns the book as a whole. We shall not be concerned with the possible sources of isolated pericopes or even with those which may lie at the root of the series of separate elements, such as the 'summaries' and in particular the great missionary sermons of Peter and Paul; the present work is restricted to the question of continuous sources as it occurs when dealing with certain groupings of pericopes of which such sources explain the interconnection. The subject is big enough and important enough to warrant a careful examination.

The primary objective of a survey of the progress of research is to promote further research. It does not aim at dispensing scholars from making their personal investigations, but seeks to make such investigation easier for them by guiding them through the labyrinth of opinions and by directing their attention to more recent and more important studies. Specialists, however, are not the only ones to profit by a survey of this kind. I have learnt with pleasure that my survey published in 1950 was useful to teachers of Scripture who were not able to consult a whole library of books in preparing their courses. It is because I have had them in mind, rather than the specialists, that I have not been content with summing up the conclusions of biblical scholars, but have drawn attention to what seemed interesting and what did not seem so. It was not necessary to enter into long-standing and out-of-date disputes, but I have not hesitated to do so to a considerable extent in the case of more current hypotheses in order to take up a definite position in the matter, indicating in what respects such hypotheses seem to me interesting and where they seem to be weak. I venture to think that no one will resent these intrusions and that they will not divert me from my objective, which is not to demonstrate a thesis but to supply information. Again, it is for the convenience of the reader that I have not used algebraic symbols and have reduced abbreviations to a minimum.

Like my earlier works, this book has had the advantage of the kindly interest of the Right Reverend Dom Theodore Ghesquière, who was good enough to read the manuscript and has suggested many modifications of language which give greater clarity to what I have tried to say. I ask him to be so kind as to accept this acknowledgement as the expression of my respectful gratitude. Likewise my cordial gratitude goes out to the Benedictine nuns of the priory of Bethany who helped in the correction of the proofs.

JACQUES DUPONT, O.S.B.

Abbey of Saint André
  29th February 1960

INTRODUCTION

BEFORE SETTING out the conclusions to which scholars have come on the question of the sources used in the Acts of the Apostles, it will be useful to see their research in relation to the critical work as a whole that has been done on the Book of Acts. In his extensive commentary, E. Haenchen[1] gives a very clear historical survey, which has earned praise from R. Bultmann[2]; his divisions are confirmed by a parallel survey by E. Trocmé.[3] He distinguishes three periods, corresponding to three main points of interest: the period of Purpose-Criticism (*Tendenzkritik*), that of Source-Criticism and that of Form-Criticism.

1. The whole aim of Purpose-Criticism (*Tendenzkritik*) was concentrated on discovering the intention of the author of Acts in composing his work; it endeavoured to reveal the 'tendencies'

[1] E. Haenchen, *Die Apostelgeschichte* (Kritischexegetischer Kommentar über das N.T., III, 12th ed.), Göttingen, 1959, pp. 13–47. This 12th edition of the commentary in the Meyer series is the 3rd of Haenchen's work, the 1st (10th) having appeared in 1956. It may be questioned whether the division I have adopted gives sufficient place to the research which, during the last twenty years especially, has been done on the theology of Acts. This inconvenience has little importance from the point of view of this book.

[2] R. Bultmann, 'Zur Frage nach den Quellen der Apostelgeschichte,' in *New Testament Essays: Studies in Memory of T. W. Manson*, Manchester, 1959, pp. 68–80; cf. p. 68.

[3] E. Trocmé, *Le 'Livre des Actes' et l'Histoire* (Etudes d'Histoire et de Philosophie Religieuses, 45), Paris, 1957, pp. 1–19. The writer did not know of Haenchen's work at the time when he was producing his own. The following is the arrangement of his historical sketch: 1. Initial research (about 1800–40); 2. The Tübingen age (about 1840–80); 3. The 'Pilgrimage to the Sources' (about 1880–1905); 4. Return to the work 'to Theophilus'—a period which could be called 'the age of Harnack' (about 1905–30); 5. Contemporary period, characterized in the literary sphere by the triumph of the methods of form-criticism (from about 1930). Apart from the last subdivision, this arrangement corresponds to that of the excellent historical survey of M. Goguel, *Introduction au Nouveau Testament*, vol. III, *Le Livre des Actes* (Bibl. historique des religions), Paris, 1922, pp. 37–72. A more or less similar general impression would easily be gathered from a small but valuable work which, however, contains very little on the sources of Acts—W. Bieder, *Die Apostelgeschichte in der Historie: Ein Beitrag zur Auslegungsgeschichte des Missionsbuches der Kirche* (Theol. Studies, 61), Zurich, 1960.

which can be discerned in the course of the narrative. The golden age of this work was that of the Tübingen school, with F. Chr. Baur and Ed. Zeller,[4] who saw in the Acts of the Apostles a tendentious history, the aim of which was to reconcile two antagonistic conceptions of Christianity, that of Peter and that of Paul.[5] Their hypothesis was much discussed and other explanations were put forward. According to some, the author of Acts was pursuing an apologetic purpose and had chiefly in mind non-Christian readers whose sympathy he sought to win. In the view of others, the book aimed at nothing more than to instruct Christian readers and perfect their religious development.[6]

2. Source-Criticism (*Quellenkritik*) sought primarily to discover the sources which Luke used to compose his account.[7] The first

---

[4] F. Chr. Baur—various articles in the *Tübinger Zeitschrift für Theologie* in 1831, 1836, 1838, and above all the important work *Paulus, der Apostel Jesu Christi*, Stuttgart, 1845. Ed. Zeller—several articles in the *Theologische Jahrbücher* from 1848 to 1851, and in particular 'Die Apostelgeschichte nach ihrem Inhalt und Ursprung Kritisch untersucht', Stuttgart, 1834.

[5] People have pointed out, not unreasonably, the apparent relationship which exists between this theory and the philosophical system of Hegel, with its pattern of thesis, antithesis and synthesis. F. Chr. Baur was a contemporary of Karl Marx. Both apply to history a specifically Hegelian conception, deriving much more from logical presuppositions than from the simple observation of facts. Cf. B. H. Streeter, *The Four Gospels. A Study of Origins*, London, 1924 (reprinted 1956), p. 544.

[6] Details and references at the beginning of my article on the question of Luke's intention in deciding to compose Acts: 'Le salut des Gentils et la signification théologique du Livre des Actes', *New Testament Studies*, 1959/60, VI, pp. 132–55: cf. 132–4.

[7] The history of this research has often been traced. It will be sufficient to instance W. Heitmüller, 'Die Quellenfrage in der Apostelgeschichte', *Theologische Rundschau*, 1899, II, pp. 47–59, 83–95, 127–40; A. Bludau, 'Die Quellenscheidungen in der Apostelgeschichte', *Biblische Zeitschrift*, 1907, VII, pp. 166–89, 258–81; E. Jacquier, *Histoire des livres du Nouveau Testament*, vol. III, Paris, 1908, 4th ed., 1912, pp. 64–80; F. Prat, 'Les sources des Actes des Apôtres', *Recherches de Science Religieuse*, 1913, IV, pp. 275–96; A. Loisy, *Les Actes des Apôtres*, Paris, 1920, pp. 17–50; M. Goguel, *Introduction au Nouveau Testament, III, Le Livre des Actes* (Bibl. hist. des religions), Paris, 1922, pp. 37–72; A. C. McGiffert, 'The Historical Criticism of Acts in Germany', in F. J. Foakes Jackson and Kirsopp Lake, *The Beginnings of Christianity*, Part I, *The Acts of the Apostles*, vol. II, *Prolegomena II: Criticism*, London, 1922, pp. 363–95; E. Jacquier, *Les Actes des Apôtres* (Etudes Bibliques), Paris, 1926, pp. cxxxvii–clxiii; A. Vitti, 'L'ultimo decennio di critica sugli Atti degli Apostoli', *Biblica*, 1931, X, pp. 235–42. In addition, see the surveys already mentioned given by Haenchen and Trocmé. I know only by name the study of A. Theissen, *Zur Quellenkritik der Apostelgeschichte*, Bonn, 1934 (cf. Kümmel, *Theol. Rundschau*, 1942, p. 162, n. 2).

attempts in this direction go back to the end of the eighteenth century.[8] A little later, Fr Schleiermacher and E. A. Schwanbeck worked out hypotheses which are still worth examination.[9] The outstanding period of source-criticism, however, really only opened with B. Weiss and his *Introduction to the New Testament* (1886).[10] For about twenty years attempts at dissection were multiplied, reaching their culminating point with the work of A. Harnack (1906, 1908 and 1911).[11] This in turn served as a point of departure for a whole series of new researches which have brought the methods of source-criticism down to our own times.

3. Form-Criticism (*Formgeschichte*) arose partly from the discouragement produced by the uncertain and contradictory results of source-criticism and of the methods of literary analysis which were its instrument. Rather than insisting on the discovery of sources which proved elusive, it has turned its attention to the small traditional units which have found a place in the narrative; its aim was to retrace the pre-history of such units, as determined by the laws of the literary form to which they belong; it sought also to determine precisely the processes of composition which enabled the author to utilize already existing materials to make them contribute to the expression of his personal views.[12] Formulated from the begin-

[8] The works of B. L. Königsmann (1798), J. A. Bolten (1799), W. K. L. Ziegler (1801) will be referred to later.
[9] Fr Schleiermacher's course on Acts was published in 1845, after the author's death. It will be discussed later, as also the work of E. A. Schwanbeck published in 1847.
[10] B. Weiss, *Lehrbuch der Einleitung in das Neue Testament*, Berlin, 1886, pp. 569–84. The importance of the change which occurred at this time was clearly seen and defined by V. Rose, 'La critique nouvelle et les Actes des Apôtres', *Revue Biblique*, 1898, VII, pp. 325–42.
[11] A. Harnack, *Lukas der Arzt, der Verfasser des dritten Evangeliums und der Apostelgeschichte: Eine Untersuchung zur Geschichte der Fixierung der urchristlichen Über Lieferung* (Beiträge zur Einleitung in das N.T., I), Leipzig, 1906; *Die Apostelgeschichte* (Beitr. zur Einl. in das N.T., III), Leipzig, 1908; *Neue Untersuchungen zur Apostelgeschichte und zur Abfassungszeit der synoptischen Evangelien* (Beitr. zur Einl. in das N.T., IV), Leipzig, 1911.
[12] Haenchen distinguishes two phases in the application of form-criticism to Acts: in the first (1923–45), the interest is centred on the small units of the book; in the second (after 1945), attention is directed more to the composition, i.e. to the personal work of the author in the presentation of the materials he had at his

ning of the century by the leaders in the field of study of comparative religion,[13] this school of thought finds its primary application as regards the Acts of the Apostles in the famous work of Edward Norden, *Agnostos Theos* (1913); M. Dibelius has made use of this and in various works E. Haenchen follows it systematically. Parallel work[14] is being done in America,

---

disposal. This division corresponds to that generally used in connection with research on the Synoptics: form-critical period (between the two wars), and *Redaktionsgeschichte* period (since the last war). In the case of Acts, the change is, however, much less marked, and the personal share taken by the author in the composition of his work is continually impressed on the reader's attention. In reality, Haenchen's presentation merely reproduces the trend of the works of M. Dibelius. For the first phase of the application of form-criticism to Acts, Haenchen cites only one study that is really significant: M. Dibelius, 'Stilkritisches zur Apostelgeschichte', in *EYXAPIΣΘPIÒN: Studien zur Religion und Literatur des Alten und Neuen Testaments H. Gunkel dargebracht* (Forschungen zur Rel. und N.T., 36), vol. II, Göttingen, 1923, pp. 27–49. S. E. Johnson, 'A proposed Form-Critical Treatment of Acts', *Anglican Theological Review*, 1939, XXI, 22–31, should also have been mentioned. Without having consulted Dibelius's article, Johnson endeavoured to classify the materials contained in Acts, taking his pattern from the literary types defined by Dibelius in his *Formgeschichte des Evangeliums* (*From Tradition to Gospel*, New York, 1935). The second phase of form-critical research was inaugurated by a series of studies by Dibelius, who returned to Acts in his later years; articles published since 1939 and collected into one volume by H. Greeven: *Aufsätze zur Apostelgeschichte* (Forschungen zur Rel. und Lit. des A. und N.T., 60), Göttingen, 1951 (English translation 1956). With the name of Dibelius must be classed here that of Haenchen himself. To Haenchen, Bultmann gives the credit for having systematically applied the method elaborated by Dibelius to the interpretation of Acts as a whole (R. Bultmann, art. cit., p. 68).

[13] We are thinking particularly of the passage in R. Reitzenstein, *Hellenistische Wundererzählungen* (1906, p. 99) referred to by H. J. Cadbury, *The Making of Luke-Acts*, 2nd ed., London, 1958 (1st ed. New York, 1927), p. 142; in the same place, references to P. Wendland (1907), O. Weinreich (1909), P. Fiebig (1911). See also the investigations of A. Dieterich (1903 and 1905) cited by E. Norden, *Agnostos Theos: Untersuchungen zur Formgeschichte religiöser Rede*, 4th ed., Stuttgart, 1956, p. 143 (1st ed. appeared in 1913). The fresh trend of New Testament research also owes much to the example given by H. Gunkel in his studies on the Old Testament: cf. M. Dibelius, *Die Formgeschichte des Evangeliums*, Tübingen, 1919: 3rd ed., 1959, p. 5.

[14] 'Parallel work.' The ignorance on both sides is often astonishing. I have instanced the case of S. E. Johnson, who has applied to Acts the principles of the method defined by M. Dibelius, in ignorance of the research by which Dibelius himself carried out this work. The excellent book *The Making of Luke-Acts*, published in 1927 by H. J. Cadbury, nowhere mentions the name of Dibelius although it uses very similar methods. The situation is no better on the German side. Desirous of illustrating the discourses in Acts by those found among ancient historians, Dibelius (*Aufsätze*, p. 125, n. 3) mentions that the subject has been touched upon by Cadbury in vol. V of the *Beginnings of Christianity*, pp. 405 f. This passage merely sums up the conclusions of more thorough investigations which Cadbury published in vol. II of

where one of the best specialists on the Acts of the Apostles is to be found, namely H. J. Cadbury.

An assessment of the studies devoted to the sources of the Acts of the Apostles should not be directly concerned with the investigations of form-criticism. In fact, however, the use of this method leads to results which are not without importance for the question with which we are dealing. It is permissible to think that its influence is not irrelevant to the discredit with which the study of the sources of the first part of Acts is today burdened. In a more positive way, Dibelius and several exegetes of the same school believe it is possible to establish, in accordance with the criteria of their own method, the existence of a source which, in the second part of the book, may have served as a basis for the account of Paul's voyages. Thus the trend of form-criticism does not entirely exclude the question of the sources and it is not without interest to take account of the particular angle from which it approaches the matter.

The plan of the present survey derives from the situation I have just summarized. I have divided it into two principal parts of which the first presents the results of the works which derive from the methods of literary analysis characteristic of source-criticism, while the second is concerned with studies which take the form-critical standpoint. There seem to be other advantages, too, in making this division. Part I deals with hypotheses which have often long been known, even if they have appeared again in recent studies; Part II is concerned with an approach to the problem which is of more recent date. Further, the works which I have grouped in the first part of this book concern chiefly the first half of Acts, whereas those in the second part directly concern the narratives of the second half of Acts.

Beginnings (pp. 7–29) and in *The Making of Luke–Acts*. Is not the first step in any historical research to inform oneself of the present state of the question one intends to study? A particularly striking example of a disquieting symptom will be found in: C. W. Carter-R. Earle, *The Acts of the Apostles* (The Evangelical Commentary), Grand Rapids, 1959. This bulky commentary abounds in references and supplies a lengthy eight-page bibliography. It only cites, however, works published in the U.S.A., with a few exceptions in favour of British publications. Scholarship cannot come to terms with such isolationism.

In this way we shall achieve many advantages—methodological, chronological and systematic. It is hardly necessary to say that there are, on the other hand, certain inconveniences,[15] and that in practice more than one compromise has had to be made. Each part will open with a chapter which is not strictly appropriate. Chapter I discusses theories which explain the compilation of Acts from an earlier work which is not strictly speaking a source. Chapter V treats of the 'we-passages' which should be ranged among those sources discerned by source-criticism but which constitute the hypothesis on which the work of form-criticism is based. It should be added that the boundaries between the 'Antioch source' which is in question in Chapter IV and the travel diary discussed in Part II are fairly elastic. It seems to me that it should be admitted that in a subject like this, no division can be wholly acceptable from every point of view. I have explained the advantages which have led me to prefer the one I have chosen. The index of authors at the end of the book will help readers to find those works which this plan has not set in the particular place where they might be looked for.

[15] Logic, which is very rightly dear to the disciples of St Thomas, has not been used to the fullest possible extent: we willingly grant this point to P. Zerafa, O.P., who draws attention to the defect in an otherwise favourable review (*Angelicum*, 961, XXXVIII, pp. 93–95).

Part One

SOURCE-CRITICISM

I

A SINGLE SOURCE

O F A L L the hypotheses on the sources of Acts the simplest is certainly that which confines itself to a single source. If we extend this single source to Acts as a whole, the latter appears as the result of a re-editing which has transformed an earlier text to a greater or lesser degree. We shall first of all consider the writers who have put forward an explanation of this kind; the question whether the basic writing which is invoked really deserves to be called a source matters little. We shall then examine the systems which, under rather varied forms, restrict the use of a basic document to the first part of the book. Luke, these writers think, made use of a history of the early Church from the beginnings to the Apostolic Council, modifying it sometimes considerably, sometimes slightly.

The following chapters will examine the hypotheses which require several sources to explain the composition of the first part of the book—parallel sources (II), complementary sources (III), and, particularly, one principal source among others according to certain writers, the 'Antioch' source (IV).

A Re-edited Work

In 1890, M. Sorof[1] believed he could distinguish two different hands in Acts. In its first form, attributed to Luke, the work contained a brief introduction on the community in Jerusalem, an account of the martyrdom of Stephen and of the founding of the community of Antioch, then the story of the spread of the Gospel in the pagan world thanks to the missionary activity of Paul; for the compilation of chapters 13 and 14, Luke used a

[1] M. Sorof, *Die Entstehung der Apostelgeschichte*, Berlin, 1890.

document in which Barnabas occupied the first place. This original work was then subjected to a complete recasting, attributable to Timothy, who made numerous additions, some borrowed from a legendary writing composed in praise of Peter (1.3–2.12; 3–4; 5.1–11; 8.5–40; 9.32–11.17; 12.3–23), others of his own invention. The hypothesis involved minute excisions which do not make it any the more acceptable.

In 1894 the classical philologist A. Gercke[2] reacted against the dissection of the text. In his opinion, the work written by Luke and chiefly devoted to the story of Paul's missions was completely reshaped at the beginning of the second century by an editor who left out part of the text and made interpolations to the extent of making it unrecognizable.[3] Ed. Norden's remarks (1913) on the composition of Acts[4] are an extension of those of Gercke. The book begins with a prologue which Norden had the unfortunate idea of reconstructing in its primitive form (it was the period when people were putting arms and legs on ancient statues that had been mutilated). The anacoluthon of the prologue comes from the fact that the editor judged it preferable to omit the second part, thus removing a programme of events which no longer fitted in with his own conception and substituting for it a long interpolation that gave new details about our Lord's ascension into heaven.[5] Luke's work must have ended where Acts ends today, namely before the trial and martyrdom of Paul. By its literary form it is to be classed with classical 'Memoirs' to which the Biblical books of Esdras and

---

[2] A. Gercke, 'Der δεύτερος λόγος des Lukas', *Hermes*, 1894, XXIX, pp. 373 ff.
[3] Th. Mommseiff acceded to this view: 'Die Rechtsverhältnisse des Apostels Paulus', *Zeitschr. für die neutest. Wiss.*, 1901, II, pp. 81–96 (cf. p. 87, n. 1).
[4] 'Zur Komposition der Acta Apostolorum' = Anhang I, in *Agnostos Theos*, pp. 311–2.
[5] In reality it would seem that the anacoluthon was much less shocking to genuine Greeks than to twentieth-century purists. In this connection see the remarks of F. Dornseiff, 'Lukas der Schriftsteller. Mit einem Anhang: Josephus und Tacitus', *Zeitschrift. für die neutestl.* Wiss., 1936, XXXV, pp. 129–55 (cf. pp. 134ff). This writer refers to Pindar, who knew his Greek and did not improvise. In line 62 of the *Second Olympic* he begins a protasis: 'If someone knew . . .'; the phrase is continued exorbitantly (until line 91) and, having finished it, the poet neglects the apodosis to begin a new phrase. It should be added that the procedure employed in Acts has this obvious advantage: the plan of the book will be traced not by the writer, but by Jesus himself (1, 8).

Nehemias likewise belong. Side by side with narratives written in the third person, it contained passages in the first. The 'we-sections' in the rewritten Acts preserve the traces of this form.

A. Loisy (1920)[6] took up Norden's hypotheses and made them the key to his interpretation of Acts—

> Luke the physician, whom the epistles mention, made it his business to compose a history which was truly unique of its kind, namely a religious legend which was true and sincere so far as human history and religious legend can be; this history has been disgracefully tampered with in both its parts—for, if the Gospel has been less badly treated than Acts, it has none the less been considerably corrupted. So far as we can judge from what remains of his work, Luke had a cultured mind, as a writer he was sufficiently expert, above all he was conscientious.[7] . . . The writer who made of the second book to Theophilus the work ultimately canonized under the title of *Acts of the Apostles*, has not left his name to posterity. We have good reason to believe that he could not and did not want to do so. He was in possession of a work that was priceless, completely authentic, and bearing the name of the one who had written it, and so he proposed to do nothing less than to transform it profoundly, while at the same time leaving it under the patronage of its first author. In these days such a procedure would be judged severely and even at that time could not have been considered completely honest, since measures were taken to hide it. . . . The editor of Acts was an impostor and one who was not entirely unconscious of the reprehensible nature of the work he had set his hand to and of how damaging it was to his sincerity.[8]

Where are we to find this dishonest impostor (whom Loisy pursues with tenacious hatred), except among the leaders of the Roman Church who alone were in a position to cause the genuine work to disappear?

---

[6] Norden's explanation is taken up, with a few modifications, by O. Stählin in the report he devotes to Acts: W. Schmid-O. Stählin, *Wilhelm von Christ's Griechischer Litteraturgeschichte*, 5th edition, vol. II, 2nd part, Munich, 1913, pp. 967–71.

[7] A. Loisy, *Les Actes des Apôtres*, Paris, 1920.

[8] pp. 89ff.

Did he act as a private person, on his own responsibility? One would like to think so. The contrary, however, is more likely. This apologia of general interest, almost political in spirit, written probably in Rome, as the work of Luke, and in the spirit of the community in Rome,[9] was very probably not the work of an individual taking the risk, on his own initiative, of promoting an idea which might or might not make its way. It would seem rather to be an officially contrived piece of writing, and the fact that Luke's authentic work has disappeared without leaving a trace is thus more easily explained. This work could not have been very widely known except, probably, in Roman circles. The authentic book must have been systematically replaced by the spurious book. . . . The writer of Acts can thus be suspected of belonging to the leaders of the community in Rome. . . . What we find displeasing in this sort of falsity and fraud which the book of Acts represents is somewhat attenuated so far as the person of the principal agent is concerned—it is the expression of a policy of which he was only the interpreter.[10]

This extreme position adopted by Loisy was not calculated to attract the sympathies of critics to his theory. As far back as 1921, M. Goguel emphasized the weaknesses of this approach. In the first place he drew attention to Loisy's arbitrary manner of defining the original work of Luke—

The original Acts, such as M. Loisy conceives it, could very well be no more than the creation of his own imagination

[9] pp. 104ff.

[10] This detail recalls the explanations of O. Pfleiderer *Das Urchristentum, seine Schriften und Lehren in geschichtlichem Zusammenhang beschrieben*, 2nd ed., vol. I, Berlin, 1902, pp. 534ff and 547–9 (the second edition is a complete recasting of the first, in one vol., published in 1887). According to Pfleiderer, the author of Acts had at his disposal memoirs of journeys composed by Luke which formed a continuous account of the missionary journeys and captivity of Paul. This document would form the basis of the work from ch. 13; the short account of 11.19–30 would constitute its introduction. This source was treated very freely and tendentiously by the author, a Hellenistic Christian of the beginning of the second century, probably a member of the Church of Rome. He had doubtless discovered in the archives of that Church the valuable document he mishandled. The narratives of ch. 1–12 would seem to rest only on oral traditions, and on the writer's creative imagination. See also Pfleiderer, *Die Entstehung des Christentums*, 2nd ed., Munich, 1907 (= 1st, 1905), pp. 207ff. It should be noted that it is already on account of the 'tendentious' character of Acts that the composition of the work is set in Rome by E. Zeller, *Die Apostelgeschichte* (1854), pp. 364–76.

which he effected by stripping the work as it now stands of all
its defects. By dint of imagining what Acts *should* have been,
so that it might fit in with what the historians wanted to find
in the work, M. Loisy ended by taking his dream for
reality. . . .[11]

There is a further weakness in the notion he formed of the work
accomplished by the writer—who completely disfigured the
work of Luke, not only Acts but also the third Gospel, and who
succeeded in substituting his own work for the original to the

[11] pp. 105ff. Loisy took up the same ideas in the introduction to his work *Les
Actes des apôtres. Traduction nouvelle avec introduction et notes* (coll. 'Christianisme'),
Paris, 1925, pp. 9–67. This introduction consists of two chapters. Loisy first of all
concerns himself with the 'Second Book to Theophilus', which has been composed
by Luke; he then examines 'Les Actes des apôtres', a tendentious recasting of
Luke's work. In his later publications Loisy changed his mind on one point—the
writer to Theophilus could not have been Luke or a companion of Paul, for he was
not earlier than the beginning of the second century; the re-editing must have been
made shortly before 140, the date at which Marcion found the third Gospel more
or less in the state in which it has come down to us. Cf. *La naissance du christianisme*,
Paris, 1933, pp. 54–58; *Les origines du Nouveau Testament*, Paris, 1936, pp. 152–207.
Very similar conceptions are found in Ch. Guignebert, *Le Christ* (L'évolution
de l'humanité, 29 bis), Paris, 1948, pp. 50–59. According to him 'the majority of
liberal critics admit, since Norden's study, that our version is not the first, but that
it is the work of a man who also revised the third Gospel, giving to both books the
same colour, and the appearance of being the two volumes of a single work' (p. 52).
This summing-up of opinions was the result of agreement between H. J. Cadbury
(*The Making of Luke–Acts*, pp. 9–11), B. H. Streeter (*The Four Gospels*, pp. 520f)
and M. Goguel (*Introduction au N.T.*, III, p. 43); we shall discuss the opinions of
these writers, which are very different from those attributed to them. Guignebert
would place the first version of the book between 100 and 115, the second between
130 and 140; the first editor doubtless had at his disposal more ancient sources, but
the modifications he introduced into them prevent their being identified and the
historian can only try to reconstruct them according to what he considers was their
probable form. In connection with these opinions, others could be quoted, much
more revolutionary, to be found in P. L. Couchoud–R. Stahl, 'Les deux auteurs
des Actes des Apôtres', *Rev. de l'Hist. des Rel.*, 1928, xcvii, pp. 6–52. It is possible
to recognize two different hands in the writing of Acts; one of the editors calls the
Holy City 'Jerusalem', the other 'Hierosolym', the one speaks of those who 'fear
God', the other of those who 'adore God', etc. The first editor might have been
Marcion, the second, one who had been likewise charged with a revision of the
Pauline epistles. It is useless to linger over such fantasies. Nor do we think it
necessary to spend time over the extreme views of G. A. van den Bergh van
Eysinga, 'Iets over bronnenscheiding in de Handelingen der Apostelen', *Nieuw
Theologisch Tydschrift*, 1923, XII, pp. 274–98; 'Nog iets over bronnenscheiding in
Handelingen', *ibid.*, 1929, XVIII, pp. 146–64; 'Bronnenscheiding in Handelingen
17–28', *ibid.*, 1930, XIX, pp. 124–38; 'Over schryver en tyd der Handelingen',
ibid., pp. 228–40; *La littérature chrétienne primitive* (Coll. 'Christianisme'), Paris,
1926; L. Couchoud–G. A. van den Bergh van Eysinga–R. Stahl, *Premiers écrits
du christianisme* (Ann. d'hist. du christianisme), Paris, 1930.

extent that the latter has disappeared without leaving a trace.[12] Goguel studies a few episodes, showing the improbability of the re-editings which Loisy attributed to the writer—the account of the evangelization of Samaria by Philip, that of the conversion of Paul, of the Antioch incident, of Paul's trial. The attitude with which the writer who composed the theological passages is credited is also improbable—

> M. Loisy admits that if certain parts of Acts at least present us with a Christology which seems rather rudimentary and still very close to Judaism, it is because the author has voluntarily eliminated all the secondary elements, those which could not claim a direct connection with Judaism and be accepted by it. This would presuppose that the writer knew what were the conditions in which the primitive Christology was formed and could distinguish that professed at the beginning of the second century from that accepted in the first community at Jerusalem. It is impossible to admit such an hypothesis. It is certain that in the second century everyone was convinced that his own form of Christology had always been taught by the Church and was that which Jesus himself expressly taught. It would have been necessary for the writer of the revised version of Acts to have had the mentality of a modern critic to have been able to carry out—at least so far as Christology is concerned—the work that M. Loisy's theory presupposes.[13]

For Loisy's hypothesis, Goguel substituted another, slightly more complex[14]—the work composed by Luke was rewritten by the person whom Goguel calls 'the writer to Theophilus', who 'utilized Luke's account at the same time as other data. Perhaps he did not entirely grasp the nature of the book, and he abridged it in a way that often cannot be regarded as happy,

---

[12] M. Goguel, 'La critique actuelle des Actes et le commentaire de M. Alfred Loisy', *Rev. d'Hist. et de Philos. Rel.*, 1921, I, pp. 446–63.

[13] p. 458.

[14] 'It would be very surprising if no trace of the original work had been preserved and if it had been entirely supplanted by the re-editing' (p. 458, n. 1). Loisy attributes to the dignitaries of the Roman Church a power which is clearly exaggerated.

combining with it much less trustworthy traditions'.[15] The work of the 'writer to Theophilus' has not come down to us in its original form—'a clumsy interpolator has mutilated the prologue so that he could introduce the account of the ascension';[16] it is possible that he also made other alterations.

In the commentary which he published in the same year in which Loisy's appeared, J. de Zwaan suggested a much more moderate hypothesis.[17] To explain the disparities in Acts, he supposes that Luke, writing about 75–80, did not finish his work; under Trajan, about 110, an editor published it after having made a few slight alterations. In 1924 de Zwaan repeated his explanation which would make Acts a posthumous work;[18] he set out to show that it takes account of a series of circumstances which characterize the composition of the book. In a study in 1950 devoted to the 'summaries' in Acts, P. Benoit[19] shows a certain sympathy for this hypothesis; a

[15] p. 458. Goguel has repeated his criticisms against Loisy in his *Introduction au Nouveau Testament*, III (1922), pp. 344–53. Other points are raised by A. W. F. Blunt, *The Acts of the Apostles* (The Clarendon Bible), Oxford, 1923, pp. 27f; Kirsopp Lake, *The Preface to Acts and the Composition of Acts*, in *The Beginnings of Christianity* I/V, London, 1933, pp. 1–7 (cf. 4–7).

[16] See in particular *Introduction au N.T.*, III (1922), pp. 170 and 352.

[17] J. de Zwaan, *De Handelingen der Apostelen*. (Coll. Tekst en Uitleg), Gröningen —The Hague, 1920, pp. 11–14.

[18] 'Was the Book of Acts a Posthumous Edition?', *Harv. Theol. Rev.*, 1924, XVII, pp. 95–153.

[19] P. Benoit, *Remarques sur les 'sommaires' des Actes 2, 42 à 5*, in *Aux Sources de la Tradition chrétienne. Mélanges offerts a M. Maurice Goguel* (Bibl. Théol.), Neuchâtel— Paris, 1950, pp. 1–10. Several writers had already drawn attention to the composite character of the 'general descriptions' of Acts 2.42–47; 4.32–35; 5.2–16. Benoit's analyses set out in a convincing manner the limits of the interpolations (2.43–45; 4.33; 5.12–14) and show that each of them borrows its characteristics from two other accounts, even (in the case of 2.43 derived from 5.11) from the immediate context of these accounts. To what are we to attribute these modifications? 'Can the editor who has intervened so clumsily perhaps be Luke himself? It would seem difficult to admit this . . . or was it he who, while putting the final touches to his book, rewrote the summaries in the way we have just analysed? The clumsiness of these revisions prevents us from adopting the latter opinion. There is a further point—the language of these additions presents several peculiarities which dissuade us from attributing them to Luke. Finally, the manifest exaggeration of 5.13a; which contradicts 13b–14; suggests more zeal than skill to improve upon the data of Luke. Such seems indeed to have been the intention of the editor who composed these interpolations; he wanted to strengthen the summaries of Luke the better to adapt them to the double rôle, preparatory and generalizing, which they play in relation to the narratives . . . And at the same time the additions improve upon the generalizing character of the primitive accounts . . . The intervention of an

more recent article, however, tends in a different direction.[20]

In 1942, W. G. Kümmel[21] pointed out that the critics seemed to have abandoned the theory which made of the Acts of the Apostles the much-altered edition of an earlier work. This is certainly the clearest result of the relentlessness with which Loisy developed this theory.[22]

---

editor touching up Luke's work should not surprise us if we remember that the book of Acts presents many other inconsistencies in style or in the arrangement of the facts' (pp. 7–10). P. Benoit concludes by linking his explanations with the hypothesis of de Zwaan: 'Certain critics have sought to see in Acts an imperfect and unfinished work to which Luke was not able to put the finishing touches and which was edited by someone among his friends or disciples. This plausible hypothesis perhaps receives confirmation from the literary analysis suggested in these pages' (p. 10). While recognizing the interest of Benoit's literary remarks, W. G. Kümmel (in his survey 'Das Urchristentum', *Theologische Rundschau*, 1954, XXII, pp. 207ff) considers that they do not provide sufficient foundation for the conclusions which their author thinks he can draw from them. In fact, (1) no proof is given of the non-Lucan character of the language of these interpolations; (2) it is not easy to see the motive which urged the author to make these additions (to strengthen the summaries?); (3) these summaries, even if we add to them the other inconsistencies which can be found in other passages of Acts, form too narrow a basis to make necessary the hypothesis of an editorial rewriting of Luke's work. It is better to be satisfied with attributing the lack of unity of the summaries to the fact that they generalize various concrete facts. Mention should also be made of H. Zimmermann, 'Die Sammelberichte der Apostelgeschichte', *Biblische Zeitschrift*, 1961, N. F., V, pp. 71–82; the author distinguishes a primitive source (2.41, 44a, 46, 47; 4.32b, 34, 35; 5.11, 12, 15) which Luke developed at the time of the final version as a consequence of his personal preoccupations.

[20] P. Benoit, 'La deuxième visite de St Paul à Jérusalem', *Biblica*, 1959, XL, pp. 778–92. We shall return to this study when discussing the 'Antioch source'.
[21] W. G. Kümmel, 'Das Urchristentum', *Theologische Rundschau*, 1942, XIV, pp. 81–93 and 155–73; see p. 167. In 1939, O. Bauernfeind observed that the works of Spitta and Loisy explaining Acts, the one by a fusion of two sources, the other by the writing of an original Acts remodelled in a hagiographical and legendary sense, have led to a negative result; the existence of a source which would have exercised in relation to Acts a rôle similar to that of the Gospel of Mark in relation to Luke's cannot be proved: *Die Apostelgeschichte* (Theol. Handkomm. zum N.T., V), Leipzig, 1939, pp. 8–9.
[22] In regard to the rewriting which the work of Luke may have undergone after its completion, it is perhaps not without interest to draw attention to the study of Ph. H. Menoud, *Remarques sur les textes de l'ascension dans Luc-Actes*, *Neutestamentliche Studien für Rudolf Bultmann* (Beihefte zur Zeitschr. für die neutestl. Wiss. 21), Berlin, 1954, pp. 148–56. Menoud is in disagreement with a fairly widespread opinion (we have already met this in the case of M. Goguel, and it is again found in Ed. Meyer, H. W. Beyer, W. G. Kümmel, *Theol. Rundschau*, 1948, XVII, p. 9, n. 1; M. Dibelius, *Aufsätze*, p. 165, n. 3) according to which the account of the Ascension was only introduced into Acts by way of a late interpolation. The principle of a different explanation is indicated by Kirsopp Lake, who questions the epilogue of Luke's Gospel and the first verses of Acts: Luke 24.50–53 was a later addition,

A Single Source in the First Part

B. Weiss's survey of the sources of Acts in 1886[23] marks the beginning of a period of active research. First, he pointed out that the first half of the book bears a strong Hebrew character; by this it is marked off from the second part, whose language is more Greek and so comes closer to that of the prologue of the

dating from the time when the Gospel was separated from Acts; Acts 1.1–5 had been completely disfigured by editorial changes, traces of which the textual tradition seems to retain. (*The Beginnings of Christianity*, I/V, pp. 3f). H. Sahlin went one step further: the third Gospel and Acts originally formed only a single book, Acts 1.6ff being directly linked with Luke 24.49; the epilogue to the Gospel (Luke 24.50–53) and the introduction to Acts (1.1–5) are two additions going back to the time of the compilation of the New Testament: *Der Messias und das Gottesvolk. Studien zur protolukanischen Theologie* (Acta Seminarii Neotestamentici Upsatoiensis, XII), Uppsala, 1945, pp. 11–18). Menoud takes up this theory again, endeavouring to corroborate it by fresh observations tending to show that the language of the offending verses does not coincide in every particular with that of Luke. In this way the story of the Ascension is saved, but at the price of a conjecture which raises more difficulties than it solves. This solution, indeed, explains neither the new data in the introduction to Acts (notably the mention of forty days) nor the singularities of its style; it does not account for the Lucan character of the offending passages or for the parallelism which makes the epilogue to the Gospel the pendant of that to Acts, or finally for the passage which situates in the Temple the final scene of the Gospel and makes of it the introductory scene of Acts. Add to this that the link between Luke 24.49 and Acts 1.6 is not perfect: the episode given in Luke 24.33–49 takes place inside a house, the Ascension recounted in Acts 1.6–12 takes place in the open air, near Jerusalem, on the Mount of Olives (cf. W. G. Kümmel, *Theol. Rundschau*, 1944, XXII, p. 196). Finally, Luke might well have had valid reasons for dividing his work into two volumes—practical reasons, since the copying on two rolls of average size presented advantages over the use of one excessively long one; and there were reasons coming from the narrative itself, the first part being exclusively devoted to Christ, the second to his representatives. M. Menoud points out to us and has given us permission to say that he has partially modified the explanations he put forward in 1954; they have been taken up by E. Trocmé (*op. cit.*, pp. 31–34) with certain new considerations which do not seem to us to make this hypothesis any the more probable. As regards Luke 24.50–53, the hypothesis of an interpolation maintained by Menoud (see also A. N. Wilder, 'Variant Traditions of the Resurrection in Acts', *Journal of Bibl. Lit.*, 1943, LXII, 307–18: cf. 311) has been taken up by H. Conzelmann, *Die Mitte der Zeit. Studien zur Theologie des Lukas* (Beitr. zur hist. Theol., 17), 3rd ed., Tübingen, 1960, p. 189, n. 4; it has been criticized in a very interesting way by P. A. van Stempvoort, 'The Interpretation of the Ascension in Luke and Acts', *N.T. Studies*, 1958/59, V, 30–42, (cf. 35). See also J. G. Davies, *He Ascended into Heaven*, London, 1958, p. 41, n. 5; E. Haenchen, *Apostelgeschichte*, 12, p. 107, n. 3; E. Graesser, 'Die Apostelgeschichte in der Forschung der Gegenwart', *Theol. Rundschau*, 1960, N.F. XXVI, pp. 93–167 (cf. p. 113, n. 3).

[23] B. Weiss, *Lehrbuch der Einleitung in das Neue Testament*, Berlin, 1886, pp. 569–84.

work addressed to Theophilus.[24] Having discovered traces of
Paulinism in the third Gospel,[25] Weiss accepted without
difficulty the idea that the author, having been a companion of
Paul, composed the second part from oral information and from
his personal memories. The language of the first part, on the
contrary, suggests more readily the use of sources. A literary
analysis led him to think that these chapters rest on a single
Judaeo-Christian source, recounting the history of the primitive
community from the election of Matthias to the Apostolic
Council. This source, he thought, had undergone numerous
editorial changes, which create difficulties of interpretation,
while at the same time they attest the use of a basic document
with which they are not always in harmony. Additions were
made, among them the group of Pauline sections which
naturally link up with the information given in the second part.
Such are: 9.1–30; 11.19–30; 12.25; 14.28.[26]

After admitting a single source in the first part of the book,
Weiss asked himself if the same hypothesis could be retained for
the second. The presence of 'we-sections' would not constitute a
difficulty against this explanation, since the source would not
necessarily be limited to these passages; the existence of interpolations and of recastings would tell in favour of this hypothesis.
But all attempts to ascertain the source, to determine its content
and character, have been unsuccessful. Then there is the use of

---

[24] Analogous consideration in A. C. Headlam, *Acts of the Apostles*, in J. Hastings,
A Dictionary of the Bible, I, Edinburgh, 1898, pp. 25–35 (cf. 34). Headlam appears
to be very sceptical about the possibility of identifying the sources used by Luke,
who puts the mark of his own style on everything he adopts, thus modifying all
efforts to determine the characteristics which should distinguish his sources. He
recognizes, however, following B. Weiss, that the first part of Acts has a more
Aramaic flavour, the second being composed in a style more purely Greek. This
difference suggests that the first chapters are based on a written source.

[25] Cf. Weiss, *op. cit.*, pp. 550–3.

[26] Similar explanations in W. Hadorn, *Die Apostelgeschichte und ihr geschichtlicher
Wert* (Bibl. Zeit- und Streitfragen, 2nd series, facs. 6), Lichterfelde—Berlin, 1906,
pp. 12–18; the first part of Acts seems to have used a Judaeo-Christian source
connected with the 'Discourses and Acts of Peter'; this source would underlie
1.15–16; 2.1–11, 14–36; 3.1–5.42; 9.32–42; 10.1–11, 18; 12.1–23. The same source
or a source of the same kind would have supplied the material for ch. 6–8. The
writer (Luke, the companion of Paul, who speaks in the first person of the events
in which he took part) does not limit himself to transcribing his sources; he has
set the mark of his language and his style on them.

the 'we'. To justify this by referring it back to a source is not sufficient. Luke did not work like a craftsman in mosaics; he did not slavishly copy the text of his sources; he recast and adopted them to his own narrative. If this 'we' is not a sheer fabrication, we are forced to think that the author used it to signify that he was among Paul's companions for the events which he reports in the first person. We must therefore make up our minds to attribute the whole of the second part of Acts to a companion of Paul. The curious mixture of detailed accounts and of incomplete pieces of information is sufficiently explained by the fact that this companion only found himself at Paul's side from time to time; the unevenness of the composition, which is a fact, can be easily understood if we suppose that the writer took personal notes which he afterwards used for the composition of his work, giving them a new turn to adapt them to his purpose and making various additions from his personal memories or from traditions he had come across in the meantime. This process would account for the small changes which upset the normal sequence of the narrative and for the presence of pericopes whose adventitious character is undeniable.[27]

In 1890 and 1891, P. Feine[28] set out his views on the composition of the synoptic Gospels and on that of the first part of Acts. Mark, he thought, derived from an earlier 'gospel' which Matthew also used, as well as another source which principally contained discourse; Luke had at his disposal the earlier 'gospel', the Gospel of Mark, the source of the discourses used by Matthew, and in addition a document which he alone possessed, his *Sonderschrift*. Pericope by pericope, Feine studied all the passages of the third Gospel which he thought should be attached to this particular source.[29] Luke was not satisfied with transcribing his source, he modified it; but the

[27] Acts 13.6–12; 14.8–18; 16.1–8, 25–34; 17.19; 20.7–12, 16–38; 21.8–14; 23.26–30; 25.14–21, 24–27; 28.17–23, the discourses and fragments of least importance.

[28] P. Feine, 'Die alte Quelle in der ersten Hälfte der Apostelgeschichte', *Zeitschr. für prot. Theol.*, 1890, XVI, pp. 84–133; *Eine vorkanonische Ueberlieferung des Lukas in Evangelium und Apostelgeschichte. Eine Untersuchung*, Gotha, 1891. Our résumé is based on the second work.

[29] Luke 1.5–2.52; 3.10–14, 23–38; 4.14–30; 5.1–11; etc.

modifications are not such that they would prevent recognition of certain characteristic features of the basic document. Now, this document does not end where the Gospel narrative ends; it continues to chapter 12 of Acts. To discover its character, it is sufficient to remove the longest additions made by Luke: Acts, 6–7; 8.25–40; 9.1–30; 11.24–30.[30]

In 1909, E. de Faye[31] thought he had discovered one single document underlying the accounts in the first part of Acts (ch. 1–14). A detailed analysis made it possible to eliminate a series of secondary characteristics or passages: what was left was homogeneous: 2.4, 5, 7, 12, 13, 14–40 (this discourse must in the source have been no more than an outline); 2.41a, 52, 44a, 46, 47; 3.1–11, 12–26 (outline); 4.5–22, 24–31 (probably); 4.33, 36, 37; 5.1–11, 12b; 6.1–6, 8–12a; 7.2–53 (outline); 7.54, 57; 8.1, 4; 11.19–30; 12.25; the greater part of ch. 13 and 14. On the church of Jerusalem and the martyrdom of Stephen this source contained only what was essential; its specific purpose was to tell the story of the beginnings, development and missionary effort of the church of Antioch. The document must have been presented as the annals of Christianity in Antioch. All that has been added to it does not presuppose written sources; oral traditions, with no guarantee of historicity, would suffice to explain it.[32]

---

[30] More recently E. Hirsch likewise wished to discover in the beginning of Acts the prolongation of a *Sonderquelle* used by Luke in his Gospel (the source, Lk. II, which could again be called the Gospel according to Cleophas). The first form of the hypothesis is as follows: the accounts of Luke 24 (including the conclusion: vv. 50–53) were immediately followed by the story of Pentecost, the descent of the Holy Spirit and the sermon of Peter (*Frühgeschichte des Evangeliums*, vol. II, *Die Vorlagen des Lukas und das Sondergut des Matthäus*, Tübingen, 1941, pp. 280–3 and 427). Thus in a new form: by means of a few corrections to be introduced into Acts I, it is possible to recognize in it the continuation of Luke 24; the account of the pilgrims of Emmaus prepares the way for that of the election of Matthias, the new apostle being in point of fact one of the two travellers. (*Frühgeschichte des Evangeliums*, vol. I, *Das Werden des Markusevangeliums*, 2nd ed., Tübingen, 1951, pp. XXX–XXXIX). It is not worth spending time over conjectures of this kind.

[31] E. de Faye, *Etude sur les origines des églises de l'âge apostolique* (Bibl. de l'Ecole des Hautes Etudes, Sciences religieuses, 23), Paris, 1909, pp. 27–93.

[32] Mention may be made here of the study of H. Waitz, 'Die Quelle der Philippusgeschichten in der Apostelgeschichte, 8.5–40', *Zeitschr. für die neutestl. Wiss.*, 1906, VII, pp. 340–55. A detailed investigation has enabled Waitz to eliminate from this passage a certain number of extraneous additions (8.10; 14.18a, 19b); what remains shows a language which is strongly Hebrew in character, the

Taking up again in 1920–1 a suggestion which was not new,[33] L. Dieu[34] linked his hypothesis directly with that of Weiss; the single source which the latter thought he could establish as the basis of the first fifteen chapters of Acts would simply be the continuation of the Gospel of Mark. The proof consisted in singling out points of contact between this Gospel and the first part of Acts;[35] it has convinced no one, except of the fact that such an approach does not lead to any result.

---

reflection of a source which is clearly very ancient. It would seem indeed that this source did not mention Philip; the only person in question must have been Peter. This chapter must then be restored to the 'Acts of Peter' which is continued in 9.32ff, and which seems to have formed the chief sources of Acts 1–12.

[33] From Zöckler (Die Apg. 2, 1895, p. 156), Wendt (Die Apg. 8, 1899, p. 19), and Goguel (Introd. au N.T., III, 1922, p. 55), we learn that this explanation had already been put forward by R. Scharfe, Die petrinische Strömung in der neutestamentlichen Literatur, Berlin, 1893: bringing out different points of contact of chs. 1–12 of Acts with I Peter and the Gospel of Mark, Scharfe concluded that the composition of these chapters was based on a written account from the hand of Mark (pp. 53f, 113ff, 150). For a more cautious position see F. Blass, Acta apostolorum, sive Lucas ad Theophilum liber alter, Göttingen, 1895, pp. 10f: the hypothesis is here limited to Acts 1.1–8; 2; 9.31–11.18; 12, 1–23. In English, the Marcan origin of the narratives of the first part of Acts has been advocated by C. A. Briggs, New Light on the Life of Jesus, Edinburgh, 1904, pp. 135f; F. C. Burkitt, Earliest Sources of the Life of Jesus, Boston–New York, 1910, pp. 79f; id., Christian Beginnings, London, 1924, p. 83. Another hypothesis which should be set on record: the first five chapters of Acts derive from a Johannine source. Such is the explanation of R. B. Rackham, The Acts of the Apostles (Westminster Commentaries), London, 1901: 8th ed., 1919, p. XLIII; it will also be found in E. M. Blaiklock, The Acts of the Apostles. An Historical Commentary (The Tyndale N.T. Comm.), London, 1959, p. 19.
[34] L. Dieu, 'Marc, source des Actes? Ch. I–XV', Rev. Biblique, 1920, XXIX, pp. 555–69; 1921, XXX, pp. 86–96.
[35] L. Dieu extends his hypothesis to the first two chapters of the Gospel of Luke: 'L'évangile de l'enfance, dans saint Luc, serait-il de saint Marc?', Rev. d'Hist. Ecclés., 1928, XXIV, pp. 571–95. Here is the hypothesis that would account for the Marcan character of Luke 1–2 and Acts 1–15, that Mark had planned a general work on the origins of Christianity. Before having had time to finish his work, he read to his friends the central chapters of the book; they were immediately passed on to others. Mark was thus faced with this situation: his book had been published before being completed. Learning at that time of the projects of Luke whose talent he highly esteemed, Mark gave him his complete manuscript. Luke thus had at his disposal a definitive edition which had not yet been published, having been anticipated by the partial edition which has come down to us under the name of Mark. It is interesting to compare these suggestions with those of C. S. C. Williams. The latter likewise establishes a connection between Acts and Mark, without, however, making Mark a source properly so-called of Acts. Luke would have composed a first sketch of his Gospel, at a time when he did not know the work of Mark. It was after coming into possession of that work that he wrote Acts; what Mark relates of Jesus thus exerted its influence on the accounts of Luke

The hypothesis presented in 1916 by C. C. Torrey[36] made more of a stir and gave rise to much discussion.[37] The first fifteen chapters of Acts, he suggested, contain a series of difficult and almost incomprehensible passages, but, to give meaning to them, all that is necessary is to re-translate the Greek word for word into Aramaic; all the difficulties come from the fact that the writer of Acts did not grasp the exact significance of certain Aramaic expressions. The first part of Acts was thus the Greek translation, clumsy in places, of an Aramaic writing into which Luke introduced the accounts of the second part of the book, which were written directly in Greek. It would seem that Torrey was not wrong in drawing attention to the semitisms of Acts. But he certainly pushed much too far his explanations as to the mistranslations of the first part of the book, and he was wrong

---

concerning the apostles. Once the composition of Acts was finished, Luke undertook the revision of his Gospel, using Mark, but taking care to omit in the Gospel what had already been referred to in Acts. See 'The Date of Luke-Acts', *Expository Times*, 1952/53, LXIV, pp. 283f; *A Commentary on the Acts of the Apostles* (Black's N.T. Comm.), London, 1957, pp. 12f (see also H. G. Russell, 'Which was written the first, Luke or Acts?', *Harvard Theol. Rev.*, 1955, XLVIII, pp. 167–74).

[36] As far back as 1799, J. A. Bolten suggested that Acts was based on one or several sources of Aramaic composition and that Luke acted as translator and commentator (*Die Geschichte der Aposteln von Lukas übersetzt und mit Anmerkungen versehen*, Altona). C. C. Torrey's theory on the first fifteen chapters of Acts has been presented in the pamphlet *The Composition and Date of Acts* (Harvard Theol. Studies, I), Cambridge, Mass., 1916. See also by the same writer: 'Facts and Fancy concerning Acts', *Amer. Journ. of Theol.*, 1919, XXXIII, 61–86, and 189–212; *Documents of the Primitive Church*, New York, 1941; 'The Aramaic Period of the Nascent Christian Church', *Zeitschr. für die neutestl. Wiss.*, 1952/53, XLIV, pp. 205–23. A similar view is expressed by W. J. Wilson, 'Some Observations on the Aramaic Acts', *Harvard Theol. Rev.*, 1918, XI, pp. 74–99; *id.*, 'The Unity of the Aramaic Acts', *ibid.*, pp. 322–35.

[37] Among attempts to focus the question may be instanced: F. J. Foakes Jackson, 'Professor C. C. Torrey on the Acts', *Harvard Theol. Rev.*, 1917, X, pp. 325–61; B. W. Bacon, 'More Philological Criticisms of Acts', *Amer. Journ. of Theol.*, 1918, XXXII, pp. 1–23; F. C. Burkitt, 'Professor Torrey on "Acts" ', *Journ. of Theol. Studies*, 1919, XX, pp. 320–9; H. J. Cadbury, 'Luke Translator or Author?', *Amer. Journ. of Theol.*, 1920, XXXIV, pp. 436–50; E. J. Goodspeed, 'The Origin of Acts', *Journ. of Bib. Lit.*, 1920, XXXIX, pp. 83–101; J. de Zwaan, in *Beginnings of Christianity*, vol. II (1922), pp. 44–65; F. J. Foakes Jackson, K. Lake, *ibid.*, pp. 141–8; A. W. F. Blunt, *The Acts of the Apostles* (1923), pp. 25f; G. Kittel, *Die Probleme des palästinischen Judentums und das Urchristentum* (Beiträge zur Wiss. vom A. und N.T., 3rd series, vol. I), Stuttgart, 1926, pp. 56–58; H. F. D. Sparks, 'The Semitisms of the Acts', *Journ. of Theol. Studies*, 1950, N.S. I, pp. 16–28; A. W. Argyle, 'The Theory of an Aramaic Source in Acts 2, 14–40', *ibid.*, 1953, N.S. IV, pp. 213f.

in neglecting the analogous phenomena which are found in the second part. He should also have taken account of the passages in a Greek that is permeated with Biblical expressions reminiscent of the Septuagint.[38] Again, this hypothesis has incurred the reproach of according too complete a unity to the first part of Acts and of failing to recognize the real unity of the entire book. Useful, perhaps, for explaining certain particular instances,[39] the hypothesis cannot be retained as an explanation of the origin of the Acts of the Apostles.

Several writers, however, allow to Torrey's hypothesis other merits than that of offering a principle for solving certain difficult passages. G. Kittel[40] considered that Torrey had shown the probability of the existence of an Aramaic source for Acts 1–12, whether or not this contribution of Aramaic tradition was to be attributed to a single source or to several. J. de Zwaan[41] thought that Acts 1.3–5, 16, and 9.31–11.18, derived from the same Aramaic document. W. L. Knox[42] speaks with

---

[38] The influence of the Greek Bible on the language of Luke is particularly emphasized by H. F. D. Sparks, art. cit., 'The Semitisms of St. Luke's Gospel', *Journ. of Theol. St.*, 1943, XLIV, pp. 129–38; 'Some Observations on the Semitic Background of the New Testament', in *Studiorum Novi Testamenti Societas*, Bulletin II (1951), pp. 33–42.

[39] In this connection we should like to draw attention to the new hypothesis by which W. A. Beardslee seeks to throw light on the episode of Matthias (Acts 1.15–26) by means of the texts of the Qumrân—'The Casting of Lots at Qumrân and in the Book of Acts', *Nov. Test.*, IV/4, Dec. 1960 (published October, 1961), pp. 245–52. Here are the writer's own words: 'Luke's source told of the decision of the community, using the metaphorical language which is evidenced from Qumrân. Luke understood its theological meaning, that this was God's choice, not man's; and in shaping his story he objectified the mechanism of the divine choice in a literal casting of lots, a practice particularly familiar, for the choice of responsible officials, in the tradition of the Gentile world' (p. 251).

[40] *Loc. cit.*

[41] *De Handelingen der Aposteln*, p. 11; cf. *Beginnings* II, p. 50.

[42] Among the sources which Luke uses after the manner of a compiler there must have been 'a very semitic source' which supplied him with the history of the Church of Jerusalem—such is the opinion of W. L. Knox in *Some Hellenistic Elements in Primitive Christianity* (Schweich Lectures 1942), London, 1944, p. 7. The writer is less positive in *The Acts of the Apostles*, Cambridge, 1948, pp. 8f, 18–22 and 39. He begins by discussing Harnack's hypothesis, seeing in the first chapters of Acts two parallel accounts of the same events. Stated thus, this explanation is not wholly convincing; it could, however, be the case that having collected his information from people who spoke Aramaic, Luke did not realize that he had been supplied in certain cases with two versions of the same event. Whatever may be the value or otherwise of this point Knox considers that Torrey's theory is reasonable, on condition that it be restricted to the first five chapters of the book; they are

hesitation of a written source for the narratives of Acts 1.2–5.16.[43]

H. Sahlin[44] consciously presented his hypothesis as a revised form of Torrey's. A Judaeo-Christian, probably of Syrian origin, perhaps a native of Antioch, composed a work on Christian origins about the year 50. In content, this 'Proto-Luke' corresponds to Luke 1.5—Acts 15.33. Its first part was written in Hebrew (Luke 1.5–3.7a), the rest in Aramaic. About 60–65 a Hellenic Christian, doubtless Luke, the companion of Paul, incorporated this work in the apologia which he wanted to compose in Paul's favour. He was not content with translating the original work, as Torrey thought; he recast it fairly freely, adding to it not only the accounts of the second part of Acts but also, in the first part, everything which relates to Paul or makes mention of him.[45] These explanations have not met with great acceptance.[46]

---

based on an Aramaic source or documentation. He concludes (p. 39) that the first half of Acts is not based on written sources, except perhaps ch. 1–5 (excluding the majority of the discourses). It is possible that the source used in these chapters recounted the same trial before the Sanhedrin twice and that there was a question of a miraculous escape, the historical value of which is doubtful. It is also possible that this whole section is based on oral traditions collected by Luke himself; the doublets would come from the fact that he did not realize that the two trials before the Sanhedrin had in actual fact been only one.

[43] R. R. Williams adopts a more definite position in *The Acts of the Apostles* (The Torch Bible Commentaries), London, 1953, pp. 21f: 'For Acts 1–5.16; an Aramaic source is thought to have been established', as does E. Trocmé, *Le 'Livre des Actes' et l'Histoire* (1957), p. 165: 'The presence of aramaïsms due to faults of translation seems established for Acts 1.1–5.16, and 9.31–11.18; and they are possible also in certain other fragments of ch. 1–15. They attest the presence there of Aramaic, thus Palestinian and very probably ancient sources' (cf. pp. 191f). What these authors considered as 'established' is still very much open to question.

[44] *Der Messias und das Gottesvolk* (1945).

[45] Luke's work would have later undergone a final transformation, of which we have already spoken; when it was included in the canon, it was split in two and the end of the Gospel added (Luke 24.50–53) and the introduction to Acts (1.1–5).

[46] The best critical examination seems to us to be that of P. Benoit in the *Revue Biblique*, 1947, LIV, 287–91.

II

PARALLEL SOURCES

SIDE BY SIDE with the writers who explain the composition of the Acts of the Apostles by appealing to a more ancient work, a rough outline representing either wholly or in part the present book, others think it is possible to explain the composition of the text which has come down to us by presenting it as the result of the combination of two earlier accounts. Originally this hypothesis was extended to the work taken as a whole. Harnack retained it for the first chapters only. In that form the value of the hypothesis has been challenged by Joachim Jeremias. It has recently appeared again, however, under a new aspect, in a study by Bo Reicke.

Origins of this Hypothesis

The theory of the two sources of the Acts of the Apostles began with a work published by F. Spitta in 1891.[1] Spitta made a series of observations for which there is some justification. He pointed out, for instance, that on the occasion of Pentecost, the coming of the Holy Spirit was accompanied either by ecstatic manifestations of the glossolalia or by a miracle of speaking with tongues (polyglossia). He then reconstructed an original narrative which mentioned only glossolalia (2.1a, 4, 12ff), and a second where only polyglossia is found (2.1b–3.5–11).[2] Or again the martyrdom of Stephen is presented sometimes as a

[1] F. Spitta: *Die Apostelgeschichte, ihre Quellen und deren geschichlicher Wert*, Halle, 1891.
[2] A good methodological criticism in K. L. Schmidt, *Die Pfingsterzählung und das Pfingstereignis* (Arbeiten zur Religionsgeschichte des Urchristentums, I, 2), Leipzig, 1919, pp. 23f: before distinguishing sources in order to extract an historical nucleus from them, we must first ask ourselves what the writer meant to say, and in what way he himself thought of the event.

S.A.–B

popular lynching (6.1–6, 9–12a; 7.2–54, 57–58a; 9.1b–2), sometimes as the result of a formal trial (6.7–8.12b–15; 7.1, 55–56,
58b–60; 8.1a, 3). The Ascension is recounted twice (Luke
24.44–53 and Acts 1.4–14), as is also the second visit of Paul to
Jerusalem (Acts 11.27–30; 12.25; and Acts 15). By indicating
details of this kind in the whole work, Spitta thought he could
show that, from one end to the other, the text was an amalgam
of two different sources, A and B; the contribution of the editor,
who provided the transitional passages, being relatively slight.
Source A, used up to ch. 24 of the Gospel, then in Acts 1.15ff
and to the end of the work, comprised in particular the we-
sections; it is the account of an eyewitness, Luke, and has very
great historical value. Source B which has been added to it is a
popular account, with a weakness for legends; it is late (after 70)
and scarcely deserves credence. The fusion of the two documents
was probably made at the end of the first century by a more or
less impartial editor.[3]

In 1895, J. Jüngst[4] put forward a modification of Spitta's
theory, the general plan of which he kept: a genuine source A,
probably coming from Luke; source B, popular and legendary,
Judaeo-Christian in origin, a continuation of the special source
of the third Gospel. Jüngst disagreed with Spitta particularly in
limiting source B to the first half of Acts (up to ch. 12, adding a
few points from ch. 15); he disagreed with him also in that he
attributed a much greater share to the editor. The latter, a contemporary of Trajan or Hadrian, was pursuing a very definite
apologetic purpose; he was seeking to prove that Christianity
had the right to enjoy the status of a *religio licita*; the needs of
his theory led him to introduce a good number of new elements,
particularly in the second part of the book.

[3] Spitta applies to Acts a procedure very similar to that which he had applied
to the Apocalypse two years earlier (*Die Offenbarung des Johannes*, Halle, 1889):
there he distinguished three sources, more or less parallel, juxtaposed by an editor
who contented himself with joining passages together and touching them up
slightly.
[4] J. Jüngst, *Die Quellen der Apostelgeschichte*, Gotha, 1895. The final pages (221–
6) sum up the result of the analyses in a clear and detailed picture; there are three
columns, the first containing elements attributable to source A, the second those
which link up with source B, the third those which depend on the editor.

In 1899, in the new edition of his commentary, H. H. Wendt[5] considered that 4.1–22 and 5.17–42 were probably two parallel accounts relating to the same event; the second account, 5.17ff, had been overladen with complementary traditional data, among which was a story of miraculous deliverance (5.18–20), duplicating that recounted in 12.3ff. Harnack reiterated this theory in an expanded form.

Harnack's Hypothesis

In the work he published in 1908,[6] Harnack examined methodically the question of the sources of Acts. What were the criteria for determining the sources used by Luke? Harnack considered that it was not possible to take either vocabulary or style as a basis: they were everywhere the same; if Luke used sources, he merely reproduced them in his own language and imposed his personal stamp upon them.[7] Another inadequate criterion he thought to be the discrepancies in the narrative, its inaccuracies, imprecisions, hiatus, contradictions; the same difficulties are found in all parts of the book, and clearly indicate a certain negligence on the part of the writer.[8] Once these inapplicable criteria were removed, Harnack thought it was impossible to prove that the second part of Acts (from 15.36) was based on sources; at most one could think that Luke made use of personal notes, or a travel journal, to narrate the events in which he took part in Paul's company, and was prepared to complete these notes in accordance with the information he gleaned from the lips of other witnesses of this period.[9] In order to form an opinion as to the origin of the accounts in the first part of Acts, the only criterion on which we can rely is that of the setting (*Schauplatz*) of the traditions related, and, in a subordinate way, that of the personages in whom these traditions showed a particular interest;

[5] H. H. Wendt, *Die Apostelgeschichte* (Kritisch-exegetischer Komm. über das N.T., III, 8th ed.) Göttingen, 1899, p. 30. Wendt published the first edition of his commentary in 1880, the second in 1888; that of 1899 is the third. It is this last edition we have consulted.
[6] *Die Apostelgeschichte*, pp. 131–88.
[7] pp. 131f.
[8] See the lengthy analyses on pp. 159–77.
[9] Cf. pp. 131 and 177–82.

these narratives, in fact, were founded on traditions which were both local and personal.[10] A first group of traditions was distinguished by an Antiochene setting[11]—ch. 13–15, to which must be added 11.19–30; 12.25, were written from a point of view which was that of the Church of Antioch. These narratives presuppose the account of Stephen's martyrdom (6.1–8.4), to which they were linked by 11.19. Since Luke probably overstressed the importance of Paul, it was possible to think that in the beginning these Antioch traditions were particularly concerned with two persons: Stephen and Barnabas. The presence of 'Saul' was doubtless only mentioned in a subordinate way. Going a step further, Harnack considered that these traditions reached Luke in the form of a written document—the Antioch source, to which he attributed considerable historical value.[12]

The other traditions of the first part of Acts had a Jerusalem setting (apart from 9.1–28, which constituted a separate tradition).[13] One distinction, however, was imperative: in 8.5–40; 9.29–11.18, and 12.1–24, the town of Caesarea occupied a prominent place; this group could be designated under the name of Jerusalem-Caesarea.[14] There remain ch. 1–5. Here Harnack distinguished a homogeneous group, in which all the episodes were closely linked: 3.1–5.16.[15] Set against this group, the accounts of ch. 2 and 5.17–42 seemed to him like a doublet; the events they recounted were identical with those of 3.1–5.16, but presented under a more legendary and less coherent form.[16] The parallelism is further accentuated if ch. 12 is joined to the

---

[10] Cf. p. 132.

[11] pp. 134–9.

[12] At least from 13.4 (pp. 153ff).

[13] p. 139.

[14] pp. 139f.

[15] pp. 142–4. Harnack shows a slight hesitation over 5.1–11.

[16] pp. 146–8. The idea that there are two parallel developments in ch. 2–5 is not new. For proof of this, see Ed. Zeller, 'Die Apostelgeschichte, ihre Composition und ihr Charakter', *Theol. Jahrbücher*, 1805, IX, 375f; *Die Apostelgeschichte nach ihrem Inhalt und Ursprung Kritisch untersucht*, Stuttgart, 1854, p. 378. The Marburg professor, who is also one of the leaders of the Tübingen school, proposes a division which does not correspond exactly with Harnack's. The two symmetrical groups (among which there would also be a continuity) are represented by 2.42–4.31 and 4.32–5.42. In each group first a flattering picture of the community is given (2.42–47; 4.32–37), then the detailed account of a miracle (3.1–10; 5.1–11),

group 3.1–5.16. The miraculous deliverance of the apostles in 5.19ff was a doublet of the deliverance of Peter in ch. 12.[17] Harnack gave to 3.1–5.16 the name of source A; this source, he thought, extended to the narratives of Jerusalem-Caesarea: 8.5–40; 9.29–11.18; 12.1–24. These narratives related to two chief persons: Peter and Philip; Luke probably received the source from Philip, or rather from his daughters.[18] Would this source be in the form of a written document? Harnack judged this probable for ch. 3–4 and 12; the rest could have been transmitted orally.[19] Taken as a whole, this group of traditions deserves a favourable verdict as history. The situation is quite different as regards source B, which was not perhaps in the form of a document and which Harnack judges adversely.[20] Nor has he any greater esteem for the recent traditions reproduced in ch. 1.[21]

In his explanations of the composition of ch. 2–5 of Acts, Harnack took his inspiration from the scheme of Spitta and of Jüngst[22]—source A is excellent and source B is bad. He differed from his predecessors, however, by giving to the word 'source' a vaguer meaning, in limiting the parallelism of the sources to three chapters, in presupposing that Luke juxtaposed his sources in large sections instead of distributing them over one single narrative which would use each of their elements individually. The procedure he credits Luke with is certainly more in conformity with his manner of proceeding in the Gospel.

It would be tedious to enumerate the different systems which, following Harnack and modifying him to a greater or lesser

---

finally the story of a persecution (3.11ff; 5.17ff). The conclusions Zeller draws from this parallelism concern not the sources used by Luke, but his procedure for setting out his material. In 1897, J. Weiss was already criticizing this way of dividing up the narratives (*Ueber die Absicht*, p. 7).

[17] p. 145.
[18] pp. 150ff. We should also have to think of Mark (ch. 12) and of Silas.
[19] pp. 184–6.
[20] pp. 152f and 182–4.
[21] Practically assimilated to the traditions of group B; cf. pp. 164–6 and 174.
[22] Harnack does not quote them. He sometimes makes vague allusions to the labours of his predecessors, but only refers to them (especially Wellhausen) for points of detail of his analyses.

degree, have adopted the principle of tracing two parallel sources in the narratives of the first part of Acts.[23] It will be sufficient to cite the explanations of F. J. Foakes Jackson and Kirsopp Lake in vol. II (1922) of the monumental work on Acts which they edited.[24] Of ch. 1–5, they attribute to source A:

[23] A pupil of Harnack, R. Schütz, has undertaken to complete the work of his illustrious master—first of all in two articles: "Ἰερουσαλήμ und Ἱεροσόλυμα im Neuen Testament', *Zeitschr. für die neutestl. Wiss.*, 1910, XI, pp. 169ff; *Das Quellenproblem der Apostelgeschichte*, in *Harnack-Ehrung* (Beiträge zur Kirchengeschichte), Berlin, 1921, pp. 44ff; then in *Apostel und Jünger. Eine quellen kritische und geschichtliche Untersuchung über die Entstehung des Christentums*, Giessen, 1921 (cf. pp. 15–66). He distinguishes two principal sources in Acts and designates them in accordance with the feature which seems to him to characterize them best: source A (ἀπόστολος) which concerns the apostles, source M (μαθητής) which treats of the disciples. To source A must be attached the whole of ch. 1–5; the discourse of Stephen 7.2–47; the mention of the apostles in 8.1; the journey of Peter and John to Samaria, 8.14–25; Paul in Jerusalem, 9.27f; Peter among the Gentiles, 9.31–11.18; the information given in 11.19b, according to which only the Jews would be preached to; the apostolic assembly, 15.1–33; the circumcision of Timothy and the publication of the Jerusalem decree, 16.3b–4; the baptism of the disciples of John, 19.2–7; Paul's vow, 21.20–27a. To source M is to be attributed 6; 7.48–8.13; 8.26–9.26; 9.29–30; 11.19–14.28; 16.1–21.19; 21.27b. It seems pointless to enter into further detail. In his 'Kritische Analyse der Apostelgeschichte' (*Abhandlungen der Königl. Ges. der Wiss. zu Göttingen, Philol-hist. Kl.*, N.F. XV/2, Berlin, 1914), J. Wellhausen only occasionally deals with the question of sources. In the section with which we are concerned, the 'summaries' in Acts 2.43–47; 4.32–37; 5.12–16; are considered as transitional passages. Between the first and second summaries, the narrative of 3.1–4.31 constitutes a single section (not without traces of modifications); after the third summary, the narrative of 5.17–42 is only another version of the facts recounted in ch. 3–4. Finally 6.1–6 constitutes the sequel to 4.32–5.11 (pp. 10–11). E. de Faye sees in 3.1–4.32 and 5.12–42 two parallel accounts; the narratives of Pentecost (2.1–16) and of Stephen's martyrdom amalgamate two irreconcilable versions of the same facts—*Etude sur les origines des Eglises de l'Age apostolique*, Paris (1909), pp. 27–72f; *Les Actes des Apôtres*, in *Le Nouveau Testament: traduction nouvelle d'après les meilleurs textes, avec introduction et notes* ('Bible du Centenaire', IV), Paris, 1928, pp. 177–9. Similar views are expressed by M. Goguel, *Introduction au N.T.*, III (1922), pp. 172–96; *Jésus et les origines du christianisme*, II, *La naissance du christianisme* (Bibl. hist.), Paris, 1946, pp. 491–4; Ed. Meyer, *Ursprung und Anfänge des Christentums*, vol. III, Stuttgart, Berlin, 1923, pp. 144ff. On W. L. Knox, cf. *supra*, p. 31, n. 42—A. W. F. Blunt (*The Acts of the Apostles*, 1923, pp. 24f) remains sceptical as to the exact delimitation of the sources of the first part of Acts; he prefers to speak of different collections of narratives connected with Jerusalem and Antioch, but without excluding the possibility of doublets: ch. 2 and 4.31–37 recounting the same event, similarly 4.1–22 and 5.17–42 (p. 25, n. 1; pp. 152 and 154).

[24] *The Beginnings of Christianity*, I/II, pp. 137–57. See what Kirsopp Lake had already written on the sources of Acts in his article *Acts of the Apostles*, in J. Hastings, *Dictionary of the Apostolic Church*, vol. I, Edinburgh, 1915, pp. 22–25. With the slight differences which a presentation to the general public necessitates, the same explanations again appear in the commentary of F. J. Foakes Jackson, *The Acts of the Apostles* (The Moffatt N.T. Commentary), London, 1931 (8th impression, 1951): cf. pp. 24, 44, etc.

3.1–4.35; to source B: 1–2 and 5.17–42. They are unwilling to pronounce on the attribution to A or B of 4.36–37 and 5.1–16. They consider that the same scheme has been followed in the ensuing chapters. Two parallel sources recount the martyrdom of Stephen—in one it is attributed to a popular rising (6.9–11; 7.54–58a), in the other, to a sentence passed by the Sanhedrin (6.12–14; 7.58b–60).[25] Two divergent traditions recount the foundation of the church of Caesarea: the first attributes it to Philip (8.3–40), the other to Peter (9.32–11.18). The same visit to Jerusalem of Paul and Barnabas is reported twice—firstly following an Antioch tradition (11.19–30), then according to a Jerusalem tradition (15.1–41). Ch. 16.1–5 is probably a summary of the journey recounted in ch. 13–14: it would then be necessary to consider 16.6ff as the immediate sequel to 14.24.[26]

H. W. Beyer's commentary (1932)[27] differs even further from Harnack. He considers that the account of Pentecost already combines two sources (2.1–4.12–13 and 2.5, 11). For the follow-

---

[25] We have come across a similar explanation but with a different distribution of the verses in F. Spitta, *Apostelgeschichte* (1891), pp. 96ff. See also M. Goguel, *Introduction au N.T.*, III (1922), pp. 194f, *id.*, *Jésus et les origines du christianisme*, II, *La naissance du christianisme* (1946), pp. 496–8; O. Bauernfeind, *Die Apostelgeschichte*, p. 108. It is worth drawing attention to a recent study which marks very clearly a trend foreign to the preoccupations of the *Literarkritik*—J. Bihler, 'Der Stephanus-bericht (Apg. 6.8–15; und 7.54–8.2)', *Biblische Zeitschrift*, 1959, N.F., III, pp. 252–70. The first part endeavours to show that all this information was put together and edited by Luke, who has stamped it with the imprint of his personal preoccupations, of his literary procedure, and of his theological ideas. The second part strives to identify the additional material repeated in this compilation; it is possible to recognize in it (1) a theme referring to the persecution which strikes the prophets, the martyrs and the just; (2) an echo of the declaration of Jesus on the substitution of a new Temple for the old one, as well as the recalling of the saying of Jesus on the coming of the Son of Man; (3) a theme which derives from the context of the charismata: the Spirit produces a higher wisdom and calls forth visions; (4) the geographical list of 6.9. It is clear that an analysis of this kind does not fit in with the notion of a compiler contenting himself with combining two pre-existing documents.

[26] This is the hypothesis set out by Ed. Schwartz, 'Zur Chronologie des Paulus' in the *Nachrichten der königl. Gesellschaft der Wiss. zu Göttingen*, Phil.—hist. Kl., 1907, pp. 263ff. Foakes Jackson and Kirsopp Lake only support this theory, however, with considerable reserve, stressing that the proof of this reconstruction is yet to be found. It crops up again in M. H. Shepherd, 'A Venture of Source Analysis of Acts,' in *Munera Studiosa* (Essays presented to W. H. P. Hatch), Cambridge, Mass., 1946, pp. 92–105.

[27] H. W. Beyer, *Die Apostelgeschichte* (Das N.T. Deutsch 5), 8th ed., Göttingen, 1957, pp. 15f and 28f.

ing chapters he takes up again a very old division,[28] believing that two parallel sources can be recognized in 2.42–4.32 and 4.32–5.42.

In the commentary he published in 1934, J. A. Findlay[29] took his inspiration both from Harnack and from Foakes Jackson–Kirsopp Lake. To the source coming from Jerusalem, to which Mark's name could be attached, he attributes ch. 1; 3–4; 5.1–16; 12.1–23; 15.1–31. To the Caesarean source, with which the name of Philip is associated, 2; 5.17–42; 6–8; with hesitation, 9.31–11.18—which could come from the Marcan source. Finally, to the Antioch source is attributed: 9.1–30; 11.19–30; 12.24–14.28; 15.36–16.9. The result of this redistribution is that 2.41 is a doublet of 4.4 and that Paul's visit to Jerusalem which is in question from an Antioch viewpoint in 11.27–30 and 12.25 is historically identical with that mentioned in ch. 15 from the Jerusalem angle.

In the work of M. Albertz (1952)[30] another echo of the theory of the two sources can be recognized. In speaking of the 'sources' of Acts, this writer does not approach them from the point of view of literary criticism; he seeks to determine not the documents that Luke used, but the origin of the information he collected. Harnack divided up his information according to the places to which it referred; Albertz linked his with persons. He distinguished the traditions relating to the Eleven, those deriving from the holy women,[31] those that can be attributed to the relatives of Jesus,[32] and, in addition, from ch. 6 onwards, the traditions coming from Hellenistic circles.[33] The traditions of

[28] We have already come across this in Ed. Zeller (1850 and 1854); it will be found also in F. Overbeck in the 4th ed. of W. M. L. de Wette, *Kurze Eklärung der Apostelgeschichte* (Leipzig, 1870, pp. 45f), and again in G. Hoennicke, *Die Apostelgeschichte* (Ev.—theol. Bibl. Leipzig, 1913), p. 25.

[29] J. A. Findlay, *The Acts of the Apostles. A Commentary*, London, 1934; we have used the 3rd ed., 1946: see pp. 49–52.

[30] M. Albertz, *Die Botschaft des Neuen Testamentes*, I. *Die Entstehung der Botschaft*, II. *Die Enstehung des apostolischen Schriftenkanons*, Zurich, 1952, pp. 261–71.

[31] Albertz attaches to this group the passages in Acts mentioning women characters—2.17, 18; 6.1; 9.37–41; 12.1–17; 16.13–18, etc.

[32] In particular James, the brother of the Lord.

[33] Albertz divides these traditions into three groups: (a) those connected with Philip (6–8 and 10.1–11.18); (b) those relating to the foundation of the Church of Antioch (11.19–30; 12.25); (c) those which reflect personal reminiscences of Paul.

the Eleven supply the substance of the first five chapters; in fact, they all go back to a single person, Peter. These narratives in which Peter occupies the first place must have reached Luke through the agency of Mark. It is useless to appeal to a written text, as Luke knew Mark very well and had every facility for ascertaining from him all he himself knew of the facts and deeds concerning Peter during the early days of the Church. Such would be the source from which we get the story of the election of Matthias (1.12–26), those of Pentecost (2.1–41) and of the cure of the lame man, with the events that followed (3.1–4.31), finally that of the death of Ananias and Sapphira (5.1–11); the two 'general pictures', 2.42–47 and 4.32–37, can be attached to the same tradition. On the other hand, the narrative of 5.12–42, which recounts facts so similar to those of ch. 4, does not appear to come from Peter or be attributable to Mark. Albertz does not expressly say that this section is only a doublet of the tradition relating to Peter; but the manner in which he presents it tends to make us think that that is the way he interprets it. In substance his hypothesis remains fairly close to that of Harnack.[34]

The theory of J. Schmitt (1953)[35] can only be remotely attached to the system of the two parallel sources. It distinguishes two series of elements in the first chapters of Acts: (1) 'primitive and perhaps Jerusalem elements', represented by 3.1–4.31; 5.12–42, as also by 5.1–11; (2) other elements coming from Hellenistic circles which underlie the Lucan narrative, 2.1–21, 36–47; 4.32–37, to which could be joined the discourse of 2.22–36, a passage originally independent. These two groups of fragments possess a real unity, thanks to the imprint they received from Hellenistic theological thought, influenced especially by Deuteronomy. The work accomplished by the writer remains under the influence of the Hellenistic circle.

---

[34] Harnack is not mentioned; but Albertz's work gives no references.

[35] J. Schmitt, 'L'Eglise de Jérusalem ou la "Restauration" d'Israel d'après les cinq premiers chapitres des Actes', *Rev. des Sc. Rel.*, 1953, XXVII, pp. 209–18. The writer announced (p. 212, n. 1) a further article to justify his positions on the literary problems of the first chapters of Acts; to our knowledge, this article has not been published. The study on which we are basing ourselves does not indicate the reasons which motivate a somewhat unusual classification of the traditions.

Criticism of J. Jeremias

Harnack's explanations would not have met with the success they did—whether under their original or under modified forms—if the narrative of the Acts of the Apostles had not supplied them with some foundation. That the data are capable of different interpretations can readily be seen from the lack of agreement in the hypotheses presented by those who think that Luke used two parallel sources. In Harnack's system, each of the two sources begins with the account of a miracle—in the one case the miracle of Pentecost (2.1–13), in the other, that of the cure of the lame man (3.1–10); this analogy is certainly very vague and it is difficult to see how it can form the basis of a parallelism in the proper sense of the term. After the miracle follows a great missionary discourse by Peter (2.14–36; 3.11–26). The relationship between these two passages is unmistakable. We cannot, however, ignore the fact that Peter's missionary discourses all have a certain resemblance;[36] this makes it necessary to extend the parallelism to the discourses of ch. 4, 5 and 10. Further, it is with the inaugural discourse of Paul (ch. 13) that the discourse of Pentecost has the deepest affinity. Thus we do not merely find ourselves in the presence of two, but of six parallel discourses. The only valid explanation will be that which can be applied to the series taken as a whole.[37] No

---

[36] This point has been very well developed by C. H. Dodd, *The Apostolic Preaching and its Developments*, London, 1936 (new edition, 1944; numerous reprints). See also W. L. Knox, *The Acts of the Apostles* (1948), pp. 17f, 20f; J. Schmitt, *Jésus ressuscité dans la prédication apostolique. Etude de théologie biblique*, Paris, 1949, pp. 3–36; B. Gärtner, 'Die Missions predikan i Apostalgärningarna', *Svensk Exegetisk Aorsbok*; 1950, XV, pp. 34–54; E. Schweitzer, 'Zu den Reden der Apostelgeschichte', *Theol. Zeitschr.*, 1957, XIII, pp. 1–11; E. Trocmé, *op. cit.*, pp. 207–12; B.M.F. van Iersel, '*Der Sohn' in den synoptischen Jesusworten. Christusbezeichnung der Gemeinde oder Selbstbezeichnung Jesu?*, Leyden, 1961, pp. 31–51; U. Wilckens, *Die Missionsreden der Apostelgeschichte. Form—und tradikonsgeschichteliche Untersuchungen* (Wissenschaftliche Monographien zum A. und N.T., 5), Neukirchen Kreis Moers, 1961, p. 9.

[37] Harnack connects the discourses of ch. 3, 4 and 10 with source A; with source B, those of ch. 2 and 5; the discourse of ch. 13 does not in any case belong to the Antioch source, where it was introduced in error and it seems to be simply a composition by Luke (*Die Apostelgeschichte*, p. 155). On this subject, see the important remarks in J. Schmitt, *Jésus ressuscité*, pp. 30ff, who, however, lays himself open to the same objection in his 1953 article: there the discourses of ch. 3, 4 and 5 are attributed to the same Jerusalem group, whereas the discourse of ch. 2 is not only linked to the Hellenistic tradition, but also divided into two parts originally independent (*Rev. des Sc. Rel.*, XXVII, p. 212, n. 1).

one would think of looking for six different versions of the same discourse. It is more likely that they are to be related to the documents which gave Luke his information about the original apostolic preaching. Thus they prove nothing as to the existence of two parallel sources.[38]

After the discourse Luke mentions the success obtained: 3,000 were converted at Pentecost (2.41), a number raised to 5,000 after the cure of the lame man (4.4). The parallelism is undeniable, but it stops at that; on the one hand it should be noted that the interest in the numerical increase of the Church recurs in a whole series of passages in Acts,[39] and on the other, that the 'general pictures' of 2.42–47 correspond to those of 4.32–35 and 5.12–15, thus falling outside the scheme of the two parallel sources. Like the missionary discourses, these 'general pictures' require their proper explanation, which the hypothesis with which we are concerned cannot provide.[40] Then comes the imprisonment of the apostles (4.1–3 and 5.17–21a, which mentions a miraculous deliverance) and their summons before the Sanhedrin (4.5–22; 5.21b–41). We shall return to this parallel later. The sequel scarcely shows any further correspondence—source A applies only in 4.31–5.11; one has to be very undemanding to discover a symmetry between the final passages—5.12–16 and 5.42.

All things considered, the only point which justifies us in speaking of parallelism or a doublet lies in the double arrest of the apostles and their two appearances before the Sanhedrin. Are we really dealing here, in spite of considerable divergences, with two versions of the same event? Repeating and emphasizing

[38] We substitute these remarks for those by which J. Jeremias endeavours to destroy Harnack's hypothesis. He contents himself with remarking that the discourses of ch. 2 and 3 differ in the occasion that has given rise to them (Pentecost and the cure of the lame man) and in their contents, adding that Peter must have preached more than one missionary sermon ('Untersuchungen zum Quellenproblem der Apostelgeschichte', *Zeitschr. für die neutestl. Wiss.*, 1937, XXXVI, pp. 205–21: cf. p. 205).

[39] Acts 2.41, 47; 4.4; 5.14; 6.1, 7; 9.31; 11.21, 24; 16.5. J. Jeremias (*art. cit.*, p. 205, n. 5) points out that 2.4 forms the introduction to a 'summary' and that 4.4 likewise has the character of a 'summary'.

[40] In addition to the study of Jeremias (*art. cit.*, pp. 206–8), see that, already cited, which P. Benoit has devoted to these 'general pictures' in the *Mélanges Goguel* (1950).

a remark of K. Bornhäuser,[41] J. Jeremias showed in 1937[42] that there was a continuity between these two narratives; far from being a repetition, they complete each other. To realize this it must be remembered that the Jewish law only allowed a breach of the law to be punished if the culprit were aware of the consequences of his act. In practice, immediate prosecutions could only be made against those who had done their Rabbinical studies; in the case of the ordinary people, they first had to be given a legal admonition before witnesses and could only be prosecuted in the case of a relapse into crime. This procedure, attested by other passages in the New Testament,[43] provides an explanation of the relationship existing between ch. 4 and ch. 5 of Acts. After having stated in exact terms that the Sanhedrin took the apostles for 'illiterate and ignorant men' (v. 13), ch. 4 relates that they concluded that it was necessary to give them a legal caution, putting them on their guard ($\dot{a}\pi\epsilon\iota\lambda\dot{\epsilon}\omega$, v. 17)[44] against the penalty they would draw down upon themselves by continuing their preaching.[45] This caution is explicitly recalled

[41] K. Bornhäuser, *Studien zur Apostelgeschichte*, Gütersloh, 1934, p. 58 (see earlier in the *Neue Kirchl. Zeitschrift*, 1922, XXXIII, pp. 332ff). The remark completes the criticisms addressed to Harnack by K. L. Schmidt, *Die Pfingsterzählung*, pp. 24–27: apart from the scenes that deal with the summons before the Sanhedrin, this writer shows that there is no occasion to speak of parallelism in regard to what remains: 'summaries' which repeat themselves, discourses which form a section apart, all this in connection with a few anecdotes which, though they vary, should be left as they are.

[42] *Art. cit.*, pp. 208–13.

[43] Thus we can understand the development between Mark 2.23–28 and 3.1–6, and that implied by the juxtaposition of two terms in Acts 9.1: Saul was breathing out threats ('$\dot{a}\pi\epsilon\iota\lambda\hat{\eta}s$: the legal warning) and destruction ($\phi\acute{o}\nu o\nu$: the punishment of habitual criminals) against the disciples of the Lord. We are also reminded of the pattern in Matt. 18.15–17: private reproaches, reproaches before witnesses, excommunication; an analogous pattern in 1 QS v, 25–vi, 1; the reprimand before witnesses should precede legal action (cf. CD IX, 2–18).

[44] $\dot{a}\pi\epsilon\iota\lambda\acute{\eta}$ recurs in v. 29. E. Trocmé remarks in this connection (*op. cit.*, p. 103, n. 2): 'If we admit this interpretation of the double appearance before the Sanhedrin, the prayer in Acts 4.24–30 receives a special emphasis: Peter and John, duly warned of what awaits them if they continue their preaching, ask with "their own", that is the whole group of the Twelve (as J. Dupont, "Notes sur les Actes des Apôtres", *Revue Biblique*, 1955, pp. 45ff, has shown) with which they are closely interdependent, for the superhuman strength to announce the Word without taking account of the "warnings" ($\dot{a}\pi\epsilon\iota\lambda\acute{a}s$) of the Jewish authorities.' In the legal language of the Rabbis, this warning is called the hatrâ'âh.

[45] See again v. 21. The members of the Sanhedrin had not found the means to inflict a penalty on the apostles ($\mu\eta\delta\acute{\epsilon}\nu$ $\epsilon\dot{\nu}\rho\acute{\iota}\sigma\kappa o\nu\tau\epsilon s$ $\tau\grave{o}$ $\pi\hat{\omega}s$ $\kappa o\lambda\acute{a}\sigma\omega\nu\tau a\iota$ $a\dot{\nu}\tau o\acute{\nu}s$), and

at the beginning of the debates of ch. 5 (v. 28); it is that, in effect, which enabled the Sanhedrin to envisage the prosecution—the apostles were condemned to scourging with rods (v. 40).[46]

The explanations of Jeremias make the theory according to which Acts 2–5 has recounted the same events twice on the basis of two different sources fall to the ground. But can these explanations be substantiated? W. G. Kümmel thinks so;[47] he considers that Jeremias has shown that the two scenes in which the apostles appear before the Sanhedrin have not the same significance, and that since his explanation it is scarcely possible any longer to maintain the hypothesis of two parallel accounts juxtaposed in Acts 2–5. E. Trocmé[48] also considers that Jeremias has supplied the key to the two appearances of the apostles before the Sanhedrin; at most it may be wondered whether Luke clearly grasped the precise import of the Jewish procedure which his narrative presupposes rather than sets forth. It seems to us clear, indeed, that Luke has not taken much trouble to penetrate the mysteries of rabbinical jurisprudence, or to help his reader to penetrate them. Thus it is true to say that Luke's presentation does not perfectly correspond to the way in which Jeremias reconstructs the events from the text. On this point we can admit that E. Haenchen[49] is right. We shall not follow him, however, when he simply rejects Jeremias's interpretation. It should rather be thought that this interpretation applies to a

---

in the face of the attitude of Peter, determined to obey God rather than men, they contented themselves with a fresh threatening warning (προσαπειλησάμενοι). Cf. Jeremias, pp. 212ff.

[46] A mitigated form of an acquittal in a criminal trial which the enemies of the apostles would have liked to end in a capital sentence (v. 33: ἐβούλοντο ἀνελεῖν αὐτούς) the intervention of Gamaliel, representing the the Pharisees' party, did not allow the Sadducees (4.1; 5.17) to obtain what they wanted. The solution adopted by the Sanhedrin according to Acts 5.40 is practically the one that Pilate put forward in regard to Jesus in Luke 23.16: release after a punishment which would serve as correction.

[47] *Theologische Rundschau*, 1942, XIV, p. 169. See also V. Wilckens, *Die Missionsreden*, p. 9, n. 5.

[48] *Op. cit.*, pp. 102f.

[49] pp. 212–15 of the 1956 edition, or 209–11 of the 1959 edition (revised and taking account of the work of Bo Reicke, which will be discussed later).

state of tradition earlier than that of the compiling of Acts; the fact that Luke places the events in a different light from that they had originally does not imply that an explanation supported by certain indications in the text and by knowledge of what actually were the legal customs of the Jews is valueless for the exegete who would discern the form in which a particular tradition reached Luke.[50] If Haenchen rejects the exegesis of Jeremias, it is because it seems to him to give too great a unity to the series of pericopes in ch. 4 and 5 of Acts, whereas he can only see them as disconnected fragments.

To the objections that Bo Reicke[51] raises against Jeremias, we must give rather more attention—clearly their intention is to bring back into favour the idea of the two parallel accounts relating to the same events.[52]

[50] Haenchen makes a concrete objection: Jeremias sees in the information of 4.13: καταλαβόμενοι ὅτι ἄνθρωποι ἀγράμματοι εἰσιν καὶ ἰδιῶται a remark which assumes its full meaning in the context of a legal prescription requiring a previous warning to persons in this particular case. Haenchen replies: the verse links this indication not with the necessity of a warning but with the consternation that the παρρησία of the apostles causes the magistrates. This assurance is astonishing on the part of men without culture. The remark is perfectly true. But no one will dream of assigning to a tradition earlier than Luke this idea of the apostolic παρρησία, a feature which characterizes his editing (cf. Acts 2.29; 4.13, 29.31; 9.27, 28; 13.46; 14.3; 18.26; 19.8; 26.26; 28.31) and is generally applicable to Paul, but also attributed to the Twelve; the use of this term is typically Pauline and Lucan (Mark uses it once, John nine times, but in a different sense). On the other hand, it must be admitted that the manner in which Luke characterizes the apostles is harsh, ἀγράμματοι καὶ ἰδιῶται (particularly as coming from him; note that D omits the second term) and runs counter to the care he generally takes to surround them with respect. It is not arbitrary to wonder if, in using such expressions, Luke was not depending on an earlier tradition; but it is not to a tradition of this kind that he owes the idea of παρρησία, which seeks to give a meaning to the remark on the apostles' lack of instruction. Supposing this remark had been found in an earlier tradition, it must have been related to another context; Jeremias has indicated a legal context which gives it an entirely satisfactory import.

[51] Bo Reicke, Glaube und Leben der Urgemeinde, Bemerkungen zu Apg. 1-7 (Abhandlungen zur Theol. des A. und N.T., 32), Zurich, 1957, pp. 108-10. The writer presented his hypothesis for the first time in the article 'Den äldsta jerusalemforsamlingens liv enligt tvenne parallela traditioner', Svenska Jerusalemforeningens Tidskrift, 949, XLVIII, pp. 37-42.

[52] A theory developed particularly on pp. 15f and 108-14. A word must be said of G. H. C. Macgregor, The Acts of the Apostles (The Interpreter's Bible, IX), New York—Nashville, 1954, pp. 17f and 81. Rather inadequately informed as to the present state of the questions (for example, he does not know the study of Jeremias), this writer seeks to reconcile the explanations of Harnack with those of Torrey: the doublets of ch. 2-5 create a strong presumption in favour of two parallel written sources and a source coming from Jerusalem can only have been written in

The Observations of Reicke

Reicke divides the narratives of the first chapters of Acts not according to the manner of Harnack, but according to that of Beyer[53]—on the one hand, 2.42–4.31; on the other, 4.32–5.42. Between these two series he discovers a remarkable symmetry:[54]

First theme: the common life (2.42–47; 4.32–5.14)

1. Common life—2.41 and 4.32–37;
2. The assembly is in fear—2.43a and 5.1–11;
3. Signs and wonders—2.43b and 5.12a;
4. Common life—2.44–47a and 5.12b;
5. Favour of the people—2.47b and 5.13;
6. Increase of the community—2.47c and 5.14.

Second theme: persecution by the Sadducees (3.1–4.31; 5.15–42)

1. Miraculous cure(s)—3.1–11 and 5.15–16;
2. Preaching in the Temple—3.12–26 and 5.17–21a;
3. Arrest of the apostles—4.1–4 and 5.21b–26;
4. Appearance before the Sanhedrin—4.5–7 and 5.27–28;
5. Peter's defence—4.8–14 and 5.29–33;
6. Private deliberation of the Sanhedrin—4.15–16 and 5.34–39a;
7. Sentence of the tribunal—4.17–20 and 5.39b–40a;
8. The apostles set at liberty—4.21–22 and 5.40h;
9. Thanksgiving—4.23–30 and 5.41;
10. The preaching continues—4.31 and 5.42.

Aramaic. Let us also quote as a reminder a writer of whom we have scarcely had occasion to speak, since he has been little concerned with the kind of problems to which this study is devoted: F. F. Bruce, *The Acts of the Apostles. The Greek Text with Introduction and Commentary*, 2nd ed., London, 1952; *Commentary on the book of the Acts. The English Text with Introduction, Exposition and Notes* (The New London Comm. on the N.T.), London—Edinburgh, 2nd ed. 1956. The same is true of the commentary, already cited, of C. W. Carter and R. Earle (1959). As to that of C. S. C. Williams (1957), it gives a few indications on the opinions in question, but without taking up any personal position.

[53] Reicke does not cite it, but refers us to his predecessors, Ed. Zeller and F. Overbeck.

[54] Developed at length in pp. 55–108.

Equally close resemblances show that ch. 3–5 rests on two parallel traditions coming down to Luke in a finally completed form. Their divergences justify us in thinking of a more or less prolonged oral transmission; it is not possible to arrive at certainty as to their being put into writing before the composition of Acts. Between these two traditions Luke has endeavoured to indicate a continuity; that, however, is only a matter of literary arrangement. 'It is doubtful whether the apostles were arrested twice in succession in the way indicated. The double description finds its most probable explanation in the simple fact that Luke happened to have these two traditions at his disposal; he repeated them not because he had a predilection for doublets, but primarily because he needed narrative material to fill up a relatively long interval.'[55]

Reicke finds himself obliged to refute the hypothesis of Jeremias.[56] In ch. 4 and 5 he sees two stages of a homogeneous juridical process, and therefore the hypothesis is clearly not compatible with the imposing structure that is presented to us. Reicke makes two objections—(1) it is arbitrary to exclude the 'summaries' which describe the life of the community and concern oneself only with the rest; (2) ch. 4 does not speak of a legal caution but of an arrest and trial; the high priests, of whom it is said that they were 'filled with envy' (5.17), would not have had recourse to a procedure so favourable to the accused. Moreover, the caution normally followed quite a different form—it was given in private, by two witnesses who had surprised the culprits in the act of committing the crime.[57]

These objections seem to us weak and insufficient to invalidate the explanation of Jeremias. (1) Jeremias brings forward valid reasons (see also P. Benoit) to justify the special treatment which must be reserved for the 'summaries' in 2.42–47; 4.32–35, and 5.12–15; these three 'general pictures' are closely related

[55] p. 113.
[56] p. 108, n. 43.
[57] The second objection is repeated by Haenchen (*Die Apg.*, p. 209). Like Reicke, he considers as self-evident the fact that the apostles incurred no serious danger in appearing before the Sanhedrin, and that the warning should have been made in private by two witnesses, at the very moment when the apostles were guilty.

and raise identical literary problems. It is not possible to insert them in the pattern of two parallel traditions. The same remark applies to the examples of apostolic preaching in 3.12–26; 4.8–12, and 5.29–32. (2) Jeremias accepts the perspective of a criminal trial, emphasizing the indication of 5.33—ἐβούλοντο applies to the examples of apostolic preaching in 3.12–26; ἀνελεῖν αὐτούς. Reicke admits that in this case the warning might have been necessary; but, he says, the animosity of the Sadducees would not have led them to adopt this procedure. To this it may be replied that this animosity (the trait is very characteristic of Luke)[58] did not dispense them from reckoning with the Pharisees, who also formed part of the Sanhedrin. For want of a previous warning, the first trial could not lead to a condemnation; the warning would thus be given before the whole Sanhedrin—an extraordinary procedure, but one imposed by the circumstances. Jeremias has indicated the features in ch. 4 which justify us in thinking that this was what was actually done.

So far the hypothesis of Jeremias does not seem to have met with criticism which would necessitate our rejecting it, and with it the idea that the two appearances of the apostles before the Sanhedrin constitute two stages of the same legal proceedings. As to Reicke's imposing symmetrical structures, it seems to us superfluous to discuss them in detail—they will awaken no interest—at least, for the honour of professional scripture scholarship, it is desirable they should not do so.[59]

---

[58] ἐπλήσθησαν ζήλου. πίμπλημι is employed twenty-four times in the N.T.: twice by Matthew, thirteen times by Luke in his Gospel and nine times in Acts; for ζῆλος cf. Acts 7.9; 13.45; 17.5 (no instance in the Synoptics; found once in John in another sense). Let us recall, from the point of view of the method to be followed, that we have made a similar point in regard to the argument that Haenchen draws from the use of the word παρρησία.

[59] We must also mention a curious note by A. E. Häfner, 'The Bridge Between Mark and Acts', *Journ. of Bibl. Lit.*, 1958, LXXVII, pp. 67–71. The writer sets out from a twofold presupposition: (1) the presence of two distinct sources underlying Acts 2–5, the argument (Harnack on the one hand, Foakes Jackson–Kirsopp Lake on the other) only bearing on the detail of what is to be attributed to these sources; (2) since the Gospel of Mark does not end with Mark 16.8, there is a case for looking for its prolongation in the first chapters of Acts, more particularly in the passages derived from source A. One difficulty comes to the fore: there is no link between Mark 16.8 and Acts 3.1ff. Häfner, in point of fact, seeks to show that

The attempts made up to the present to explain the composition of Acts, or of considerable sections of the book, by the combination or juxtaposition of two parallel sources have not led to convincing results.

---

the 'bridge' or intermediate link between these two passages is to be found in Acts 1.13–14. This reconstruction of the primitive sequence of the end of Mark calls for two remarks: (1) the apostles had not left again for Galilee for the good reason that the women had not transmitted the angel's message (Mark 16.7); (2) faith in the Resurrection was born not as a result of apparitions of the risen Christ, but of the miracle of Acts 3.1ff; men noticed, not without surprise, that the name of Jesus was capable of effecting a cure, and from that it was concluded that Jesus was alive. This torrent of conjectures shows more imagination than critical sense. We cannot take seriously this tradition about the Resurrection which would ignore all the apparitions, contrary to all the traditions which have come down to us, beginning with I Corinthians 15.5. As regards the angelic message which the women had not transmitted (but of which the evangelists were, however, aware) Häfner has overlooked the fact that it constitutes a simple reminder of what Jesus had said to his intimate followers before his Passion: Mark 14.28; from the literary point of view, these two indications in Mark 14.28 and 16.7 appear to be the preparation of the account of an apparition in Galilee and it is legitimate to think that it was with that that the Gospel ended.

III

COMPLEMENTARY SOURCES

THE DISTINCTION which we have established between hypotheses which explain the composition of Acts by the juxtaposition of two parallel sources and those which presuppose a
combination of complementary sources, only approximately
corresponds to the opinions expressed by scholars. We have, for
instance, ranked Harnack among those who believe there were
parallel sources; we are thus emphasizing the characteristic
feature of his interpretation of ch. 2–5 of Acts. In the following
chapters (6–15), however, he prefers to see an amalgam of
complementary sources: Antioch source (6.1–8.4; 11.19–30;
12.25–15.35), Jerusalem-Caesarea source (8.5–40; 9.29–11.18;
12.1–24), probable extension of the Jerusalem source A (3.1–
5.16), lastly a private source which supplied the account of
Paul's conversion (9.1–28). This division offers further parallels,
11.27–30 and 15.1–35, appearing as two accounts of the same
event, the one from the Jerusalem and the other from the
Antioch viewpoint. With Foakes Jackson and Kirsopp Lake it
would also be possible to speak of two parallel traditions concerning the foundation of the Church of Caesarea, the one
attributing this foundation to Philip, the other to Peter. Taking
it by and large, however, the hypothesis of parallel sources is
often completed by an appeal to complementary sources. We
admit quite frankly that our distinction is not adequate; it
simply helps to bring to the fore what seems to us to constitute
a more particular characteristic of the hypotheses grouped
together in this way.

The Earlier Theories

It is possible to begin this survey with the first attempts at distinguishing sources in Acts, at the end of the eighteenth century. In 1798, B. L. Königsmann[1] thought we should conclude from Luke's prologue that the author of the third Gospel and of the Acts was not to be ranked among the eyewitnesses of the events he narrates; he would thus not be the same person as the writer who says 'we' in certain passages of Acts—the 'we' passages are evidence of the use of a source. The diversity of style likewise attests that the narratives of Acts were based on different sources; Königsmann did not seek to determine them further. In 1801, W. K. L. Ziegler[2] suspected the presence of a varied documentation behind the narratives of the first part of Acts. In regard to the information concerning Peter, he recalled that the Fathers speak of 'Acts of Peter' and of a 'Gospel of Peter'; the accounts of the martyrdom of Stephen and the conversion of Paul come from written sources. Fr Schleiermacher[3] did not believe any more than Königsmann did that Acts was composed by a companion of Paul. He thought that an unknown compiler, working during the last years of the first century, used written sources coming from Jerusalem, Antioch and Ephesus and a travel diary, probably composed by Timothy (whence the 'we' of several passages of the second part of the book); and that a source, translated from the Aramaic by Hellenists, supplied the missionary discourses.

In 1847, E. A. Schwanbeck[4] endeavoured to arrive at a greater accuracy in the distribution of sources. The compiler of

---

[1] B. L. Königsmann, *De fontibus commentariorum sacrorum qui Lucae nomen praeferunt deque eorum consilio et aetate*, Altona, 1798. We have not been able to consult this study, but have summarized it according to A. C. McGiffert, *art. cit.*, p. 385.

[2] W. K. L. Ziegler, 'Ueber den Zweck, die Quellen und die Interpolationen der Apostelgeschichte', in *Gablers neuestes theologisches Journal*, 1801, VII, pp. 125ff. Article summarized at second hand.

[3] Schleiermacher published his conclusions on the third Gospel and its sources in 1817–*Ueber die Schriften des Lukas, ein kritischer Versuch*. His course on the Acts of the Apostles was not published until after his death—*Vorlesungen über Einleitung ins Neue Testament* (Sämtliche Werke, 1/8, Berlin, 1845, pp. 344–79). Schleiermacher took up his stand against the conclusions of the Dutch exegete J. C. Riehm, *Dissertatio critico-theologica de fontibus Actuum Apostolorum*, Utrecht, 1821, who attributed to Luke, the companion of Paul, the composition of all the second part of Acts; in the first part, centred on Peter, Luke would use different sources, which it is no longer possible to identify in detail.

[4] E. A. Schwanbeck, *Ueber die Quellen der Schriften des Lukas, I. Ueber die Quellen der Apostelgeschichte*, Dannstadt, 1847. Not having been able to consult this work and

Acts used (1) a biography of Peter (1–6.7; ch. 8; 9.31–11.18);[5] (2) a biography of Barnabas (4.36–37; 9.1–30; 11.19–30; 12.25–14.28; 15.2–4); (3) an account of Stephen's martyrdom (6.8–7.59; 8.2); (4) memoirs drawn up by Silas (from 15.14 to the end).[6] H. A. W. Meyer[7] accepts the idea of a source (doubtless in Hebrew) concerning Peter, of another concerning Stephen and of a mission narrative (ch. 13–14, etc.) which perhaps formed part of the story of Stephen; but he rejects the idea of a special writing devoted to Barnabas.[8]

In 1886 Bernard Weiss opened the second phase of the source-criticism, and it was in 1891 that F. Spitta inaugurated the system of the two parallel sources A and B. As far back as 1893, Johannes Weiss,[9] son of Bernard, took his stand in favour of Spitta, but introducing such modifications as to transform the

---

judging the summaries of Foakes Jackson–Kirsopp Lake (*Beginnings*, II, p. 123), McGiffert (*ibid.*, p. 387), Haenchen (*Apg.* 24), insufficient, we have based ourselves on the analysis of Ed. Zeller, *Die Apostelgeschichte* (1854), pp. 490ff (see in particular 494f). In this connection we should like to draw attention to another writer, somewhat neutral but well informed on the works of his predecessors—O. Zöckler, *Die Apostelgeschichte als Gegenstand höherer und niederer Kritik* in *Griefswalder Studien. Theologische Abhandlungen Hermann Cremer*, Gutersloh, 1895, pp. 107–45; more briefly, in *Die Apostelgeschichte* (Strack–Zöckler's Komm. zu den hl. Schriften A. u. N.T., B. Neues Testament, II Abt., 2 Heft.), 2nd ed., Munich, 1895, pp. 150–6.

[5] Zeller wrote—ch. 8, ch. 9, 11–13, 18 (p. 495). This is clearly a mistake. Foakes Jackson–Kirsopp Lake (*loc. cit.*), followed by Jacquier (p. cxxxviii) have made a further one in correcting it—ch. 8 and ch. 11, 1–18; a glance at the context shows that the correct reading is ch. 8 and ch. 9.31 to 11.18.

[6] 15, 3–13 is a passage drawn from other sources. A much simpler explanation is presented by H. Ewald, *Geschichte des apostolischen Zeitalters* (Geschichte des Volkes Israels, VI), 3rd ed., Göttingen, 1868; *Die Bücher des Neuen Testaments*, vol. II, 2nd ed., Göttingen, 1872—Luke, the physician, compiled Acts; for the first part he had at his disposal two Judaeo-Christian sources: a history of Peter, fairly homogeneous (ch. 1–5; 8.5–40; 9.32–11.32), a history of Stephen and of Saul, more composite (6.1–8.4; 9.1–31).

[7] H. A. W. Meyer, *Kritisch-exegetisches Handbuch über die Apostelgeschichte* (Krit.-exeg. Komm. über das N.T., 3 Abt.), 3rd ed., Göttingen, 1861, p. 12.

[8] In 1885, A. Jacobsen attributed to a *Barnabasquelle* the basis of ch. 13–15: *Die Quellen der Apostelgeschichte*, Berlin, 1885, pp. 16–21.

[9] J. Weiss, 'Das Judenchristentum in der Apostelgeschichte und das sogenannte Apostelkonkil', *Theol. Studien und Kritiken*, 1893, III, pp. 480–540; see also *id.*, 'Die Chronologie der Paulinischen Briefe', *ibid.*, 1895, V, pp. 252–96. We have only an indirect knowledge of these two articles. On the other hand, we have been able to consult *Ueber die Absicht und den literarischen Charakter der Apostel-Geschichte*, Marburg, 1897 (Weiss seeks to disregard the question of sources), and *Das Urchristentum* of which the first part appeared in Göttingen in 1914 (Weiss summarizes on p. 7 the idea he has formed of the sources of Acts and on pp. 195ff the reasons for seeing two

hypothesis entirely. He attributes to source B the whole of the
narratives in Acts 1–5. Source A, Antiochene or Hellenistic,
only appears from ch. 6 onwards. It was in ch. 15, the specific
subject of his study, that J. Weiss thought the two sources could
be seen to meet, A supplying vv. 1–4 and 12, B vv. 5–11 and
13–33 (the names of Paul and Barnabas in vv. 22 and 25 to be
suppressed). Even in this ch. 15 it is impossible to speak of
properly parallel sources, for the account borrowed from source
B is concerned with an event later than that originating from
source A. We are thus dealing with two complementary sources.
The Antioch source underlies 6.1–8.4; 11.19–30; 13–14, a few
verses of ch. 15; it seems to be continued in the travel diary
which forms the basis of the second part of the book. Source B,
Judaeo-Christian in inspiration, supplies 1–5; 9.31–11.18 (Weiss
hesitates for 9.1–30), ch. 12 and a part of ch. 15.[10]

---

sources in ch. 15). An American edition of this work has been published by F. C.
Grant: *Earliest Christianity*. A History of the Period A.D. 30–150 (Harper Torchbooks), vol. I, New York, 1959 (see p. 9 and pp. 261–3).

[10] We must mention for sake of completeness the somewhat complicated
hypothesis suggested by C. Clemen, *Die Chronologie der Paulinischen Briefe ausf neue
untersucht*, Halle, 1893, pp. 58–61; 'Die Zusammensetzung von Apg. 1–5', *Theol.
Studien und Kritiken*, 1895, V, pp. 297–365. Clemen thought he could identify three
principal sources and three different editors. At the outset, a *History of the Hellenists*,
which recounted the martyrdom of Stephen and the foundation of the Church at
Antioch (the substance of 6.9–8.1; 11.19–21, 24a, 26). After it had been rewritten
and interpolations had been introduced, this document was inserted in a *History of
Peter*, which at the same time grouped other minor narratives relating to the community in Jerusalem, to the institution of deacons, to the episodes of Simon Magus
and of the Ethiopian eunuch (the main content of ch. 1–5; 6.7, 8, 11–15; 7.37–60;
8.2, 4–13, 18–24, 26–40). Another group would have as its basis travel recollections
edited by Luke in the 'we' style; added to by a certain number of legendary
anecdotes, these recollections would have been incorporated in an *Itinerary of Paul*,
which must itself have served as a basis for the composition of a *History of Paul* (the
content of 9.1–31 and ch. 13 to the end). To the original editor are attributed the
additions made to the *History of Paul* (14.8–18; 16.23b–34; 17.18–33; 18.12–17;
19.11–13, 15–41; 20.17–35). Then a Jewish-minded editor, working between the
years 97 and 117, collected in a single work the *History of Peter* and the *History of
Paul*, not without adding to it a number of new elements (9.32–43; 10.1–11, 18;
15.1–4, 13–18, 20–22; 16.1–3; 20.20b–26; 22.1–16, 19–21; 23.1–10; 24.10–21;
28.16–29). Finally, an anti-Jewish editor undertook a complete remodelling of the
work at the time of Hadrian; he made use of the Pauline epistles, of Flavius
Josephus, and again added a series of episodes; his imprint was recognizable in
9.1–31; 12.1–25; in certain elements of ch. 13–14; in 15.5–12, 19, 23–33, 41; 19.4,
6, 14; 20.19b, 25–35, 38a; 23.25–30, etc. It should be noted that Clemen shows

In a series of articles published in 1895 and 1896, A. Hilgen-feld[11] thought he had discovered three sources behind the Acts of the Apostles: (1) Acts of Peter, Judaeo-Christian in inspiration (1.15–5.42; 9.32–42; 11.2D; 12.1–23); (2) Acts of the Seven, of Hellenistic inspiration (6.1–8.40); (3) Acts of Paul, written in Antioch, probably by Luke (vestiges of them would be found in 7.58b–8.1a, 3; 9.1–30; 11.27–29; and in ch. 13–28). These three sources were probably revised and considerable additions made to them by an editor anxious to show that Paul was perfectly in agreement with Peter and with Peter's conception of Christianity.

J. de Zwaan, in 1920,[12] distinguished three sources in the first part of Acts: (1) a document written in Aramaic underlies 1.3–5.16 and 9.31–11.18, composed shortly before the Jewish revolt; (2) a Caesarean tradition, to which should be attached 8.4–40; 12.1–24. Luke must have received it during his stay in Caesarea, about 57–59, and it is doubtful whether it reached him in a written form; (3) a tradition associated with Antioch and Jerusalem supplied 5.17–8.3; 11.19–30; 12.25–15.35; doubtless a simple oral tradition,[13] and difficult to date (between 50 and 70?). In addition to these three sources, Acts makes use of material coming from Luke: 9.1–30 and from 15.36 to the end. As it contains the 'we' passages, this material must go back to the years 56–62. Luke used all these data to compose, towards 75–80, the outline of the book that he wanted to publish. He did not have the opportunity to put the final touch

---

himself more reserved in his work *Die Apostelgeschichte im Lichte der neueren text, quellen und kritischen Forschungen*, Giessen, 1905 (cf. pp. 15–35). See also *Paulus, sein Leben und Wirken*, vol. I, Giessen, 1904, pp. 169ff—the first part of Acts used a source which is only perceptible in certain passages (especially 7.58ff and 11.19), whereas another source is more clearly manifest in the second part of the book.

[11] A. Hilgenfeld, 'Die Apostelgeschichte nach ihren Quellenschriften unter-sucht', *Zeitschr. für wissenschaftl. Theol.*, 1895, XXXVIII, pp. 65–114, 186–217, 384–446, 481–516; 1896, XXXIX, pp. 24–78, 177–216, 351–87, 517–57. See again the same review 1899, XLII: *Das Aposteldekret nach seinem ursprünglichen Wortlaut* (pp. 138ff); *Nachwort zu Acta apostolorum graece et latine* (pp. 382ff).
[12] *De Handelingen der Apostelen*, pp. 10–15.
[13] Except for the discourse of Stephen, ch. 7, which seems to be based on an Aramaic source.

to it and publish his work; an editor took charge of this, under Trajan (about 110), after a revision which gave Acts the form in which it has come down to us.[14]

In 1909, E. de Faye admitted only a single written source behind the first fourteen chapters of Acts;[15] in 1921, he admitted two other sources side by side with this fundamental source.[16] It is to a written source, more recent in origin, that the idea must be attributed that Pentecost was accompanied by a miracle of tongues (2.2, 3, 6, 8, 11), that community of possessions was obligatory in the early Church (2.44, 45; 4.32, 34, 35), and that Stephen was judged before a tribunal (6.12b–15; 7.55, 58b, 59). The third source supplied more highly developed accounts, such as those of 8.4–40; 9.32–11.18; 12.1–24. The editor, finally, has not hesitated to touch up his sources and make interpolations in them; we can recognize the idea he has

---

[14] Much more cautious positions in the voluminous monograph of A. Wikenhauser, *Die Apostelgeschichte und ihr Geschichtswert* (Neutestl. Abhandlungen, VIII 3–5), Munster—W., 1921, pp. 81–87. In view of the enormous mass of concrete and specific information contained in Acts, it is probable that the composition of the work is based, at least in part, on written notes. As regards the first part of the book, Wikenhauser thought it possible to distinguish six groups of traditions in the text—(A) the primitive community (1.1–5.42); (B) the episode of Stephen (6.1–8.3); (C) the pericope of Philip (8.4–40); (D) the conversion of Paul (9.1–30); (E) a journey of Peter's (9.32–11.18); (F) the history of the Church of Antioch (11.19–30; 12.25ff). These groups have each their own point of view; the links which bind them together are loose. It would seem more or less normal to attribute a particular origin to each of them; in this sense, it is possible to speak of a Jerusalem tradition, a Hellenistic, Caesarean, Antioch tradition. . . . But have we the right to speak of written sources? It is possible, even probable, that Luke received a certain amount of this information in written form; but it is impossible to arrive at real certainty in a given case. None of the hypotheses offered is convincing and Wikenhauser gave up trying to present a new one. He showed himself favourable to the idea that the discourse of Stephen might be supported by a written source. Wikenhauser returned to the question in his commentary—*Die Apostelgeschichte* (Regensburger N.T., 5), Ratisbon, 1938 (3rd ed. reviewed 1956, pp. 11ff). The source containing the discourse of Stephen could have contained the whole episode 6.1–7.60; moreover, ch. 2–5 are probably based on written information. Wikenhauser again devoted a paragraph to the sources of Acts in his *Einleitung in das Neue Testament*, Freiburg-im-Breisgau, 1953 (4th ed., 1961, pp. 232–4). At the present time it is realized that it is impossible to prove the use of written sources in the first half of Acts; people prefer to admit that the author used a certain number of particular traditions, certain of which had perhaps already been fixed in written form.

[15] See above, pp. 23f.

[16] 'De la valeur documentaire du livre des Actes', *Revue d'Histoire et de Philosophie Religieuses*, 1921, I, pp. 301–16.

formed of the apostolic age (for instance 2.41; 6.7; 14.23; the whole of 5.17–42; 9.1–30; ch. 15 and the discourses).

Cerfaux's Theories

In 1936, L. Cerfaux[17] undertook, from a close examination of the texts, a new examination of Harnack's hypothesis; this brought him to conclusions that were both subtle and complicated. In the first part of Acts he recognized a single document forming a coherent whole with clearly marked features— the section 2.41–5.40. Side by side with this document, a whole group of traditions linked with Caesarea; this group is not homogeneous. Cerfaux distinguished in it C^1 (1.15–2.40), which would seem to be based on a written source; C^2 (8.1b–13.26–40), for which Luke seems to have had at his disposal notes which he made at Caesarea; C^3 (9.1–30) constituted by oral traditions; C^4 (9.31–10.48) using a document; and C^5 based on oral information. Two passages seem to derive from a 'Hellenistic dossier' supplying material which was already composite: 5.41–8.1a and 11.19–30. Finally, a Galilaean tradition in 1.1–14 should be mentioned. The compiler has put his stamp everywhere; a few passages are more particularly attributable to him: 8.14–25; 11.1–18.

The most important point of this reconstruction is without doubt the existence of a single descriptive document reproduced, with slight modifications, in the section 2.41–5.40. Cerfaux took up the study of this section again in an article in 1939.[18] The examination of the vocabulary revealed the literary imprint of Luke, but also certain features which seem to indicate the use of documents imposing certain terms which Luke himself would not have chosen. The manner of citing the Old Testament and the evidence we have of Paul's way of quoting

[17] L. Cerfaux, 'La composition de la première partie du Livre des Actes', *Ephem. Theol. Lov.*, 1936, XIII, pp. 667–91. Reproduced in *Recueil Lucien Cerfaux, Études d'exégèse et d'histoire religieuse de Mgr. Cerfaux* (Bibl. Ephem. Theol. Lov., VI–VII), vol. II, Gembloux, 1954, pp. 63–91.
[18] L. Cerfaux, 'La première communauté chrétienne à Jérusalem (Act: II, 41–V, 42)', *Ephem Theol. Lov.*, 1939, XVI, pp. 5–31. Reproduced in *Recueil Cerfaux*, II, pp. 125–6.

in general suggest the same explanation. Other features again point in the same direction—abundance of topographical or historical detail, archaic conceptions and formulae, etc. These data bring us again to the same concrete background, that of Hellenistic Judaism, and more particularly, of the Hellenistic Judaism of Jerusalem. It is the vocabulary of the Hellenists which is reflected in the chapters which Luke has devoted to the primitive community. We are therefore led to conclude

> that he edited his book in accordance with the recollections of the community in Jerusalem. Yet a precise enumeration of the sources and the exact delimitation of their outlines is impossible. It seems to us, however, that we can arrive at the conclusion that Luke made use of written documents. Beneath the style proper to the author of Acts, we can perceive in the section under consideration an unusual vocabulary and turns of phrase; the theology and technical information it contains are just as unexpected. The vocabulary and material of the ideas expressed thus belong to the Hellenistic Judaeo-Christian community. They were at Luke's disposal, probably in passages already written and preserved by the community, narratives, descriptive 'summaries', propaganda and apologetic discourses. . . . In the background of these pieces, there existed a whole literary activity which consisted in collecting from the Old Testament Messianic texts . . .; liturgical prayers, connected both with Jewish liturgical prayers and with the more important Messianic texts, were formulated. . . . This quite primitive literature has left its mark on this particular section of Acts. . . . Since the first part of Acts has preserved certain documents, it is possible to make contact with them, but not of course to define them precisely.[19]

The difference which can be discovered between the positions adopted by Cerfaux in 1936, at the time when, criticizing

---

[19] *Recueil Cerfaux*, II, pp. 155f. Note here the way in which the question of the sources of the first part of Acts is envisaged, somewhat summarily, by W. Barclay, *The Acts of the Apostles* (The Daily Study Bible Series), 2nd ed., Philadelphia, Pa, 1955, pp. xviii–xix. Luke must have had access to two sorts of 'sources'—(a) the recollections preserved in the church of Jerusalem (ch. 1 to 5 and ch. 15), in that of Caesarea (8.26–40 and 9.31–10.48) and in that of Antioch (11.19–30 and 12.25–14.28); (b) episodes concerning the great figures of the Church must have already formed narrative cycles: Acts of Peter, John, Philip, Stephen.

Harnack, he more or less adopted the points of view of the person he was criticizing, and those he maintained in 1939 (and since that date),[20] seems to us highly significant. At the outset, there is talk of a written document, clearly defined, forming a homogeneous whole and marked by characteristic features.[21] At the end of this discussion we are concerned exclusively with a varied documentation going back to a milieu which we seek to discover, whilst at the same time we realize it is impossible to delimit written sources.[22] The evolution which has taken place in this research and in the way of approach to the questions is due, in large part, to the introduction of the methods of form-criticism.

Trocmé's Explanations

Dedicated to the memory of M. Goguel, the work published in 1957 by E. Trocmé[23] is again largely indebted to the methods of

[20] Cf. L. Cerfaux–J. Dupont, *Les Actes des Apôtres* (La sainte Bible . . . de Jerusalem), 2nd ed., Paris, 1958, pp. 8f; L. Cerfaux, 'Les Actes des Apôtres', in A. Robert–A. Feuillet, *Introduction à la Bible*, vol. II, *Nouveau Testament*, Tournai, 1959, pp. 337–74 (cf. pp. 349–55).

[21] Two recent writers have not proceeded beyond this stage, accepting the conclusion to which Cerfaux came in 1936 without any knowledge of the study he published in 1939—C. S. Dessain, 'The Acts of the Apostles', in *A Catholic Commentary on Holy Scripture*, London, 1953, pp. 1019 and 1026; A. Hastings, *Prophet and Witness in Jerusalem. A Study of the Teaching of Saint Luke*, London, 1958, pp. 25 and 125f.

[22] W. G. Kümmel (*Theol. Rundschau*, 1942, XIV, p. 168) severely criticizes the article published by Cerfaux in 1939. Like Cerfaux, he admits that the account of the primitive community in Acts contains information and characteristics that are ancient. What he has against Cerfaux is that he sought to establish the existence of a continuous written source coming from the primitive community, of which Luke made use. The long passage we have cited shows on evidence that Kümmel has misunderstood Cerfaux's intention. His criticisms would be understandable if it were a question of the 1936 article; they are scarcely justified so far as that of 1939 is concerned. The same remark applies to J. Keulers, *De Handelingen der Apostelen* ('De boeken van het N.T.', IV), 2nd ed., Roermond–Maaseik, 1952, p. 12, who, against Cerfaux, expresses the most serious doubts as to the possibility of establishing the existence of a major written source, basing himself on literary peculiarities. The same thing again in J. Renié, *Actes des Apôtres traduits et commentés* ('La Sainte Bible . . .' L. Pirot–A. Clamer, IX/1), Paris, 1949, pp. 21f. Admitting the probability of written documents, he attacks Cerfaux and his view of the sources of the first part of Acts, by stressing that Luke revises and rewrites his documents too much for it to be possible to delimit them with accuracy. This seems also to be Cerfaux's thought, which a too extensive recourse to lexicographical arguments has perhaps put on the wrong track.

[23] *Le 'Livre des Actes' et L'Histoire*. The question of the sources of ch. 1–15 is studied in pp. 154–214.

literary criticism in favour at the beginning of this century. Trocmé thinks he can recognize a certain number of sources in the first part of the Acts.[24] Ch. 3–5 are based on a written homogeneous document; Luke revised this and added to it the discourses, the 'summaries' and the episode of Ananias and Sapphira (5.1–11). In its two sections, ch. 1 reproduces traditions which have been treated fairly freely. Ch. 2 is based on a source; besides minor touches, Luke added to this the geographical list of vv. 7–11, which comes from another document, and the discourse of vv. 22–36 which, like the other missionary sermons, goes back to special documentary sources.[25] In 6.1–7, Luke made use, not without distorting its meaning, of a Hellenistic source. Then comes a series of pericopes which derive from a single source: 6.8–15; 7.55–8.3; 9.1–30; the martyrdom of Stephen and the conversion of Paul were thus joined in the document (Pauline) of which Luke made use to recount these events. Luke was not satisfied with inserting the discourse of Stephen and the story of Philip; he has modified his source and inserted additions in it, such as the episode of Ananias in the story of the conversion of Paul (in practice, 9.1–30 combines, with editorial amplifications, an account of a vocation and that of a cure). In ch. 8, vv. 26–40 depend on a Hellenistic tradition, whilst vv. 5–25 result from the combination of two distinct traditions.[26] From 9.31–13.3, Luke uses a long series of quite small traditional fragments,[27] completing them by pieces of his own composition. From 13.4 onwards, he uses a 'diary' which supplies at least the outlines of the narrative to the end of the book;[28] the apostolic assembly of ch. 15 could be linked up with

[24] Let us recall that Trocmé considers as 'established' the presence of Aramaic sources for Acts 1.1–5, 16, and 9.31–11.18; perhaps also for other fragments of ch. 1–15 (see above, p. 29, n. 43).

[25] Cf. pp. 207–9.

[26] On this point Trocmé took his inspiration from a conjecture of O. Bauernfeind, *Die Apostelgeschichte* (1939), p. 170 (and not pp. 79ff). One of the two accounts opposed Saul to Barjesus, the other Paul to Elymas; the account mentioning 'Paul' could be attached to the 'diary' (pp. 155f).

[27] From 9.31–11.18—three anecdotes relating to Peter; the third combines a 'legend' with a document recounting a vision, without counting the additions of Luke. 11.19–30 is made up of two fragments of the Antioch tradition. In 12.1–23, Luke utilizes a 'legend'. 13.1–3 is another fragment of the Antioch tradition.

[28] We shall again refer to the 'diary' in ch. VII of this study.

some indication of this 'diary', but vv. 5–12 and 23–29 are probably borrowed from a private document.

To sum up: Trocmé seeks to identify a very varied set of documents in which we can recognize two consecutive sources— the one which underlies the two appearances of the apostles before the Sanhedrin (ch. 3 to 5) and that which connects Paul's conversion with the martyrdom of Stephen (ch. 6 to 9). It is our impression that the analyses on which the suggested recon-struction is based will not meet with much favour.[29]

---

[29] F. C. Grant gives a few explanations of the sources of Acts in his work *The Gospels. Their Origin and their Growth*, London, 1959, pp. 126f (an American edition was published in 1957). He distinguishes five groups: (1) an ancient tradition, probably coming from Jerusalem or Judaea and centred on Peter: 1.12–5.42; 9.31–11.18; 12.1–23; (2) a tradition centred on Stephen which could be attached to the Hellenistic group of Jerusalem: 6.1–8.1a; (3) a tradition which seems to have its roots in Caesarea and which concerns Philip: 8.1b–40; (4) an Antioch tradition relating to 'Barnabas and Saul': 4.36f(?); 11.19–30; 12.24–14.28 and from 15.1–16.5; (5) Pauline material—9.1–30; a part of 12.24–14.48 and from 15.1–16.5; the whole of 16.6–28.31.—A fairly simple distribution, as can be seen—but how far can we speak of sources as such? Grant replies: Luke must have possessed a written set of documents (the hypothesis would seem particularly imperative for the dis-course of Stephen in ch. 7; it is also to be recommended in the case of the archaisms of the discourses of Peter), but he has interwoven and rewritten his sources to such a point that it is no longer possible to distinguish or identify them.

IV

THE ANTIOCH SOURCE

TWO ARTICLES which appeared in 1959, one signed by
R. Bultmann, the other by P. Benoit, have given a new lease
of life to the 'Antioch source', one of the sources identified by
the promoters of the old literary criticism. It had never been
entirely lost sight of; earlier, two studies had been devoted to it,
one by H. H. Wendt in 1925, the other by J. Jeremias in 1937.
Harnack's work[1] formed the starting-point for this research.
After having stressed that the narratives of Acts 11.19–30 and
12.25–15.35 were written from an Antioch point of view, he
pointed out that this collection of passages presupposes the
story of the martyrdom of Stephen, 6.1–8.4. Having thus de-
limited the Antioch source, Harnack added that it must have
reached Luke in the form of a written document, at least from
13.4 onwards. Among the writers who have reopened this
question, we may instance J. Weiss,[2] who attached to the
Antioch source 6.1–8.4; 11.19–30 and ch. 13–14; he thinks,
moreover, that the source could well be continued in the travel
narratives of the second part of the book. J. A. Findlay[3] gives a
slightly different distribution, attributing to the Antioch
source 9.1–30; 11.19–30; 12.24–14.28; 15.36–16.9.[4] We shall
not spend time over these different systems, preferring to reserve
our attention for the four studies which have been devoted
specifically to this source.

[1] See above, pp. 35–37.
[2] See above, pp. 53f.
[3] See above, p. 40.
[4] What J. de Zwaan (1920) said of the Jerusalem–Antioch tradition, to which
he attached 5.17–8.3; 11.19–30; 12.25–15.35, should also be recalled. See *supra*,
pp. 55ff.

The Theories of Wendt

As far back as 1899, H. H. Wendt[5] suggested the existence of a source which, though it was not called by that name, bore a considerable resemblance to the Antioch source. Starting from the we-sections, he discovered traces of rewriting which showed that the author of these sections was not to be identified with the writer of Acts; the latter has preserved the 'we' as did the compiler of the books of Esdras–Nehemias for several parts of his work taken from sources written in the first person. Just as interpolations were made in such parts, so the we-sections of Acts are inseparable from their third-person context. Wendt thus imagined as the basis of the second part of Acts a source which recounted the Pauline missions. It must already have contained the story of the first mission, reproduced with interpolations in Acts 13–14 (13.6–12.16–41, 42–52; 14.8–20); it then, he thought, continued in 15.35 (15.1–33 is a further interpolation) and supplied the nucleus of the narrative as far as ch. 21, Paul's arrival in Jerusalem. It reappeared intermittently right to the end of the book, somewhat obliterated by the additions of the compiler. This source could not have begun abruptly with ch. 13; it presupposed an account of the foundation of the Church in Antioch (11.19–21, 26b–29)[6] which in turn linked up with the story of Stephen's martyrdom (6.1–8.4). It doubtless began with a general picture of the Jerusalem community, a picture the elements of which could be found at the basis of the summaries in 2.43–47; 4.32–35; 5.12–15.[7]

Irritated by all the stir made by the hypotheses of Harnack

---

[5] *Die Apostelgeschichte*, 8th edition, revised, of Meyer's *Kommentar*; we have not been able to verify whether Wendt had already put forward the same hypothesis in the earlier editions (1880 and 1888).

[6] Wendt accepts the authenticity of the reading 'we' (D) in v. 28.

[7] In 1913, in the final edition of his commentary (9th ed. in the Meyer series), Wendt completely revised his study on the question of the sources of Acts; after his brief reference to earlier works (pp. 15–21), he provided a more exhaustive and better arranged critical exposition than in the previous edition (pp. 21–40). His conclusions, however, remained substantially the same as those of 1899. One important change (indicated on pp. IIIf)—after reading Norden's *Agnostos Theos* (1913), Wendt considered it essential to relinquish the attachment of the substance of the discourse in Athens (17.22–31) to the *Hauptquelle* of Acts.

and the scant attention paid to his own theories, Wendt defended his views again in an article published in 1925.[8] His general line of argument had not changed; we must note, however, that there was no longer any question of making the source begin before 6.1.[9] He now put the emphasis chiefly on the indications of revisions and interpolations and saw them as indirect testimony to the source which had undergone such changes.[10]

The Theories of Jeremias

In his article in 1937, J. Jeremias[11] decided to subject the hypothesis of an Antioch source as presented by Harnack to a new examination. Acts 6.1 certainly marks a break in the narrative; at the same time new terms make their appearance—Christians called 'disciples',[12] and the 'Hellenists'. The narrative takes on a different tone, giving more detailed information. All these are indications of a new source. To determine its extent we must begin by removing the interpolations with which it is overloaded. Of these Jeremias recognizes four—8.5–40; 9.31–11.18; 12.1–24 15.1–33. Thus to the Antioch source must be attributed 6.1–8.4 9.1–30; 11.19–30; 12.25–14.28; 15.35ff. It would seem that this source continues right

---

[8] H. H. Wendt, 'Die Hauptquelle der Apostelgeschichte', *Zeitschr. für die neutestl. Wiss.*, 1925, XXIV, pp. 293–305. Criticism was chiefly aimed at Ed. Meyer, *Ursprung und Anfänge des Christentums*, III (1923), who supported Harnack's conclusions without taking Wendt's criticisms into account (in the final edition of his commentary in 1913).

[9] The original account presented Stephen's death as a lynching; Luke makes of it an execution in legal form and takes care to mention the presence of Saul (p. 296).

[10] A. Steinmann mentions Antioch traditions for the accounts of 6.1–8.4; 11.19–15.35 (except ch. 12), but is unwilling to pronounce on the question of determining whether Luke received these traditions by word of mouth or in a written form—*Die Apostelgeschichte übersetzt und erklärt* ('Die Heilige Schrift des N.T.', IV), 4th ed., Bonn, 1934, pp. 9f.

[11] The article in which Jeremias criticizes the hypothesis of two parallel sources in Acts 2–5 is 'Untersuchungen zum Quellen problem der Apostelgeschichte', *Zeitschr. für die neutestl. Wiss.*, 1937, XXXVI, pp. 205–21. We are now concerned with the second part of this article: 'Die antiochenische Quelle der Apostelgeschichte und die Datierung der ersten Missionsreise' (pp. 213–21).

[12] This name appears for the first time in 6.1; it recurs twenty-eight times (twenty-nine, counting the feminine of 9.36) between 6.1 and 21.16; it is no longer found in the final chapters.

to the end of the book. It is a source of great value which must have reached the writer of Acts in written form—the interpolations that he has introduced are a proof of this. The historical corollary is that 15.1–33 is a doublet of 11.27–30; 12.25, and that the assembly of the apostles took place before the first missionary journey (13–14).[13]

Jeremias differed from Harnack, as he did from J. Weiss and H. H. Wendt, by including the account of Paul's conversion (Acts 9.1–30) in the Antioch source. He differed from Harnack, but agreed with J. Weiss and H. H. Wendt, in excluding 15.1–33. In 1939, W. Grundmann[14] accepted his explanations in the main, but showed hesitation over the attribution of 9.1–30 to the Antioch source.[15] He added that this source must have begun with an account of the community in Jerusalem or, more precisely, of the two communities, the co-existence of which is demonstrated by 6.1ff.[16]

Jeremias's method is not perfect in every respect.[17] W. G. Kümmel has rightly pointed out that it is not sufficient to expunge (from the narrative) the passages which are clearly accretions, so as to be justified in declaring that the remainder reproduces a homogeneous document.[18] Nor is agreement between the narratives sufficient to justify us in attributing them to one source; it should first be asked whether such agreement does not come from Luke's processes of composition.

[13] An explanation already put forward by Jeremias in his article 'Sabbatjahr und neutestamentliche Chronologie', *Zeitschr. für die neutestl. Wiss.*, 1928, XXVII, pp. 98–103. The reconstruction of the Antioch source such as Jeremias proposes it is referred to favourably and adopted in practice by H. Zimmermann, 'Die Wahl der Sieben (Apg. 6.1–6). Ihre Bedeutung für die Wahrung der Einheit in der Kirche', in *Die Kirche und ihre Amter und Stünde—Festgabe Kardinal Frings*, 1960, pp. 364–78 (cf. 370f).

[14] W. Grundmann, 'Das Problem des hellenistichen Christentums innerhalb der Jerusalemer Urgemeinde', *Zeitschr. für die neutestl. Wiss.*, 1939, XXXVIII, pp. 45–73.

[15] There is a possibility that 9.1–30 was afterwards attached to 7.58b (which is an interpolation) and to 8.3 (p. 55, n. 22).

[16] This source may have supplied certain information incorporated in 2.1–5.42 (p. 54, n. 21); thus perhaps 4.36f (cf. 9, 27): p. 60. Grundmann insists on the composite character of ch. 2–5 and takes very far the process of cutting up the text, basing himself partially on Spitta. See p. 49, n. 10, for ch. 2; pp. 51f for ch. 3 and 4 (3.17–26 had not the same origin as the rest: 3.1–16; and 4.1–31).

[17] *Theol. Rundschau*, 1942, XIV, pp. 169ff.

[18] The agreement between 9.30 and 11.19 is somewhat forced.

Bultmann's Theories

In his article in 1959,[19] R. Bultmann reacts against the scepticism manifested by Haenchen in his commentary on the matter of the written sources of the Acts of the Apostles.[20] In the first place he endeavours to show that it is easier to understand the composition of certain pericopes if we assume that Luke used a written source and contented himself with rewriting it—as, for instance, in his account of the matter in 15.1–35, where Paul and Barnabas are introduced after the event.[21] It is not, however, sufficient to have recourse to a written source to explain a

[19] R. Bultmann, 'Zur Frage nach den Quellen der Apostelgeschichte', in *New Testament Essays, Studies in Memory of Th. W. Manson*, Manchester 1959, pp. 68–80.

[20] A justified reaction, E. Fuchs considers, 'Meditationen zu Ernst Haenchens Kommentar über die lukanische Apostelgeschichte', *Verkündigung und Forschung*, 1958–59 (published in 1960), pp. 67–70 (cf. 68).

[21] In vv. 2.22 and 25f, as in vv. 3–5 and 12, Bultmann refers (reference incomplete and inaccurate) to W. Bousset, 'Der Gebrauch des Kyriostitels für die Quellenscheidung in der ersten Hälfte der Apostelgeschichte', *Zeitschr. für die neutestl. Wiss.*, 1914, XV, pp. 141–62. From Dibelius (*Aufsätze*, p. 89), Bultmann accepted the idea that the decree of vv. 23–29 reproduced a document. We realize, in fact, that it is addressed 'to the brethren of the Gentiles that are at Antioch and in Syria and Cilicia' (v. 23), an indication which does not fit in with the setting of Luke's account. He drew attention, finally, to the inconsistency of the first verses (1–5)—the same conflict breaks out twice, in Antioch (vv. 1–2), then in Jerusalem (v. 5); sent by the community in Antioch to obtain a decision, Paul and Barnabas seem to forget the reason for which they have come to Jerusalem (v. 4).—A further article of Haenchen's replied to these remarks: 'Quellenanalyse und Kompositionsanalyse in Act 15', in *Judentum—Urchristentum-Kirche. Festschrift für Joachim Jeremias* (Beihefte zur Zeitschrift für die neutestl. Wiss. 26), Berlin, 1960, pp. 153–64. Haenchen endeavoured to show (1) that the discourses of Peter and James (vv. 6–21) cannot be attributed to one source—the discourse of Peter presupposes the story of Cornelius such as Luke recounted it in ch. 10–11, the discourse of James is linked with that of Peter and consists essentially in an argument taken from the Septuagint; (2) that the discrepancies shown in vv. 1–5 are purely apparent: the rewriting, if account be taken of the point of view from which the narrative was composed, can be explained without difficulty; (3) that the address of the decree does not limit its scope, but on the contrary enlarges it by linking with the Church in Antioch the communities of the same origin—by mentioning these organizations of Christians, Luke was using a procedure that was familiar to him, consisting of occasionally pointing out the existence of Christian bodies whose foundation he has not recounted. There is no need, then, according to Haenchen, to appeal to written sources; this does not, however, mean that the four prohibitions were simply invented by Luke; he must have had knowledge of them from a (non-written) tradition. In conclusion, all the indications which have been taken as a basis to affirm the use of sources find a sufficient and much more satisfactory explanation in a deeper understanding of the way in which Luke composed his text, of the procedures he made use of, and of the considerations by which he was guided. The question has now cropped up again in the work of B. Gerhardson, *Memory and Manuscript. Oral Tradition and Written Transmission in Rabbinic Judaism and Early*

particular pericope; we must inquire whether or not Luke had an extensive source at his disposal which would account for the linking of the pericopes in a considerable part of the book. Following Dibelius, Haenchen admits that the account of Paul's missions partly depends on an 'itinerary' written in the first person plural. Bultmann expresses agreement, but would have liked more details as to the content of this 'itinerary', as to the pericopes which are linked with it and those which have been added to it. By itself, the use of 'we' is not an adequate criterion—Luke has extended this to passages which do not depend on the 'itinerary' and has not always retained it in those passages he took from that source. However this may be, the presence of the itinerary is unmistakable from ch. 16 onwards; it may be questioned whether it extends as far as ch. 21 (Paul's arrival in Jerusalem, and his arrest) or right to the end of the book. In particular the question of determining where this source begins must be faced. Bultmann considers that its presence would enable us to solve the difficulty raised in 13.2 by the expression 'as they were ministering to the Lord' where the subject 'they' has no explanation in the context; it would be sufficient to admit that Luke has transferred to the third person a detail that his source recounted in the first person—'as we were ministering to the Lord'.[22] At once the 'we-source' can be

Christianity ('Acta Seminarii Neotest. Upsal.', XXII), Uppsala, 1961, pp. 245–61. The debates recounted in ch. 15 of Acts can only be understood in their true meaning in the light of the customs, procedure and formulae of Palestinian Judaism; this remark makes it necessary to consider the account in Acts as a most faithful reflection of ancient traditions and invites us to take the hypothesis of written sources seriously. Gerhardson is a little venturesome in connection with 15.1— this verse sums up the subject of the debate with an accuracy and concision worthy of the best rabbinical traditions—whence the question of ascertaining whether, to compose his account, he had not material of rabbinical type at his disposal (p. 250). Let us not deprive Luke of what is justly his. It is not because the definition of 15.1 is accurate and well phrased that we should refuse to credit him with it; Luke is perfectly capable of summing up a question in a few words. What he did in 15.1 to characterize the point of view of the Judaeo-Christians, he did also in 25.16 to translate a principle of Roman law (cf. our article ' "Aequitas Romana". Notes sur Actes 25, 16', Recherches de Science Rel., 1961, XLIX, pp. 354–85.)

[22] Dann ist in V. 2 die Gemeinde als Subjekt gedacht' (p. 77). Bultmann does not seem disturbed by the fact that his conjecture gives to the verb λειτουργεῖν a

seen to be an Antioch source. We must continue to go back—
11.27–30 and 12.25 must be attached to the same source;
Bultmann admits the authenticity of the Western reading which
uses 'we' in 11.28, 11.27–30 cannot be detached from the
previous verses, 11.19–26, which have, nevertheless, been
touched up by Luke. But 11.19 is attached to 8.4, for it completes a phrase which had remained unfinished; and 8.4 presupposes the story of Stephen, which in turn presupposes the
account of the Hellenist group.

The Antioch source such as Bultmann conceives it, referring
explicitly as he does to Harnack and Jeremias,[23] was thus used
by Luke in Acts 6.1–8.4;[24] 11.19–30; 12.25. It was continued by
an itinerary composed in the first person plural, the indications
of which may be found in 13.3f, 13f, 43f, 48f; 14.1f, 4–6, 21–26;

---

meaning which, although familiar in the vocabulary of certain Christian communities, none the less seems foreign to the New Testament. The error is of the kind
that would be committed by taking the expression 'public service' in the sense of a
service rendered by the public. Etymologically, 'liturgy' does precisely mean
'public service'; such service is the prerogative of those who are invested with a
public function. Taken in the sense of worship, the word designates a minister of the
priestly type. It is in this way that Luke uses λειτουργεῖν in regard to the sacred
functions exercised by Zachary in the Temple (Luke 1.23); the same use is found
in the epistle to the Hebrews (10.11) where in addition the word is chosen to refer
to the risen Christ exercising his priestly functions in the heavenly temple (8.2, 6).
In Rom. 15.16, Paul compares himself to a celebrant (λειτουργόν) accomplishing a
priestly ministry (ἱερουργοῦντα) in preaching the Gospel. The author of the Didache
is completely in line with our text when, after having directed that hands should be
laid on bishops and deacons who are worthy of it, he adds—'for they, too, accom-
plish for you the sacred ministry of the prophets and of the teachers' (ὑμῖν γὰρ
λειτουργοῦσι καὶ αὐτοὶ τὴν λειτουργίαν τῶν προφητῶν καὶ διδασκάλων, 15.1). To
perform a 'liturgy' appertains not to the community taken as a whole, but to
sacred ministers, those whom W. Bauer calls the 'christliche Gemeindebeamten'
(Griechisch — Deutsches Wörterbuch zu den Schriften des Neuen Testaments und der übrigen
urchristlichen Literatur, 5th ed., Berlin, 1958, col. 930f). For further details on this
terminology, we may content ourselves with referring to H. Strathmann–R. Meyer,
art. λειτουργέω, Theol. Wörterb. zum N.T., IV (1942), pp. 221–380 A. Romeo, 'Il
termine λειτουργία nella grecità biblica (Settanta e Nuovo Testamento)', in the
Miscellanea Liturgica in hon. L. C. Mohlberg, vol. II ('Bibl. Ephem. Lit.', 23), Rome,
1949, pp. 467–519. The vocabulary used thus invites us to leave to the Five who
were at the head of the Church in Antioch the accomplishment of the sacred
functions of the liturgy; there is no reason for correcting the text as Bultmann
would wish to do.

[23] 'Thus I think it possible to hold to an Antioch source, such as Harnack and
later Jeremias admitted and tried to reconstruct' (p. 78). Bultmann differs from
Harnack in excluding 15.1–35, from Jeremias in excluding 9.1–30.
[24] 6.12b–15 and 7.1–53, which are interpolations, should be excluded.

then in ch. 16[25] to ch. 21, perhaps even to ch. 28. Bultmann's analyses would seem to take it for granted that a single source is in question; towards the close of his article, however, he states that he is unwilling to take up a position on the connection between the Antioch source and the itinerary and that he even considers it unlikely that these two sources ever formed a literary unity. The writer of Acts, perhaps himself from Antioch, no doubt found these two documents in the archives of the Church there.[26]

The Theories of Benoit

Like J. Weiss in his article in 1893,[27] it was through difficulties raised by ch. 15 of Acts that P. Benoit was brought to concern himself with the sources of Luke.[28] In the first place he makes a

[25] Thus the source is not continued in 15.35, but only in ch. 16, without precise indication. It may be wondered whether Bultmann accepted Schwartz's theory. It would not seem so, since in ch. 14 he extended the source to v. 26, i.e. the verse which brings the missionaries back to Antioch. Then, however, it would follow that the starting point of the new journey must likewise be Antioch? The critics who see in ch. 15 an interpolated section think they can join the two ends of the primitive document together by linking 14.24 with 16.6 or else 14.28 with 15.35; in placing himself half-way between these two hypotheses, Bultmann seems to have chosen a very uncomfortable position.

[26] In the latest edition of his commentary (1959), Haenchen has already been able to reply briefly to Bultmann. He has limited himself to two objections (pp. 75f): (1) It is difficult to see what could have urged the Antioch Christians to compose a chronicle. What interest would they have in so doing when, as Dibelius has pointed out, they were expecting the end of the world at any moment? (2) It is no less difficult to understand why the author of Acts should have tampered with an excellent source, coming from eyewitnesses of the events related. It seems to us clear that remarks of this kind would not be sufficient to compromise the hypothesis at which they are aimed; in saying this, however, we are in no sense claiming that this hypothesis should be considered as justified. With regard to the interest shown by the early Christians in connection with the traditions relative to the activity of the apostles and the foundation of communities, the study of J. Jervell, 'Til sporsmalet om tradisjons grunnlaget for Apostlenes Gjerninger', *Norsk Teol. Tidsskr.*, 1960, LXI, pp. 160–75, may be instanced. Basing himself on the indications supplied by Paul's epistles, the writer shows that the apostolic Church was interested in her own history; clearly, he cannot thereby establish the existence of written documents concerning that history.

[27] See above, pp. 76ff.

[28] P. Benoit, 'La deuxième visite de saint Paul à Jérusalem', *Biblica*, 1959, XL, pp. 778–96; reprinted in *Studia Biblica et Orientalia*, vol. II: *Novum Testamentum* (Analecta Biblica, II), Rome, 1959, pp. 210–24. Benoit does not quote J. Weiss, but refers to the distinction of sources in Acts 15, as presented by Kirsopp Lake (*Beginnings of Christianity*, I/V, p. 203); this, moreover, not without modifying the hypothesis and introducing new theories. Some of the latter bear a certain resemblance to the remarks of Bultmann instanced above (p. 105, n. 20), remarks in turn

general remark. Luke is not content with reproducing the
sources which may have come down to him as they are; he puts
his personal stamp on them and his whole work indicates a
considerable editorial activity. This state of affairs makes any
distinction between written sources and oral traditions very
difficult. 'In more than one case, however, there remain between
the different passages differences of doctrine or vocabulary
sufficiently important to enable us to think of written sources.'[29]
He makes one reservation, however, and it is an important
one—'In any case, even in the very work of editing it is clear
that Luke proceeded in stages, as he did in his Gospel, and
composed passages which he afterwards combined by means of
insertions and link passages which literary criticism should be
able to identify.'[30] Thus the immediate sources of the book are
fragments already edited by Luke; the basic documents can be
identified only in an indirect manner.

Against Jeremias, Benoit supports Harnack in regard to the
account of Paul's call, Acts 9.1–30. This passage should not be
included in the Antioch source. We should see in it a fragment
of Pauline tradition. It is again to the Pauline tradition and not
to the Antioch source that Benoit proposes to attach ch. 13–14.
It is not simply a matter of substituting a homogeneous
Pauline document reproduced just as it is, for the Antioch
source, but of recognizing in Luke's literary activity when he
composed Acts that 13–14 represents an autonomous stage in
his rewriting, a section of his dossier independent of what
precedes, which he was thus easily able to insert into the pattern
of another version. This he did skilfully, no doubt, but not
without producing a certain disruption.[31] To attach 13–14 to

---

inspired by W. Bousset (*Zeitschr. für die neutestl. Wiss.*, 1913, pp. 156–62). The
common source is doubtless J. Weiss; in this connection it is regrettable that a study
discussing Weiss's views has not attracted attention—L. Brun, 'Apostelkoncil und
Aposteldekret. Eine Untersuchung zu AG 15 und GI 2', in L. Brun–A. Fridrichsen,
Paulus und die Urgemeinde, Giessen, 1921, pp. 1–52. The writer defends the literary
unity of ch. 15 of Acts, especially of the first verses; it is only necessary to appeal to a
source for the decree (pp. 3–20).

[29] p. 780.
[30] *Ibid.*
[31] p. 783.

the general pattern, Luke made two joins to introduce these two chapters;[32] 12.25 and 15.1–2[33] to get back to the source he had abandoned in 11.30 (12.1–23 being a first insertion taken from a Palestinian tradition). Thus it would seem that in the Antiochene tradition as it reached Luke the information in 11.27–30 was immediately followed by 15.3–33 (a fragment, moreover, which is composite, conflating two distinct debates into a single account).[34] In 15.35 the version returns to the Pauline tradition abandoned in 14.28. This reconstruction allows us to realize that the journey mentioned in 11.30 is identical with that in question in 15.3ff;[35] its chronological place must be that of ch. 15, i.e. contrary to the hypothesis of Jeremias, *after* the first missionary journey.[36] In the framework of Acts, 11.30 anticipates a later event; the disruption in the chronology is sufficiently explained by reasons of literary composition.[37]

Luke thus transposes different traditions—9.32–11.18 and 12.1–23 belong to Palestinian traditions; 9.1–30; 13.3–14.28

[32] See on pp. 786f some remarks enabling this verse to be looked upon as no more than a link passage.

[33] Different literary observations justify us in speaking of the editorial character of these two verses—pp. 784f.

[34] 'It can be said roughly that v. 13 is the hinge by which we pass from one debate to the other' (p. 792, n. 3). On this distinction of two debates in the narrative of ch. 15, P. Benoit has given an explanation on several occasions—review of O. Cullman's *Saint Pierre* (*Revue Biblique*, 1953, LX, p. 567), discussion with Mgr. Cassien Bésobrasoff on 'La Primauté de Pierre dans le Nouveau Testament' (*Istina*, 1955, II, p. 308); these two studies have been reprinted in the collected work *Exégèse et Théologie*, vol. II, Paris, 1961 (see pp. 254 and 289).

[35] This is also stressed, more summarily, by J. A. Findlay (cf. *supra*, p. 40).

[36] The date of 49 suggested by Jeremias can then be admitted; in the hypothesis of Jeremias, who places the *first* journey after the council, 'we wonder where to situate this journey, since Paul's stay in Corinth in the course of the second journey very probably began as early as autumn 50' (p. 781). According to the theories of Jeremias, the date of 49 would coincide with the worst period of the famine mentioned in 11.28b. We accept this explanation ('La famine sous Claude, Actes, XI, 28', *Rev. Bibl.*, 1955, LXII, pp. 52–55) and Benoit is also in agreement; one writer, it should be pointed out, has just taken his stand in favour of the date 42/43—A. M. Tornos, 'La fecha del hambre de Jerusalén, aludida por Act. II, 28–30', *Estudios Eclesiásticos*, 1959, XXXIII, pp. 303–16; Κατ' ἐκεῖνον δὲ τὸν καιρόν en Act 12. I y simultaneidad de Act. 12 con Act. 11.27–30', *ibid.*, pp. 411–28.

[37] To explain why Luke has not placed the section 13–14 between 11.26 and 11.27, Benoit envisages various factors—the desire to alternate the traditions, insertion of the Palestinian tradition of ch. 12 in a place where the text has just turned the reader's thoughts towards Judaea, the fact that 11.27 is not separated from the parallel case recounted in 22f, duplicating a visit which in point of fact had two distinct results (pp. 789f).

and 15.35ff to Pauline traditions; 11.19–30 and 15.3–33 to Antioch traditions. Benoit's genuinely original contribution lies less in the distribution of these sources and traditions than in the idea he has formed of Luke's processes of composition. 'The sections which Luke dovetails are not so much documents received just as they were, as rewritings by his own hand, first written separately in the course of his researches and afterwards joined and fitted in by him with the help of omissions and link passages to make a complete composition'.[38] The source documents used by Luke were edited by himself in the course of his researches; each of them represents a particular tradition. These different traditions have only succeeded in exercising their influence on the final version through the editorial processes to which the different parts were subjected. Hence the difficulty we experience in grasping the particular features of each of them, and yet at the same time we receive the impression that an editorial process has been going on and that the writer has had access to documents to which he has made additions and which he joins together by means of very obvious link passages. This hypothesis—it is only an hypothesis—restores to favour a suggestion of B. Weiss (1886);[39] it would perhaps merit reconsideration on the basis of a wider investigation.

[38] p. 790.
[39] See above, pp. 25–27.

Part Two

FORM-CRITICISM

V

THE WE-SOURCE

FORM-CRITICISM is concerned with the material that has been incorporated into a narrative such as that of the Gospels or that of Acts; its aim is to classify this material according to the literary forms, then to determine the origin of each group. The way in which such material has reached the writer is here a secondary consideration. Whether he received it from an oral tradition or found some of it already in permanent written form matters little. Similarly, the fact that there may have been particular collections made up of a certain number of written fragments is not of great consequence. These different stages of the genesis of a work are of greater concern to scholars who are investigating the history of the processes of composition. For the last few years such research has aroused new interest. The particular trend of form-criticism has, however, led to the revival from a different point of view of a problem with which the specialists of the source-criticism were already faced—the problem of ascertaining whether the narrative of Paul's journeys in the second part of Acts is made up of scattered pieces of information or whether in its main pattern at least it does not derive from a source that must have been composed, by its very literary form, of a more or less lengthy series of accounts. The notion of this source and the name given to it vary from one writer to another—travel journal, memoirs, itinerary, travel diary are spoken of; in all cases what is in question is a series of events recounted briefly in their chronological order.

The research which has been carried out in this direction will be discussed in the following chapters. Such research presupposes an existing situation which it will be well to outline in the first place—thus we shall here discuss the hypotheses which in the spirit of the source-criticism have recourse to a particular source to explain the origin of several sections of Acts which in recounting events make use of the first person plural—16.10–17; 20.5–15; 21.1–18; 27.1–28, 16.[1]

The classic explanation which has always had and still has supporters, even among those scripture scholars least open to the suspicion of 'conservatism',[2] is that, by the use of 'we', the

---

[1] It is usual to speak of three we-sections. In the first, the narrator is one of Paul's companions from Troas to Philippi; the narrative continues in the third person in 17.1 (the absence of 'we' between 16.18 and 16.40 has no significance—the passage treats of incidents concerning Paul and Silas alone). The second we-section begins at Philippi, at the time when Paul was passing through the town at the end of his last missionary journey (20.5); it continues as far as the arrival in Jerusalem (21.18). It is interrupted by the Miletus discourse (20.17–38), but it is clear that the narrator had no opportunity of indicating his presence in his account of the discourse; nor has the absence of 'we' after 21.18 any significance, since the events did not call for any intervention on the part of the narrator. The third section begins at the moment when Paul leaves Caesarea and continues until the arrival in Rome (28.16); here again it is difficult to define the limit, the end of the narrative being concerned with Paul alone. Several writers think it possible to add to these three we-sections the 'we' found in 11.28 in the Western text—a reading which has been called in question and which it seems preferable to ignore.

[2] For the nineteenth century there are numerous references to German writers in A. C. McGiffert, *The Beginnings of Christianity*, I, II, p. 377. The following is what E. Renan wrote in 1866—'In many places, from v. 10 of ch. 16 onwards, the writer of Acts makes use in his narrative of the pronoun "we", thus indicating that for that particular time he formed part of the band of apostles surrounding Paul. This would seem to prove the fact. There is only one loophole, in fact, by which we may escape the force of such an argument—namely, to suppose that the passages where the pronoun "we" is found have been copied by the final editor of Acts from an earlier MS., from an original memorandum of one of Paul's disciples, of Timothy, for instance, and that the editor, through inadvertence, forgot to substitute the name of the narrator for "we". Such an explanation, however, is scarcely acceptable. At most such negligence would be understandable in a compilation that was clumsy. But the Third Gospel and Acts form a work that is well written, a work of reflection and of a certain style, written by the same hand and in accordance with a consistent plan. The two books together form a whole that is in the same style throughout, offering the same favourite expressions and the same way of quoting Scripture. A fault in the editing as glaring as that in question would be inexplicable. We are thus inevitably led to conclude that the one who wrote the end of the work is the same as the one who wrote the beginning and that the narrator of the whole is the one who wrote "we" in the passages quoted earlier . . . I continue to believe that the final editor of Acts is indeed the disciple of Paul, who says "we" in the last chapters. All the difficulties, however insoluble they may appear, should be, if not thrust aside, at least held in suspense by an argument as decisive as that which results from this word "we" . . .' (*Les Apôtres*, 3rd ed., Paris 1930, pp. xif and xivf). As the problem was stated a century ago, we could not wish for clearer explanations. Since then new factors have developed, but we shall see that writers such as A. Harnack, H. J. Cadbury, M. Dibelius, A. D. Nock and E. Trocmé continue to think that the traditional explanation remains the most satisfying.

writer of Acts is discreetly indicating his presence among the companions of the Apostle's journey. Of all the explanations put forward, this is certainly the simplest and most obvious. Many writers, however, consider it unacceptable, rejecting it for various reasons. We do not intend to dwell on the theological reasons—the differences which exist between the thought of Luke and that of Paul are emphasized, sometimes in an exaggerated and one-sided way, in order to conclude that 'Luke' cannot have known Paul;[3] our own impression is that we shall

[3] A typical example: Ph. Vielhauer, 'Zum "Paulinismus" der Apostelgeschichte', *Evangelische Theologie*, 1950–51, X, 1–15. The author puts forward four outstanding differences between Luke and Paul—(1) their attitude towards *theologia naturalis*, (2) attitude in regard to the Law, (3) Christological conceptions, (4) importance attached to the eschatological expectation. To quote one detail— Vielhauer rightly emphasizes the importance Paul attaches to the title 'Son of God' in Christology; in Acts, 'die Gottessohnschaft Jesu ist Apg. 13.33 "adoptianisch", bei Paulus metaphysisch verstanden und nie mit Ps. 2.7 begründet' (p. 11). It should be noted in the first place that Acts twice uses the title of 'Son of God', and each time to characterize the preaching of Paul (9.20; 13.33). It should further be recalled that in Rom. 1.4, Paul uses this title with specific reference to Ps. 2.7 (cf. M. E. Boismard, 'Constitué Fils de Dieu (Rom. 1.4)', *Rev. Bibl.*, 1953, LX, 5–17). Moreover, is it necessary to emphasize that in speaking of 'adoptionism' in connection with Acts and of 'metaphysics' in connection with Paul, we place their thought in a Greek philosophical context which is wholly foreign to them? (On the so-called 'adoptionism' of Acts, cf. our remarks in *Recherches de Science Religieuse*, 1948, XXXV, pp. 541–3.) A further detail—the eschatological emphasis is not the same in Paul as in Luke. To conclude from this that Luke did not know Paul, it would be necessary to begin by proving that he had necessarily to adopt Paul's ideas on this point. We should then have to show that there are absolutely no shades of meaning in Paul and in Luke which can enable us to find points of contact and that there is no evolution in the epistles. We have devoted a long study to 2 Corinth. 4.7–5.10 and Phil. 1.20–24 (Σὺν Χριστῷ, *L'union avec le Christ suivant St Paul*, I, Bruges-Louvain—Paris, 1952, pp. 115–91). In our opinion Paul took his inspiration from a Greek theme (derived from the *Phaedon*), and thus moved away from the usual framework of Jewish eschatology to envisage the happiness that can be attained by the soul detached from the body. It is clear that, if Vielhauer had found passages of this kind in Acts, he would have hastened to emphasize their incompatibility with the Pauline hope such as he defined it, seeing only one aspect of it—Paul was living in expectation of an early parousia (p. 12). Paul is more complex and, we can go so far as to say, more intelligent than the caricature we have been given of him. As to Luke, who would have nothing further to expect, since the promise was already realized (cf. p. 13), he has none the less written texts such as that of Acts 3.20–21. . . . To draw artificial distinctions of this kind seems to us very puerile. Moreover, it leaves on one side another aspect of the question— that of the points of contact which exist between Luke and Paul; we have already instanced the case of the παρρησία and it would be sufficient to refer to the dissertation of Vielhauer himself for another Pauline theme which is found in Acts, that of 'edification'. (Ph. Vielhauer, *Oikodome. Das Bild vom Bau in der christlichen Litteratur, vom Neuen Testament bis Clemens Alexandrinus*, Heidelberg, 1939). Despite the reservations of W. G. Kümmel (*Theol. Rundschau*, 1954, XXII, pp. 208–10),

not obtain convincing results in this way. Neither shall we spend time on certain difficulties of an historical order—that Luke was badly informed on certain points of the life of Paul;[4] here again there is nothing conclusive. There remain the objections of a literary nature, tending to show that the author of Acts cannot be confused with the writer who, in one of his sources, uses 'we' and ranks himself among Paul's companions. It is remarks of this kind which must engage our attention.

The Nineteenth Century Exegetes

We have already pointed out[5] that as long ago as 1798, B. L. Königsmann thought he could conclude from the prologue of the Gospel that Luke did not count himself among the eye-witnesses of the events to which he devoted his twofold work; the 'we' of the second part of Acts would thus come from one of the sources of which he made use. Königsmann did not try to define the source in question further. His merit in our opinion consists in having sensed the importance of the prologue for the interpretation of the whole work and particularly for that of the we-sections. He was unfortunately mistaken as to the significance of this prologue. We shall return to this point in connection with the work of H. J. Cadbury.

Again, the explanations of F. Schleiermacher and E. A.

Vielhauer's antitheses have made an impression on E. Haenchen who has adopted the same tactics in his commentary (pp. 99–103). An interesting reassessment by W. Eltester, 'Lukas und Paulus', in *Eranion. Festschrift für H. Hommel*, Tübingen, 1961.

[4] The chief difficulty lies in the narrative of ch. 15 or in a general way in the apparent disagreement between what Acts says of Paul's visits to Jerusalem and what Paul himself writes on this subject in the Epistle to the Galatians. But is it really necessary to accuse the author of Acts of not knowing what any companion of Paul must necessarily know? Examination of the first book to Theophilus should make us prudent. Mark (9.2) and Matthew (17.1) both date the episode of the Transfiguration 'six days after' the preceding episode; when he writes 'about eight days' Luke (9.28) was probably not in possession of any different information. The angel's message to the Holy Women—'Tell ye his disciples that he is risen. And behold he will go before you into Galilee' (cf. Mark 16.7; Matthew 28.7) becomes in Luke—'Remember how he spoke to you when he was yet in Galilee' (24.6). Luke has his own way of interpreting the story and it is not that of a modern historian; rather than correcting him we ought to try to understand what he has written.

[5] See above, pp. 52f.

Schwanbeck,[6] who thought the information in the second half of Acts could be traced back, the former to a travel diary probably written by Timothy,[7] the latter to some memoirs of Silas,[8] have thrown little light on the problem.

[6] See above, pp. 52f.

[7] The attribution of the travel diary to Timothy does not figure in the texts printed under the name of Schleiermacher; from one of his pupils, however, we know that he taught this in one of his courses of lectures. The pupil puts forward the same explanation—M. Ulrich: *Theol. Studien und Kritiken*, 1837, V, pp. 369ff; 1840, VIII, pp. 1003ff. An analogous explanation will be found in W. M. L. de Wette, *Lehrbuch der historisch-kritischen Einleitung in die kanonische Bücher des Neuen Testaments*, Berlin, 1826, p. 204 (4th ed., 1842, p. 205); cf. *Kurze Erklärung der Apostelgeschichte*, Leipzig, 1846 (4th ed., 1870, pp. XXXVIIIf). Convinced that the author of the we-passages is identical with the one who composed the work as a whole, E. Th. Mayerhoff attributed to Timothy the editing of the third Gospel and of Acts— *Historisch-kritische Einleitung in die petrinischen Schriften, nebst einer Abhandlung über den Verfasser der Apostelgeschichte*, Hamburg, 1835, pp. 1–30. In the lengthy review that he devoted to this work (*Theol. Studien und Kritiken*, 1836, IV, pp. 1026ff.), Fr. Bleek returned to the hypothesis of Schleiermacher, that Timothy was only the author of the we-fragments; he repeated and developed this explanation in his *Einleitung in das Neue Testament*, Berlin, 1862, pp. 328ff (4th ed. by W. Mangold, Berlin, 1886, pp. 440ff). The attribution of these same passages to Timothy is likewise put forward by W. Beyschlag, *Theol. Studien und Kritiken*, 1864, XXXII, 215. See also S. Davidson, *Introduction to the Study of the New Testament*, vol. II, 3rd ed., London, 1894, p. 156. In 1886, C. Weizsäcker hesitated between Timothy and Aristarchus (see *infra.*, p. 118). In 1890 M. Sorof imputed to Timothy a recasting of the work composed by Luke—*Die Entstehung der Apostelgeschichte*, Berlin, 1890. In addition to the attribution of the we-sections to Timothy, the hypothesis which refers them back to Titus is also found—L. Horst, *Essai sur les sources de la deuxième partie des Actes des Apôtres*, Strasburg, 1849; M. Krenkel, *Paulus der Apostel der Heiden*. Vorträge gehalten in den Protestantenvere in zu Dresden und Leipzig, Leipzig, 1869, pp. 214f; J. J. Kneucker, *Die Anfänge des römischen Christentums*, Karlsruhe-Leipzig, 1881, pp. 14f and 50f; A. Jacobsen, *Die Quellen der Apostelgeschichte* (Wissenschaftliche Beilage zum Programm der Friedrichs-Werderschen Gymnasiums, Ostern, 1885), Berlin, 1885, p. 24; O. Holtzmann, *Zeitschr. für wiss. Theol.*, 1889, p. 409.

[8] The attribution of the we-sections to Silas is again found in Johannes Jeremias, who bases himself on the methods of *Schallanalyse*: articles published in 1937 in the *Sächsischen Kirchenblatt*, then the work *Der Wir-Bericht in der Apostelgeschichte* (Studien des Bundes evang. Pfarrer im Dritten Reich, Land Sachsen), Dresden, 1938. The attribution to Silas often goes hand in hand with explanations which involves the doing away with one personality, either by identifying Silas with Luke (Silas comes from *silva*, Luke from *lucus*: a 'forest' or a 'wood' is practically the same thing)—thus G. Van Vloten, 'Lukas und Silas', *Zeitschr. für wiss. Theol.*, 1867, pp. 223f, and 1871, pp. 431–4, or again, E. C. Selwyn, *St Luke the Prophet*, London, 1901; or by identifying Silas with Titus—hypothesis put forward in 1864 by Fr Maercker (*Titus Silvanus und sein Wirken für das Christentum*, Meiningen), repeated in the following year by E. Graf ('Titus Silvanus. Einige Bemerkungen zu der unter diesen Titel von Prof. Freidrich Märcker in Meiningen verfassten Abhandlung, mit besonderer Rücksicht auf Act. 15.22'), in the *Deutsche Vierteljahrsschrift für Englisch-Theologische Forschung und Kritikm*, 1865, VIII, pp. 373–94). The hypothesis is again found in Fr Zimmer, 'Die Identität von Titus, Silas und Silvanus', *Zeitschr. für kirchl. Wiss. und Kirkl. Leben*, 1881, pp. 169–74; 'Woher kommt

In the Tübingen school we would call attention to Ed. Zeller (1854).[9] His study on the we-sections is very significant and had great influence. He considered that the we-passages came from one source. This explanation was the only one that enabled us to account for their discontinuity; for, supposing that the writer of Acts wanted to convey to us that he accompanied Paul, he should have used the first person in a continuous section corresponding to the period during which he claimed to have been with the Apostle. The discontinuity of the 'we' can only be explained if the writer, solely for the passages where he uses it, had a written source in the first person at his disposal. These sections, moreover, are distinguished from the rest of the work by a whole series of particular characteristics—in the first place by the accuracy of their information, although the details in question have no particular interest for the purpose of the work. There we find concrete and vivid descriptions, such as those of ch. 27 (vv. 14ff, 37ff), to an extent unparalleled throughout the rest of the book. They also have their linguistic peculiarities— constructions, expressions and words which are not found else-

---

der Name Silas', *Jahrb. für protest. Theol.*, 1881, pp. 721–3. It again recurs in W. Seufert, 'Titus Silvanus (*ΣΙΛΑΣ*) und der Verfasser des ersten Petrusbriefes', *Zeitschr. für Wiss. Theol.*, 1885, XXVIII, pp. 350–71; Seufert maintains (pp. 367ff) that this Silas–Titus is the author of the travel diary which forms the we-source of Acts. Same explanation again in E. Barnikol, *Personen-Probleme der Apostelge- schichte; Johannes Marcus, Silas und Titus. Unter suchungen zur Struktur des Apostelge- schichte und zur Verfasserschaft der Wir-Quelle* (*Forschungen zur Entstehung des Urchristentums des Neuen Testaments und der Kirche*, III), Kiel, 1931. Barnikol's interpretation is complicated by the fact that he distinguishes two Silas, the *Dekret Silas* of Acts 15 and the *Reise-Silas* of the following chapters; it is the second Silas who is to be identified with the Titus of the Epistles; we can imagine the strain which such an hypothesis must impose on the interpretation of the Epistles, where both Silas and Titus are mentioned. It is curious to note that these views, apparently so revolutionary, have arisen from preoccupations which are frankly apologetic; in the beginning it was a matter of justifying the silence with which the person of Titus is surrounded in Acts, whereas Paul presents him in the Epistles as a most valued collaborator, the one he entrusts, for instance, with restoring order in Corinth after having failed to achieve this himself. How does it come about that his name does not appear in Acts in places where he must necessarily have been present? The problem is real, but the solution proposed is clearly not acceptable. We should also mention a supporter of the attribution of the travel diary to Epaphras: J. A. Blaisdell, 'The Authorship of the We Sections of the Book of Acts', *Harvard Theol. Rev.*, 1920, XIII, pp. 156–8.

[9] *Die Apostelgeschichte*, pp. 513–16.

where in the writer's work (even if we leave out of account the nautical terms which the other narratives did not call for).[10] It is true that on the other hand these sections also contain a considerable number of features that belong to the characteristic language of 'Luke'; and they also contain a whole series of narratives, the miraculous aspect of which cannot be attributed to an eyewitness. We must conclude from this that the author of Acts has very largely rewritten and interpolated the information at his disposal; it is not without significance that the miraculous episodes are also those in which we find most of the Lucan characteristics. It cannot be questioned that the we-source did not contain only what the author of Acts has taken from it; the little of it which survives does not permit us to form an idea of its content. Everything leads us to think that this source, written by a companion of the Apostle, had Luke as its author. Developing and giving shape as they did to ideas which had already been put forward by F. Gfrörer[11] and F. C. Baur,[12] these observations of Zeller are repeated in one way or another in a great number of nineteenth-century writers.[13] In 1875, A. Hilgenfeld[14] corroborated the Tübingen thesis by introducing into the debate the parallel case of the books of Esdras and Nehemias, where several sections are written in the first person,[15]

---

[10] As regards the vocabulary, Zeller draws attention to $\mu\acute{o}\lambda\iota\varsigma$ (mistakenly written $\pi\acute{o}\lambda\iota\varsigma$), used in 27.7, 8, 16; and occurring again only in Acts 14.18; $\chi\rho\tilde{\eta}\sigma\theta\alpha\iota$, Acts 27.3, 17; and not elsewhere in Luke–Acts; the absolute use of $\tau\tilde{\eta}\ \dot{\epsilon}\pi\iota o\acute{u}\sigma\eta$ (16.11; 20.15; 21.18), used elsewhere with $\dot{\eta}\mu\acute{\epsilon}\rho\alpha$ (7.26) or $\nu\upsilon\kappa\tau\acute{\iota}$ (23.11). Among constructions we should simply like to draw attention to the case of $\ddot{o}\tau\iota$ with the infinitive—27.10 (wholly classical).

[11] F. Gfrörer, *Geschichte des Urchristentums*, Stuttgart, 1838.

[12] F. C. Baur, *Paulus der Apostel Jesu Christi. Sein Leben und Werken*, Stuttgart, 1845.

[13] It will be sufficient to mention as an example F. Overbeck in the latest edition of W. M. L. de Wette, *Kurze Erklärung der Apostelgeschichte*, 4th ed., Leipzig, 1870, pp. XXXIXff; W. Mangold in F. Bleck, *Einleitung in das Neue Testament*, 3rd ed., Berlin, 1875, and 4th ed., 1886, p. 445. A variant of this explanation will be found in W. C. van Manen, *Paulus*, I. *De Handelingen, der Apostolen*, Leyden 1890—the we-sections written by Luke were primarily incorporated in certain 'Acts of Paul' which were then fused with certain 'Acts of Peter'.

[14] A. Hilgenfeld, *Historisch-kritische Einleitung in das Neue Testament*, Leipzig, 1875, p. 607; see also the same author's remarks in the *Zeitschrift. für wiss. Theol.*, 1896, p. 189.

[15] Esdr. 7.29–9.15; Neh. 1.1–7.5; 12.31; 13.4–31. The parallel is clearly more useful than the mediaeval chronicles to which E. A. Schwanbeck thought he could have recourse.

whereas the narrative as a whole is in the third; the passages in the first person seem to be simply borrowed from memoirs.[16] This observation was not lost sight of, but writers did not always draw the same conclusions from it.

H. J. Holtzmann in 1885[17] gave a very good résumé of the question. He pointed out that the most common explanation remained that which he described as traditional and apologetic—that the narrator who says 'we' in certain parts of Acts is to be identified with the writer of the work. Three considerations favoured this opinion: (1) ecclesiastical tradition, (2) the unity of style and language which characterized the whole work, (3) the indication of Luke 1.3, where, speaking of himself in the first person singular, the writer seems to supply the key to his manner of using the first person plural in the latter part of his work. Against this explanation was that of the critics who denied identity between the narrator of the we-sections and the author of Acts. They pointed out that the latter, in so far as he has no source at his disposal, reveals a very imperfect knowledge of the apostolic age; they also insisted on the contrast between the precision and accuracy of the we-fragments and the obscurities or inaccuracies which are found elsewhere, notably in the immediate context of these fragments.[18]

The explanations put forward by C. Weizsäcker in 1886 deserve attention.[19] This writer did not think that Acts was composed before the second century. When we compare the Book of Acts with the information supplied by the epistles, the

---

[16] Hilgenfeld also instances the transfer into the first person in several places in Jeremias and he instances the case of the book of Tobit, which begins in the first person (1.1–3.6) and continues in the third.

[17] H. J. Holtzmann, *Lehrbuch der historisch-kritischen Einleitung in das Neue Testament* (Sammlung theol. Lehrbücher), Freiburg-im-B. 1886 (we have used the second edition revised and enlarged, published in 1886—pp. 406–9). Holtzmann repeats the same explanations in his *Hand-Commentar zum Neuen Testament, I. Die Synoptiker—Die Apostelgeschichte*, Freiburg-im-B., 1889, pp. 310–12: repeated without any considerable alteration in *Die Apostelgeschichte* (Hand-Commentar zum N.T., I/2), 1st ed., Tübingen Leipzig, 1901, pp. 5–7).

[18] For a representative of this standpoint in criticism on the eve of Harnack's publications, see R. Knopf, *Die Apostelgeschichte* (Die Schriften des N.T. neu übersetzt und für die Gegenwart erklärt, I/2), Gottingen, 1806, pp. 4–5 and 68.

[19] C. Weizsäcker, *Das apostelische Zeitalter der christlichen Kirche*, Freiburg i. Br., 1886. We have used the 3rd ed., Tübingen–Leipzig, 1902, pp. 199–212.

narrative shows *lacunae* and errors which are sufficient to prove that the author wrote long after the events. But the numerous and precise details he has at his disposal could only be accounted for if he possessed first-class sources. The use of written documents is particularly clear in a series of details, dry and colourless, which mention the stages of the journey. It is precisely there that we come across the we-fragments—the author of the work has preserved the style of his source. Weizsäcker was inclined to attribute this source to Timothy, without absolutely excluding Aristarchus; above all, he considered it most unlikely that this source contained anything but what the writer of Acts took from it. Thus it was a question essentially of two travel narratives—the one of a journey from Troas to Jerusalem, the other from Caesarea to Rome. In addition to this we-source, Weizsäcker suggested the presence of a source underlying short narratives which seem to be related 16.10–24, 35–39; 17.5–9; 18.7–17; 19.28–41. It also seemed to him that the travel narrative of ch. 13–14 presupposed an indication of the places visited by the missionaries. The miraculous accounts of 14.8–14; 16.25–34; 19.13–19 doubtless make use of traditions rather than written documents. It would be possible to explain the whole of the narrative of 21.18 to 26.32 in the same way, at the same time leaving the responsibility for the discourses to the author alone.

Harnack's Argument

At the beginning of this century, Harnack was the great champion of the identity of the author of the we-fragments with the author of the whole book. Without entirely neglecting the argument which could be drawn from tradition[20] and that supplied by the prologue of the Gospel,[21] he placed the emphasis

[20] He developed this in his first work *Lukas der Arzt* (1906); we have consulted this work in the English translation of J. R. Wilkinson, *Luke the Physician, the Author of the Third Gospel and the Acts of the Apostles* (New Test. Studies, I), 2nd ed., London–New York, 1909. See pp. 1–6. Harnack insists on the fact that a work bearing a dedication must necessarily bear the name of its author. We shall come across a similar consideration in M. Dibelius.

[21] *Luke the Physician*, pp. 8–11. A consideration repeated and developed by H. J. Cadbury; we shall return to it.

firmly on the linguistic argument.[22] He thought that this argument alone[23] supplied an irrefutable proof, showing that the we-passages were directly written by Luke without the use of an already existing source. These passages, in fact, do show a striking agreement with the vocabulary, syntax and style which characterize Luke;[24] they betray those points that interest him most, his literary manner of presenting the persons, countries, towns, peoples, houses, indications of time; they reveal the same negligences, the same trifling inaccuracies.[25] The case of the passages in the third Gospel which depend on Mark or on the Q source is quite different—there the style and, in particular, the vocabulary show hardly any of the characteristics of Luke.[26]

[22] To define Harnack's thought exactly, we cannot do better than to follow the résumé and modifications found in his final work on the subject—*Neue Untersuchungen* (1911), pp. 1–20. The arguments supplied by tradition and by the prologue to the Gospel are no longer in question here.

[23] 'Von den 261 Worten, die im N.T. dem Luk-Ev. eigen tümlich sind, finden sich höchstens 3 auch in den aus Q stammenden Partien seines Werks! Damit vergleiche man den Wortbestand in den Wirstücken in ihrem Verhältnis zum Ganzen der Apostelgeschichte! Diese *eine* Beobachtung musste die Kritiker überzeugen, dass die Wirstücke keine Quelle sein können' (*Neue Untersuchungen*, p. 2; the italics are Harnack's). In a more succinct form, a very similar line of argument will be found in J. C. Hawkins, *Horae synopticae. Contributions to the Study of the Synoptic Problem.* 2nd ed., Oxford, 1909, pp. 182–9. Among the oldest studies with the same trend may be instanced—S. Klostermann, *Vindiciae Lucanae, seu de itinerarii in libro Actuum asservati auctore*, Göttingen, 1866, pp. 50–56; C. F. Nösgen, *Commentar über die Apostelgeschichte des Lukas*, Leipzig, 1882, pp. 15–24; K. Schmidt, *Die Apostelgeschichte unter der Hauptgeschichtspunkt ihrer Glaubwürdigkeit*, I, Erlangen, 1882, pp. 11–91; J. Friedrich, *Das Lukasevangelium und die Apostelgeschichte, Werke desselben Verfassens*, Halle, 1890; Th. Vogel, *Zur Charakteristik des Lukas nach Sprache und Stil*, Leipzig, 1897 (2nd ed., 1899).

[24] *Neue Untersuchungen*, p. 1, summarizing the long analyses of *Luke the Physician*, pp. 26–120.

[25] *Neue Untersuchungen*, p. 1, summary of the researches which formed the subject of *Die Apostelgeschichte* (1908).

[26] So far as Q is concerned, we have already quoted (p. 84, n. 22) this remark, noting that in the New Testament, out of the 261 words proper to the Gospel of Luke, three at most occur in passages depending on Q; the details may be found in the preface to another work by Harnack: *Sprüche und Reden Jesu. Die zweite Quelle des Matthäus und Lukas* (Beitr. zur Einl. in das N.T., II), Leipzig, 1907, p. III. The way in which Luke slightly corrects his source without taking away its principal characteristics is illustrated by certain examples in *Luke the Physician*, pp. 93–96 (Luke 6.41–42; 7.6–9). For the passages derived from Mark, see *ibid.*, pp. 87–93 (analysis of Luke 4.30–37 and 5.17–24). Despite the numerous revisions made by Luke, the style, syntax and vocabulary of Mark recur everywhere in the sections which the third Gospel owes to it. It is possible for the same method to succeed in establishing that Luke 1–2 has not used sources, at any rate sources written in Greek; in these two chapters Luke is too much himself for it to be possible to admit that he depended on a pre-existing document (*ibid*, pp. 96–103).

In the we-sections, on the contrary, these characteristics are presented in such number and with such frequency that the authorship must necessarily be attributed to Luke, just as we attribute to him the occasional remarks which sometimes interrupt his narratives to recall the purpose he is aiming at or the ideas he wants to stress. Among the features which characterize Luke's manner of writing, Harnack emphasized those which show medical knowledge and a special interest in clinical observations.[27] Such features confirmed, he thought, the attribution to 'Luke, the most dear physician' (Col. 4.14) of the work as a whole and more particularly of the we-sections, written in his language and style and with his personal preoccupations.

Cadbury's Reply

Favourably received by the supporters of tradition,[28] Harnack's theories yet aroused much criticism. The objections put to him

[27] Suggestions tending to show that Luke makes use of terms coming from a medical vocabulary had already been put forward by J. Freind, *History of Physick from the Time of Galen to the Beginning of the Sixteenth Century* (1725–6); suggestions pointing in the same direction had been made by J. K. Walker in the *Gentleman's Magazine* for June 1841. The question has been taken up and treated systematically by W. K. Hobart, *The Medical Language of St Luke. A Proof from Internal Evidence that 'The Gospel according to St Luke' and 'The Acts of the Apostles' were written by the same Person and that the Writer was a Medical Man* (Dublin Univ. Press Series), Dublin–London, 1882. Hobart pushed his theory too far and without sufficient discernment; his exaggerations have not prevented the success of his explanation, reduced to more reasonable proportions—see, for instance, A. Plummer, *A Critical and Exegetical Commentary on the Gospel according to St. Luke* (Intern. Crit. Comm.), Edinburgh, 1896, 5th ed., 1922, pp. lxiii–lxvi; R. J. Knowling, *The Acts of the Apostles* (The Expositor's Greek Testament, II), London, 1904, pp. 9–11; B. Weiss and J. Weiss, *Die Evangelien des Markus und Lukas* (Krit.-exeg. Komm. über das N.T., 1 Abt., 2. Hälfte, 9th ed.), Göttingen, 1901, p. 252; Th. Zahn, *Einleitung in das Neue Testament*, vol. II, 3rd ed., Leipzig, 1907, pp. 433f. Harnack returns to the question in *Luke the Physician*, pp. 13–17 and 175–98, and in *Neue Untersuchungen*, pp. 15–18.

[28] The linguistic argument has been developed at length by E. Jacquier, *Histoire des Livres du Nouveau Testament*, vol. III, Paris, 1908; 4th ed., 1912, pp. 7–29, then in *Les Actes des Apôtres* (Etudes Bibliques), Paris, 1926, pp. LXff. Jacquier has tried to simplify the theory by presenting only one demonstration to prove that the language of Acts is identical with that of the third Gospel and that the language of the travel diary is identical with that of the other parts of Acts; as, moreover, his explanations are not set out in structural form, the result gives an impression of great confusion. The demonstration of Harnack and of Hawkins seems decisive to C. Lattey, who has given a good summary of it in *The Acts of the Apostles* (The Westminster Version of the Sacred Scriptures. The New Testament II), London, 1936, pp. XVL–XLVII. Its influence can be recognized in the introductions to the

were not always of great interest; the most important and
effective were those that came from H. J. Cadbury. In the first
place Cadbury took up the theory of Luke's medical language.[29]
To establish that Luke uses a vocabulary special to the medical
profession, it is not sufficient to discover in medical treatises a
certain number of terms used by him, we must be sure also that
these terms were not familiar to writers who were certainly not
medical men. The results of this evidence speak for themselves
—the majority of the so-called medical words selected by
Hobart can be found in writers who had no special competence
in medicine. The medical knowledge of Luke is found to be
practically on the same level as that of Flavius Josephus; it is
inferior to that of Lucian of Samosata, the rhetorician of the
second century. Further evidence[30] is to be found in the *Corpus
Hippiatricorum Graecorum* that makes use of a vocabulary that is
often very enlightening for the understanding of the vocabulary
of Luke; are we to conclude from this that Luke was a horse
doctor? These observations of Cadbury's are very telling. It is
no longer possible to use Luke's vocabulary to prove that he
was a physician. However, there is not only the vocabulary;
the numerous touches which Luke gives to Mark's narratives
likewise indicate a certain taste for clinical observation. He
shows a natural liking for medical matters and the medical
profession. Cadbury[31] thought that here again recourse to a
physician's professional preoccupations was not necessarily

majority of the popular commentaries—for instance, J. Kürzinger, *Die Apostelge-
schichte* (Echter-Bibel), *Würzburg*, 1951, p. 6; C. H. Rieu, *St Luke, The Acts of the
Apostles* (The Penguin Classics, L. 56), Harmondsworth, 1957, pp. 17 and 22f;
there is also an echo of it in the manuals, as in the notice of J. Huby for *Initiation
Biblique. Introduction à l'étude des Saintes Ecritures* (A. Robert–A. Tricot), 3rd ed.,
Tournai, 1954, p. 230.

[29] H. J. Cadbury, *The Style and Literary Method of Luke*, I. *The Diction of Luke and
Acts* (Harvard Theol. Studies, VI), Cambridge, Mass., 1919, cf. *id.* 'Lexical Notes
on Luke—Acts, II—Recent Arguments for Medical Language', *Journ. of Bibl. Lit.*,
1926, XLV, pp. 190–209. Summary of the first-mentioned study, in A. C. Clark
(who is in full agreement), *The Acts of the Apostles. A Critical Edition with Introduction
and Notes on selected Passages*, Oxford, 1933, pp. 405f.

[30] H. J. Cadbury, 'Lexical Notes on Luke-Acts, V, Luke and the Horse-
Doctors', *Journ. of Bibl. Lit.*, 1933, LII, pp. 55–65.

[31] H. J. Cadbury, *The Making of Luke-Acts*, New York, 1927 (2nd ed., London,
1958), pp. 118f, 219, 273, 338, 358.

implied—other explanations, such as care for literary style, delicacy, etc., were possible.

Cadbury was doubtless right in thinking that it is not possible to supply proof that the third Gospel and Acts were written by a physician. His remarks seriously weakened Hobart's theory. They were, however, less conclusive in their opposition to a more subtle theory, as it was defended by Harnack.[32] Since tradition represented the third Gospel and Acts as the work of Luke the physician, could not certain features of this work or certain touchings up of the Mark or Q sources, be explained by taking this traditional view into account? To show that it is not possible to prove *a priori* that Luke was a physician does not signify that it has been proved he was not one or that the hypothesis of his medical training is not helpful for the understanding of certain peculiarities of his writing.[33]

Harnack's main interest is concentrated on another point, namely to establish that the author of the we-sections is the same person as the writer of the whole work and that these we-sections are not based on any written source. Cadbury[34] readily admits that Harnack has demonstrated very clearly the unity of language between the we-passages and the rest of the book. The lack of agreement turns on the conclusions to be drawn from this observation. According to Cadbury, it merely shows that Luke has rewritten his sources to the extent of making the criterion of vocabulary or style of a passage valueless in deciding whether its composition is based on the use of a document or

[32] Cf. *Neue Untersuchungen*, p. 15. See also G. Bonaccorsi, *Primi Saggi di filogia neotestamentaria Letture scelte dal Nuovo Testamento greco con introduzione e commento*, vol. I, Turin, 1933, pp. cvf; H. Simon. J. Prado, *Praelectiones Biblicae ad usum scholarum, Novum Testamentum*, vol. II, 3rd ed., p. 7—'Locutiones medicae, quae, post Hobart, a Harnack, Zahn et aliis notatae sunt, altioris culturae ambitum non excedunt; modus tamen, quo tales voces adhibentur, medici suspicionem ingerit.'

[33] In this limited sense it would be possible to grant that there is some foundation in the criticism formulated against Cadbury by J. Moffatt, 'St Luke and Literary Criticism', *Expositor*, 1922, 8th series, vol. xxiv, pp. 1–18. See also the modification made by G. H. C. MacGregor, *The Acts of the Apostles* (1954), p. 8. Cadbury has confined himself to dealing with his adversary's position; he has not sought to enlarge the debate. The lexicographical argument does not justify us in stating that Luke practised the medical profession; nevertheless, 'if it be believed that the writer of Acts was a physician, the language of Acts offers no obstacles' (*The Beginnings of Christianity*, I/II, p. 166).

[34] Cadbury's explanations have been discussed by V. H. Stanton, 'Style and

not. Harnack claims that the linguistic characteristics of the sources are maintained in the passages of Luke where these sources are used. This is not so: in some parts of the third Gospel and of Acts independent of Mark, the vocabulary and certain constructions characteristic of Mark[35] appear with a frequency equal to or greater than that found in the parts dependent on Mark. Harnack denies the use of sources in the passages where the linguistic peculiarities of Luke are particularly numerous. The proportion of Lucan expressions, however, is the same in the sections derived from Q and in those of Luke 1–2, for which Harnack will not admit a source. Moreover, the account of the calming of the storm, borrowed by Luke 8.22–24 from Mark 4.35–39, has been so much rewritten that it contains a proportion of Lucan characteristics at least equal to that of the account of the storm in Acts 27; according to Harnack, the abundance of Lucan features makes this episode a special case of composition without the use of a source. It would thus seem that the liberty with which Luke handled his sources was too great to enable us to decide with certainty what he owed to his sources in the passages for which sources have not come down to us; this also prevents us from denying the existence of a source underlying narratives strongly marked by the author's literary character.

Authorship in the Acts of the Apostles', in *Journ. of Theol. Studies*, 1923, XXIV, pp. 361–81 (cf. pp. 374–81). Taking up the defence of the theory developed by Harnack, Stanton thought he could maintain the effectiveness of the linguistic criterion to demonstrate that there was no source underlying the we-sections, but that they were directly written by Luke in the style and with the vocabulary characteristic of his manner of writing. This article scarcely invalidates Cadbury's arguments to any extent, and the latter cannot be blamed for having maintained his positions later (*The Making of Luke-Acts*, pp. 67f). Cadbury, moreover, was not unaware that other criteria existed as well as the linguistic one used by Harnack— the existence of doublets, intrusion of foreign elements, differences of points of view . . . (*ibid*, p. 68). To Haenchen's remark (*Quellenanalyse und Kompositionsanalyse*, 1960, p. 157) noting that the text of Mark could not be reconstructed from Luke, B. Gerhardson replied: 'It is perhaps true of the wording of the text' (*Memory and Manuscript*, 1961, p. 209, n. 3). Cadbury pointed out that so far the criteria based on the content of the narrative had not led to very convincing results (*op. cit.*, pp. 68–70). It must be recognized that the handling of these arguments is difficult and requires extreme care; perhaps also sufficient work has not yet been done in this direction.

[35] In particular, the use (Semitic) of the initial καί; it is as frequent in Luke 1–2 as in the passages due to Mark.

Subsequent Developments

The line of argument developed by Harnack did not attain its objective. There is no question but that the writing of the we-sections derives from the literary activity of Luke; but that does not prove that there is no written source underlying these sections. It does not seem possible to decide the question of the sources of the second part of Acts on linguistic considerations; to do so would lead to disappointing results from a method which hoped to arrive at an almost mathematical certitude.

Thus there is nothing surprising in the fact that despite Harnack many writers continue to speak of a we-source to account for the origin of the we-passages—as, for instance, P. Wendland, in 1912,[36] who insisted on the idea that the we-fragments had undergone interpolation; thus they did not adequately represent the we-source the writer of the book had at his disposal. J. Wellhausen, in 1942,[37] thought that the author could have known only a few fragments of the we-source.

According to F. J. Foakes Jackson and Kirsopp Lake,[38] the we-sections confront the exegete with four hypotheses:

1. The writer of the travel diary is identical with the compiler of Acts and the latter used the first person to intimate his presence at the events he recounts.
2. The writer of the travel diary is not to be identified with the compiler, but his diary comprised, in addition to the we-sections, narratives in the third person, the whole constituting the main source of ch. 16–28 of Acts.
3. The author of the travel diary wrote only the we-sections, then another writer added the additional narratives which, with the we-fragments, were reproduced by the compiler of Acts in ch. 16–28.
4. The author of the travel diary wrote only the we-sections and the compiler owed the rest of the narratives to other sources.

[36] P. Wendland, *Die urchristlichen Literaturformen* (Handbuch zum N.T., I/3), 2nd, 3rd ed., Tübingen, 1912, pp. 324 and 334f.
[37] J. Wellhausen, *Kritische Analyse der Apostelgeschichte* (1914), p. 34.
[38] See in particular, *The Beginnings of Christianity*, I/II (1922), pp. 161–6.

It was to this last hypothesis that Foakes Jackson and Kirsopp Lake gave their preference.[39]

H. Windisch[40] considered that if the writer to Theophilus had really wanted to intimate his presence by the use of 'we', he should have informed his reader of the significance of this fact. Since there is no indication to show this intention, the simplest explanation remains the hypothesis of the use of the travel diary. In copying certain passages from this source, the compiler kept 'we', but omitted to mention the name of Paul's companion whose identity is concealed by this pronoun. This omission may be due to negligence; it is more probable that it is quite deliberate—the compiler retained 'we' to cover himself with the authority of the eyewitness whose notes were in his possession. Today we should condemn such a procedure as dishonest; there is nothing strange about it if we take account of the customs of the times.[41]

H. W. Beyer[42] considered that, among the sources used by the compiler of Acts,

[39] In *The Beginnings of Christianity*, I/II (1922), pp. 158–67. Same presentation of the state of the question in A. H. McNeile–C. S. C. Williams, *An Introduction to the Study of the New Testament*, 2nd ed., Oxford, 1953, pp. 102 and 106f; C. S. C. Williams, *The Acts of the Apostles* (1957), pp. 5–7, who favours the first solution (because of the linguistic arguments of Hawkins and Harnack). In favour of a we-source, see again T. W. Manson, *A Companion to the Bible*, Edinburgh, 1945, p. 116—'The last part of the book certainly incorporates a travel-diary, characterized by the use of the first person'; A. Boudou, *Actes des Apôtres* (Verbum Salutis, VII), 3rd ed., Paris, 1933, pp. 26f; J. M. Gettys, 'The Book of Acts', in *Interpretation*, 1951, V, pp. 216–30 (cf. 217); J. Knox, *Chapters of a Life of Paul*, London, 1954, p. 71, etc. A somewhat extraordinary variant of this hypothesis in F. Hielscher, *Forschungen zur Geschichte des Apostels Paulus*, Cottbus, 1925—the we-source was a narrative in which a pagan author related his journey from Puteoli to Philippi and back; the remainder supplied by Acts was due to the imagination of a Christian in Rome.

[40] In *The Beginnings of Christianity*, I/II, pp. 329 and 343.

[41] On what the literary habits of antiquity actually were, a much better-informed opinion will be found in A. D. Nock, in *Gnomon*, 1953, XXV, pp. 502f; we shall return to this. Windisch has based himself on a single example, that of the sections written in the first person in the books of Esdras and Nehemias; it does not seem possible to assimilate this case to that of Acts; mention will be made of it again in connection with Norden. Again, we may consult the opinion of another good authority on ancient literature, A. Diessmann, who considers that Luke drew on the style of sailing narratives to describe in the first person plural facts which he had experienced in person. *Paulus, Eine kultur und religionsgeschichtliche Skizze*, 2nd ed., Tübingen, 1925, p. 21.

[42] H. W. Beyer, *Die Apostelgeschichte*, 8th ed., 1957, pp. 3–4.

'the most valuable was the account of the physician Luke who accompanied Paul on the occasion of his second missionary journey from Troas to Philippi[43] and later on the occasion of his third journey from Philippi to Rome;[44] he was thus an eye-witness of the most important events.[45] His notes did not merely consist of a statement of the places where they stayed with chronological details, or, indeed, of detailed indications of all the vicissitudes of the journeys, such as the brilliant description of the exciting voyage to Rome, but they were also concerned, as is natural, with the activity of Paul and even with his discourses. It is easy to recognize this account; when it reports the events in which Luke took part personally it uses the first person plural—hence the name we-source. From this it has been concluded, rather too hastily, that this source only underlay those passages which quite by chance used "we". In point of fact these passages constitute a whole in which an eyewitness recounts what he has actually experienced. Other elements, however, have been introduced. In a search for improvement, the compiler has here and there touched up this priceless source. On the whole, however, he has reproduced it very faithfully. The proof of this lies in the fact that he has left the 'we' as it was. . . .'[46]

In the eyes of M. S. Enslin,[47] the writer of Acts is too badly informed about Paul's ministry to be the companion who composed a travel diary; this diary is only one of the sources used by the author, who probably only had it in fragmentary form. The reasons for which he preserved the 'we' are not clear.[48]

It is again the echo of the old we-source that can be recognized in the commentary that a very orthodox writer, G.

---

[43] Acts 16.9–40.

[44] Acts 20.3–28.31.

[45] Col. 4.14; Phm. 24; 2 Tim. 4.11; Eusebius, *Hist. Eccl.*, III, 4.1.

[46] The attribution of the discourses to the we-source is too exceptional an hypothesis for us to omit to call attention to it.

[47] M. S. Enslin, *Christian Beginnings*, III, New York, 1938: reprinted under the title *The Literature of the Christian Movement* (Part III of *Christian Beginnings*) in the series Harper Torchbooks, New York, 1956, p. 419.

[48] In the 'Schweich Lectures' for 1942, W. L. Knox saw in Luke little more than a compiler contenting himself with amalgamating his sources. The narrative of Paul's journeys would result from a combination—a very clumsy one, moreover—of two sources: a history of the Pauline missions, a travel diary drawn up by Luke

Ricciotti, published in 1951.[49] The we-passages must have come 'from a kind of "travel-diary" kept by Luke for his personal use.' Having already conceived the plan of composing his historical work, Luke took notes from his diary, thereby following a custom of which antiquity has left us many examples; Flavius Josephus was to do the same thing a few years later, at the time of the Jewish war. These notes were written in the first person plural.

> It was from this diary that Luke afterwards took the passages in question to transfer them just as they were to Acts. Such a literal borrowing seems to us strange today, for it allows the third and the first person to remain side by side in the narrative without giving any explanation of the abrupt change from one to the other; this procedure was not unknown in antiquity, and writings of captains, travellers, governors and magistrates have come down to us, where sometimes the first and sometimes the third person is found, according to whether the narrator was present on the occasion of the events, or not.[50]

This explanation would appear to presuppose that the travel

---

himself (*Some Hellenistic Elements in Primitive Christianity*, pp. 7–8 and 14). A fresh examination of the question led Knox to considerably different conclusions in 1948 (*The Acts of the Apostles*, pp. 15f, 52, 54–59)—the language, style and methods of revision indicate that the same hand is at the root of the story of Paul's journeys and of the accounts in which the author indicates his presence by using the 'we'. The sole written source would be the travel diary—Luke would simply have inserted his personal notes, without touching them up, in the history he composed by putting in order the information he possessed on the subject of Paul. It will be noted that these explanations leave to the 'we' the characteristic of a source feature; its maintenance, however, corresponds to the deliberate intention of the writer; who thus indicates his share in the events.

[49] G. Ricciotti, *Gli Atti degli Apostoli, tradotti e commentati*, Rome, 1951, pp. 26f. Cf. A. Penna, *San Paolo*, Rome, 1945, pp. 23–25 and 28f.

[50] In putting forward these considerations, G. Ricciotti deliberately takes up the same position as Norden. We shall see shortly that Norden appeals to the memoirs of antiquity to account for the literary form of *one* source of Acts where the first and third person were already found juxtaposed; Ricciotti invokes the same writings to explain the compiling of Acts from a source which only supplied the we-sections; this presupposes that it was written in the first person. Clearly the learned prelate has read Norden a little hurriedly and has not grasped the import of his arguments. A little farther on (pp. 40–51) he devotes a paragraph to 'The

diary supplied only the we-sections; thus again it is a matter of a we-source.[51]

The hypothesis of a we-source has left deep roots in the field of research on the sources of Acts.[52] We shall come across the traces of its influence again, more than once, in the explanations which we have still to discuss. But the methods of form-criticism clearly tend to turn our minds in another direction; therefore our attention will be devoted less to determining the source which has supplied the we-sections than to defining the literary genre to which it belongs.

---

history of criticism', without considering it necessary to go beyond the 1920s, and his investigations on the state of the questions do not ever seem to have extended far enough to bring him into contact with the name of Dibelius.

[51] We have pointed out above (p. 79, n. 7) the way in which in 1931 E. Barnikol identified Silas (at least the *Reise-Silas*) with Titus, the author of the *Wir-Quelle* of Acts. Herr Barnikol has been kind enough to send me his article 'Das Fehlen der Taufe in den Quellenschriften der Apostelgeschichte und in den Urgemeinden der Hebräer und Hellenisten', which appeared in the *Wissenschaftliche Zeitschrift der Martin Luther Universität* (Halle–Wittenberg), 1956–7, VI, pp. 593–610. This study takes for granted rather than demonstrates the existence of two major sources at the root of the Book of Acts—source P 2 (*Petrus-Philippus —Quelle*), which is the basis of ch. 1–12 and 15; source PG (*Paulusgeschichte* or *Wir-Quelle*). These two sources were supposedly amalgamated into a single book, not without undergoing many revisions on the part of an editor about 135. Barnikol attributes to this editor the long series of minor alterations which introduce into the text the idea of a sacrament of baptism, unknown to first-century Christianity. The demonstration is as surprising as the theory. . . . Barnikol has published numerous works which we have not been able to consult—a book, *Apostolische und neutestamentliche Dogmengeschichte als Vor-Dogmengeschichte* (Theologische Arbeiten zur Bibel-Kirchen-und Geistesgeschichte, VI), Halle, 1938 (the reasons for which he dates Acts about the year 135 are explained on pp. 79, 81 and 83); also a whole series of articles in the review he edits *Theologische Jahrbücher*, in particular an article published in 1957 under the title—'Die drei Phasen dei Formgeschichte der Petrus-Philippus-Quelle (P. 2) um 75–135, n. Chr'. It does not seem to us that very useful information will be found in this direction.

[52] See also C. K. Barrett, *Luke the Historian in Recent Study*, London, 1961, p. 22. In speaking of the sources used by Luke, we can consider it as a fact that the use of 'we' is not a mere fiction; it does not necessarily mean that the writer was an eye-witness; the meaning would appear to be that this writer 'had some sort of access to some sort of eyewitness material for this part of his narrative'.

VI

THE 'WE' AND 'THEY' SOURCES

FOR A long time now many writers have been convinced that the source from which the we-passages come is not co-extensive with those passages. They have pointed out, in fact, that they bear traces of touching up—additional phrases, like-wise drawn up in the first person, must have been added to the original narrative with the necessary adaptations; thus the presence of the 'we' would not be sufficient to prove that a particular passage comes from the source in question. Moreover, it is difficult to detach the we-passages from their immediate context, written in the third person; it would seem difficult to attribute a different origin to passages so closely linked—thus the source of the we-passages would also have supplied passages in 'they'. As a result of these observations, criticism was thus faced with two possibilities: that of literary criticism, normally leading to the hypothesis of the Antioch source or to one of its variants; and that of form-criticism, which sought to define the literary genre of the source used—Ed. Norden thought of 'memoirs', M. Dibelius of a travel diary. We shall first discuss Norden's suggestions as to the nature of a source document characterized by the alternation of 'we' and 'they' passages.

Norden's Hypothesis

The idea that it was memoirs that underlay the narratives in Acts relating to Paul's missions is not new. We have met it in E. A. Schwanbeck (1847),[1] who thought these narratives were based on a memorandum written by Silas. A. Hilgenfeld (1875

[1] See above, p. 79.

and 1896)[2] relates the second part of the book of Acts to certain 'Acts of Paul', in which certain sections were written in the first person depending as they did on a memorandum written by a companion of the Apostle; in preserving the 'we', the writer followed the example of the compiler of the books of Esdras and Nehemias, who juxtaposes both 'we' and 'they' sections. H. H. Wendt (1899)[3] referred to this parallel case and mentioned the *Memoiren*, the use of which would explain the presence of the 'we' in certain passages of Acts. In 1913, Ed. Norden[4] considered that the narrative of Paul's journeys was based on a ὑπόμνημα; by his study of 'memoirs' as a literary genre, he made a considerable contribution to the elucidation of this question.

From the point of view of source criticism, Norden contributed nothing new. He ranged himself on the side of the explanations of P. Wendland, tending to show that the narrative of Paul's journeys has been subjected to a certain amount of touching up,[5] which would prove that the final editor used a source. He considered as one of the best-authenticated results of the analysis of the sources the fact that the we-source contained not only we-passages but also narratives composed in the third person.[6] In this respect the alterations made to the basic writing by the compiler have not modified its specific character. Starting from these suppositions, Norden set out to look for works presenting the same characteristics as the basic writing underlying the second part of Acts, thus supplying it with a literary background. For this we have to turn to narratives of journeys, the prototype of which is the Odyssey. As far back as the fifth century this literary genre appears under two forms— the one, without any pretentions, the memoranda or re-

---

[2] See above, pp. 81f.
[3] See above, p. 63.
[4] E. Norden, *Agnostos Theos. Untersuchungen zur Formengeschichte religiöser Rede*, Leipzig, 1913 (4th ed., Stuttgart, 1956), pp. 34f and 313–31.
[5] Norden was chiefly struck by the consideration that Acts 27.9–11 might constitute an interpolation in relation to its context.
[6] H. H. Wendt's explanations are considered as decisive—it is impossible to separate 16.10ff from 16.6–9 or to establish an excision in 20.1–6.

miniscences of the writer's journey, written in the first person; the other, that of a work of literature, where the narratives are given in the third person, even if the writer witnessed the events he relates. Intended for publication, Caesar's *Commentarii* on the Gallic war are a literary work written in the third person; in content, however, they scarcely differ from the reports Caesar sent to the Senate, as Cicero had done shortly before—in these reports, intended for the archives, the general spoke in the first person. The reports of the Roman functionaries thus link up with the travel reminiscences (true or fictitious) of which Greek literature has left us a number of examples.

The composition of the ὑπομνήματα in which narratives of exciting sea voyages are not infrequent (recalling the account of Ulysses relating his misadventures to Alcinous) illustrates the case of the we-passages in Acts, particularly in ch. 27. The parallel becomes even more interesting when we find memoirs combining narratives in the first and in the third person. Norden has drawn attention to a certain number of these. There are narratives of expeditions—that of Ptolemy III Euergetes (third century B.C.) who, after having recounted the exploits of one of his commanders in the third person, continues in the first when speaking of the expedition to Syria he led himself; that of Arrianus (second century A.D.) recounting the voyage of inspection he made along the coasts of the Euxine Sea, and completing this report with the indications supplied to him by those he ordered to continue the voyage. There are also works of history in which, contrary to custom, the historian recounts in the first person that portion of events in which he has played an important rôle—Velleius Paterculus (under Tiberius) Dion Cassius (third century), Ammianus Marcellinus (fourth century), etc.; we come across this procedure again in certain apocryphal Gospels and in Acts. The procedure that is attributed to the basic document underlying the Acts of the Apostles is thus in no way exceptional; by the juxtaposition of 'we' and 'they' passages, this document is linked with a clearly defined literary type—that of 'memoranda' in which the writer adds to his personal memories (recounted in the first person) additional information on the events in which he did not take part (third person).

There remains the question of ascertaining why the writer of Acts preserved the 'we' of his source when he does not claim to identify himself with one of the companions of the Apostle. It would seem that in taking the memoirs of Luke and combining them with information from another source, he should have unified his narrative and written the whole of it in the third person.[7] Hilgenfeld[8] supplied the key to this problem by pointing out that the process of composition used in Acts is identical with that of the books of Esdras and Nehemias. Writing about 200 B.C., the writer of these books had various sources at his disposal—among others, an historical account written in Aramaic about 450 and in particular memoranda written in the first person by Esdras and Nehemias. These memoranda have been in part recorded as they were originally written, including the use of the first person. The book of Jeremias gives evidence of an analogous procedure—to the passages written by the prophet in the first person, Baruch added others which refer to Jeremias in the third person. The book of Enoch was likewise written in the first person; a later editor added passages written in the third. This way of working seems to have been fairly usual among Jewish writers. Norden thought that the compiler of Acts was more particularly inspired by the example of the writer of Esdras and Nehemias; we should thus have an explanation for a process of composition which has no analogy among the Greek historians. Taken from the memoirs of Luke, the 'we' of Acts supplied no information as to the identity of the compiler of the work; it simply revealed that his work had links with Jewish historiography.

---

[7] The problem occurs in a particularly acute form in the hypothesis, adopted by Norden, according to which the editor deleted the second part of the prologue of Acts, being unwilling to reproduce on his own account what Luke said there of the share he had taken in events. This latter part of the prologue indicated the subject of the book and at the same time justified the use of the first person in the narrative of the events in which the writer had taken part. We have already said (p. 18, n. 5) that this hypothesis has no foundation beyond the prejudices of outmoded scholarship.

[8] Cf. *supra*, p. 81.

S.A.–D

To sum up, Norden's explanation bears on two points. In the first place, it claims to account for the 'we' and 'they' source, which served as a basis for the compiling of Acts—we should think of it as a ὑπόμνημα compiled by Luke on the pattern of a literary type well known to ancient writers. Secondly, it attempts to justify the retention of the 'we' by the compiler—in preserving this feature of his source, he in no way intends to present himself as a companion of the Apostle, but to follow a manner of procedure the example of which he had found in the books of Esdras and Nehemias and which seems to have been familiar to Jewish historians.[9]

On these two points of Norden's theory, different explanations have been put forward; it seems to us that they still offer a certain interest. We would first of all draw attention to an objection of A. Wikenhauser[10] which tends to call in question the manner in which Norden explains the combination of the 'we' and 'they' sections in Acts; in actual fact, it is a matter of the exact value which should be given to the parallel cases, and in this connection it will be useful to draw attention to a parallel mentioned by F. Prat,[11] which has received very little notice.[12] We shall then examine the exegesis of the prologue of Luke as H. J. Cadbury has expounded it;[13] without attacking Norden's

---

[9] No general view on the sources of Acts is given in the commentary of E. Preuschen, *Die Apostelgeschichte* (Handbuch zum N.T., IV/1), Tübingen, 1912. The author confines himself to stressing the traces of rewriting to which the compiler subjected his collection of documents when producing his book. Before his work was printed, Preuschen was able to consult Norden's book (1913!) and add a few pages (pp. V–IX) to mark his entire agreement, particularly on the point of the literary form of the ὑπομνήματα on which the narratives of Paul's journeys depend. Norden's influence can be traced in the explanations of M. Goguel, *Introduction au N.T.*, III (1922), cf. pp. 164–71 and 258–341; see also *Jésus et les origines du christianisme*, II. *La naissance du christianisme* (1946), pp. 511–25. The writer of Acts had available an excellent source where sections written in the first person alternated with those written in the third; we must think of it as a story of the Apostle Paul and his missions and everything points to Luke as its author. The editor touched up this document and made different additions to it; later some other hand made an interpolation.

[10] Attention was drawn to this by J. Renié, *Actes des Apôtres* (1949), p. 20.

[11] The reassessments made by Wikenhauser and Cadbury were repeated by E. Trocmé, *Le 'Livre des Actes' et l'Histoire* (1957), pp. 124 and 125–7.

[12] A. Wikenhauser, *Die Apostelgeschichte und ihr Geschichtswert* (1921), p. 73.

[13] E. Trocmé, *op. cit.*, p. 124.

theory directly, Cadbury tends to interpret the 'we' of Acts in a very different way from that of the German philologist.[14]

The Parallels

Wikenhauser has pointed out that the relationship of the 'we' and 'they' sections is not the same in the case of Acts as in that of the books of Esdras and Nehemias. In the latter books the chief characters are often mentioned by name in the passages written in the third person, so that the identity of the one who is speaking in the first person in the we-passages is unmistakable; in Acts, on the other hand, the name of Luke does not appear in the accounts written in the third person, and there is no indication enabling us to identify the narrator who counts himself among the companions of Paul. Trocmé makes the consequence of this remark explicit—'If we want to maintain the theory of the imitation of the one (Esdras and Nehemias) by the other (the narrator of the we-sections), the history of the Pauline missions must be attributed to the principal person of Acts, i.e. to Paul himself.'[15]

It would seem that this observation could be extended; it applies not only to the case of Esdras and Nehemias, but to the whole of the ὑπομνήματα cited by Norden—the narrator who recounts in the first person the events in which he has taken part not only arranges so as to leave no possible doubt as to his identity but presents himself regularly as an actor in the foreground of these events. If we go by this rule, the author of the memorandum on the Pauline missions must thus be Paul in person—a consequence which clearly raises too many difficulties for us to linger over it.[16]

---

[14] Trocmé, however, adopts an explanation of this kind in what he writes on the subject of the 'diary' that Paul (supposedly) had drawn up by a secretary with the intention of using it as a help to memory (*op. cit.*, p. 138). This hypothesis will be discussed in ch. VII of this study.

[15] F. Prat, 'Un rapprochement littéraire entre la Vie de saint Siméon Stylite le Jeune et les Actes des Apôtres', *Rech. de Sc. Rel.*, 1923, XIII, pp. 554–6.

[16] H. Delehaye, *Les saints stylites* ('Subsidia Hagiographica', 14), Brussels–Paris, 1923. The life of St Simeon Stylites the Younger is studied (pp. LIX–LXXV), and a part of the Greek text edited (pp. 238–71).

F. Prat brought a rather unexpected piece of evidence to the debate. He was struck by the interest that the remarks of an illustrious Bollandist, H. Delehaye, in connection with the *Vie de saint Syméon Stylite le Jeune* (sixth century), offered for Acts.[17] The work is anonymous.[18] 'The biographer was writing for the generation that knew the Stylite. Yet he could not have taken up his pen immediately after the saint's death, for many remarkable facts have had time to be forgotten.'[19] Delehaye examines the question of sources and concludes—'We do not want to deny the use of a written source altogether; but it is not possible to demonstrate the existence of one, still less to isolate the document of which use was made.'[20] A further remark directly affects the subject with which we are concerned—'It is more interesting to note that from ch. LXX onwards the narrator, who up till then has been speaking of the disciples or brethren in the third person, begins to use the first: ἐν μιᾷ τῶν ἡμερῶν ὁ τοῦ Θεοῦ δοῦλος καλέσας ἡμᾶς. He appeals to his personal memories and places himself among the saint's disciples.'[21] What value is to be given to this appearance of the 'we'? 'It is natural enough to wonder if the somewhat brusque entry of the eyewitness in the seventieth chapter into an account which up to that point has been impersonal, is not perhaps a literary device. There is nothing to indicate this. The occurrence of ἡμεῖς, though a little unexpected, is not in the least affected and it is not continuous enough to be artificial.'[22] The *Vie* has 259 chapters; the use of 'we', appearing as it does for the first time in ch. LXX, is not consistently present—the writer speaks of the brethren of the monastery of Mount Admirable[23] sometimes in the third person, and sometimes in the first, counting himself among them. The learned Bollandist considers that this evidence should be

---

[17] John Damascene, but he alone, attributes it to Arcadius, Bishop of Cyprus (beginning of seventh century). Delehaye sets out the reasons for calling in question this suggestion.

[18] p. LXII, with quotations in support taken from the prologue.

[19] p. LXIII.

[20] *Ibid.*

[21] p. LXIV.

[22] A monastery situated in the neighbourhood of Seleucia of Pieria, the port of Antioch (cf. Acts, 13.4).

[23] p. LXIV.

accepted—'We can thus without reservation listen to the con-
fidences of a disciple well placed to ascertain the truth.'[24] This
does not mean, however, that we should trust him blindly; his
narrative, full of legendary amplifications 'is a very curious
document which must be used with the requisite discernment'.[25]
P. Delehaye does not seem to have thought of the case of the
Acts of the Apostles in the remarks he makes on the significance
of the 'we' in the Life of St Symeon. It would be unfair, on the
other hand, to blame P. Prat for having made a comparison
which seems obvious. We should like to call attention to one
point. In the critical comment he makes on the use of the first
person by the author of the *Vita*, P. Delehaye takes no account
of the indication given by the prologue of this work. On the
subject of this prologue he writes—the biographer 'makes two
divisions in the facts he recounts—some were related by others
who preceded him, whereas for part of them he states he is an
eyewitness: ὅσα τοίνυν παρὰ τῶν προηγησαμένων ἡμᾶς παραλαβόντες
ἰσχύσαμεν διατηρῆσαι καὶ ἡμας ἐθεασάμεθα αὐτόπται τούτων γενέσθαι
καταξιωθέντες ἀναγκαῖον ἡγησάμεθα γράψαι.'[26] It would seem that
the explicit claim to have been present at a part of the events
should come into the interpretation of the passages written in the
first person. This way of writing shows exactly the events of
which the narrator claims to have been an eyewitness. This
points deserves to be stressed for, in this again, the *vie* provides
a criterion for the exact understanding of the 'we' used in Acts.
The interpretation of this 'we' must take account of the claims
put forward by Luke in the prologue to his work. This is what
H. J. Cadbury has sought to throw into relief.

The 'We' Passages and the Prologue

Cadbury was not the first to think that the prologue placed by
Luke at the beginning of his work (Luke 1.1–4)[27] must be taken
into consideration in the critical evaluation of the 'we' in certain

[24] p. LXXI.
[25] pp. LXIIf.
[26] And also, secondarily, the prologue of Acts (1.1) for his use of the first person
singular.
[27] See above, p. 52.

passages of the latter part of the work. As long ago as 1789 B. Königsmann[28] based himself on the prologue in rejecting the identity of the writer to Theophilus as that of the person numbered among Paul's companions in the narratives in the first person. He thought, in fact, that in the prologue the writer expressly distinguished himself from the group of those who were eyewitnesses of the events he recounts—an erroneous interpretation according to other exegetes such as B. Weiss,[29] Th. Zahn,[30] A. Harnack[31] and B. H. Streeter.[32] A careful study of the prologue shows that the writer is presenting himself as a contemporary and eyewitness of a part of the facts he recounts and this statement indicates the importance that should be attributed to the passages he writes in the first person. Such is also Cadbury's interpretation, based on a detailed investigation of the terms of the prologue.

Before discussing this exegesis, let us begin by recognizing that it is not directly opposed to Norden's theory. Greatly concerned to rediscover the 'Lucan' form of the prologue to Acts, which according to him was clumsily amputated and altered by the 'editor', Norden showed little interest in the prologue to the third Gospel. It is clear, however, that logically, according to Norden's system, this prologue must have been written by Luke, the companion of Paul, not by the editor who subjected the original work to a rewriting. Loisy in any case recognized this without the least hesitation—'The writer who says "I" in the two prologues is the one who says "we" in the account of

[28] *Lehrbuch der Einleitung* (1880), pp. 579f.
[29] *Einleitung*, II³ (1907), pp. 373f, 412 and 432.
[30] *Luke the Physician*, pp. 8–10.
[31] *The Four Gospels* (1924), pp. 457–9.
[32] H. J. Cadbury, 'The Knowledge Claimed in Luke's Preface', *Expositor*, 1922, 8th series, vol. XXIV, pp. 401–20 (this article followed a study devoted to Luke 1.4 which stressed the juridical character of the vocabulary of this verse, in which the writer shows his apologetic intention—'The Purpose Expressed in Luke's Preface', *ibid*, 1921, XXI, pp. 431–4); 'Commentary on the Preface of Luke', in *The Beginnings of Christianity*, I/II (1922), pp. 489–510; *The Making of Luke-Acts* (1927), pp. 344–8 and 358f; '*We*' and '*I*' Passages in Luke—Acts, *New Test. St.*, 1956–7, III, pp. 128–32. Cadbury's exegesis has been taken up by J. H. Ropes, 'St. Luke's Preface: ἀσφάλεια and παρακολουθεῖν', *Journ. of Theol. St.*, 1923–4, XXV, pp. 67–71; *The Synoptic Gospels*, Cambridge, Mass., 1934. See also B. W. Bacon, 'Le témoignage de Luc sur lui-même', *Rev. d'Hist. et de Philos. Rel.*, 1928, VIII, pp. 209–26; H. Sahlin, *Der Messias und das Gottesvolk* (1945), pp. 39–47.

Paul's journeys, and this companion of the Apostle must be the physician Luke mentioned in the epistles.'[33] In fact, the hypothesis that saw in the third Gospel and in Acts the result of a complete rewriting of an original work[34] has gone out of fashion, and there is no need to regret it. Today people readily admit that the prologue comes from the hand of the writer who composed the work as a whole such as it has come down to us. In these conditions what does the prologue tell us about the identity of the narrator who speaks in the first person in the narrative of Paul's journeys?

The writer first of all takes up a position in relation to his predecessors—'Forasmuch as many have taken in hand to set forth in order a narration of the things that have been accomplished among us' (Luke I.1). 'Εν ἡμῖν: this way of speaking seems to indicate that the writer, as well as his readers, classes himself among the contemporaries of these events, or at least of certain of them.[35] He continues, defining his position in relation to other persons—'according as they have delivered them to us, who from the beginning were eyewitnesses and ministers of the word' (v. 2). Here the writer counts himself among those who have received the tradition; he does not form part of the group of those who were behind this tradition, those who have been, from the beginning, eyewitnesses and ministers of the word. This does not mean that he is not in any sense an eyewitness or minister of the word; the text merely says that he has not been so from

---

[33] *Les Actes des Apôtres* (1920), p. 89. See also, by the same author, *L'Evangile selon Luc*, Paris, 1924, p. 52 and *passim*; *Les Actes des Apôtres. Traduction nouvelle* . . . (1925), p. 12. We have seen that later Loisy abandoned this interpretation. In regard to Loisy's explanations, M. Goguel writes—'There is, it must be admitted, one argument which seems very strong in favour of the identification of the writer to Theophilus with Luke, the biographer of Paul, and consequently of the attribution to an editor of everything in the Book of Acts which cannot come from a companion of Paul. This is that it seems natural to identify the first person expressed by 'I' in the prologue with the one concealed under the 'we' of certain parts of the narrative' (*Rev. d'Hist. et de Philos. Rel.*, 1921, I, p. 457). Goguel considers, however, that identity between the eyewitness and the writer of Acts is not certain, for the reconstruction of the prologue of Acts as suggested by Norden and Loisy remains conjectural. Doubtless! But should we not take account of the preface the writer to Theophilus has placed at the head of his work?

[34] See above, pp. 17–24.

[35] Cadbury does not lay much stress on this consideration.

the beginning, without stating whether this was or was not the case afterwards.[36]

After telling his readers that he has at his disposal a series of documents—the narratives composed by his predecessors—and excellent information—the tradition he has received from those who have been eyewitnesses from the beginning—the writer speaks of himself in v. 3, which is of capital importance: 'It seemed good to me also, having diligently attained to all things from the beginning, to write to thee . . . most excellent Theophilus . . .' To grasp the meaning of this verse, it is essential to realize the exact significance of the statement in which the writer declares that he has 'followed' (παρηκολουθηκότι) all things for a long time. It is on this point that Cadbury has contributed interesting details, based on extensive research. παρακολουθέω, 'to follow closely' is primarily used in its literal meaning, which is little different from that of the simple verb ἀκολουθέω, 'to follow', in speaking of a person who follows or accompanies another. Hence its use for an event which 'follows' or 'accompanies' something else;[37] then for someone who 'follows' a rule by conforming his conduct to it, or for one who 'follows' with attention and understanding the words of an orator or the text of a book. All this is not to the point. There remains a very clearly attested meaning—'to follow' events, whether by keeping oneself informed of their progress as they develop, or by being present and taking an active part in them. This meaning can be applied to the prologue without difficulty. Is there no other acceptable meaning, however? Cadbury gives an explanation of an interpretation which a certain number of

[36] Cadbury emphasizes the fact that v. 2 does not justify us in excluding Luke from the group of eyewitnesses (*Expositor*, pp. 411–16; *Beginnings*, 497f). For his explanations which are not altogether clear we are allowing ourselves to substitute another and simpler one, by drawing attention to the ἀπ' ἀρχῆς which qualifies the 'eyewitnesses and ministers of the word'. In studying the prologue word by word, Cadbury somewhat neglects the relationship which connects the words. It should also be noted that he rightly rejects the indication that certain critics would like to find in the aorists παρέδοσαν and γενόμενοι in order to assume that the eyewitnesses were already dead at the time when Luke was composing his prologue. There is nothing to be concluded, either from the use of the aorist or of the verb παραδίδωμι so far as the date of the work is concerned. (In the contrary sense, see Loisy, *Ev. selon Luc*, p. 75—'the generation of the apostles seems to have disappeared altogether').

[37] Cf. Mark, 16, 17—the signs which 'will accompany' the believers.

exegetes have accepted and which has been adopted by the *Jerusalem Bible* 'after having informed myself of all things from the beginning'.[38] Can παρακολουθέω be used in the sense of 'to inform oneself', 'to make investigations'? Cadbury has collected a large number of uses of the verb in question—there is not a single instance in which it can have the meaning of 'to inform oneself', 'to make an investigation' on past events.[39] We might think it possible to link up this interpretation with that in which 'to follow' is taken in the sense of applying our attention to the words we hear or to the text we are reading intelligently. Such hypothesis, however, is useless for, apart from the considerable difference between the generally accepted meaning and that now put forward, the latter comes up against well-established usage—when Greek writers use παρακολουθέω in the sense of reading, what they have in mind is the reading of those for whom their work is intended, not the reading they have done in preparation for it.

Account must, moreover, be taken of the general nature of

[38] E. Osty, *L'Evangile selon saint Luc* (La Sainte Bible . . . de Jérusalem), 2nd ed., Paris, 1953, p. 27. This was already the translation adopted by M. Goguel, *Introduction au N.T.*, III (1922), pp. 114f; *Le Nouveau Testament. Traduction nouvelle d'après les meilleurs textes, avec introductions et notes*, Paris, 1929, p. 89. Similar interpretation by M. J. Lagrange, *Evangile selon saint Luc* (Etudes Bibliques), Paris, 1921, pp. 5 and 7.

[39] J. H. Moulton and G. Milligan thought this meaning could be attributed to the word in the Pap. Par. 46, 19 (153 B.C.)—cf. *Expositor*, 7th series, vol. X, pp. 286f. After Cadbury's explanations of this text (*Expositor*, 8th series, vol. XXIV, pp. 405f), they changed their opinion and, not only did they support Cadbury's interpretation, but they contributed additional confirmation—*The Vocabulary of the Greek Testament Illustrated from the Papyri and Other Non-Literary Sources*, London, 1930, pp. 485f. Others have ranged themselves on the side of Cadbury, as, for instance, J. M. Creed, *The Gospel according to St Luke. The Greek Text with Introduction, Notes and Indices*, London, 1930, pp. 4f. Other exegetes refer to him, but without having grasped the import of his line of argument—A. Loisy, *L'Evangile selon saint Luc* (1924), pp. 74f., E. Klostermann, *Das Lukasevangelium* (Handb. zum N.T., 5), 2nd edition, p. 3. There is no lack of commentators who adopt the interpretation criticized by Cadbury without seeming to be aware that it is open to discussion—cf. F. Hauck, *Das Evangelium des Lukas* (Theol. Handcomm. zum N.T., III), Leipzig, 1934, p. 17; J. Schmid, *Das Evangelium nach Lukas* (Regensburger N.T., 3), 3rd ed., Ratisbon, 1955, pp. 30f. P. Schubert, 'The Structure and Significance of Luke', 24, in *Neutestamentliche Studien für Rudolf Bultmann* (Beihefte zur Zeitschr. für die neutestl. Wiss., 21), Berlin, 1954, pp. 165–86 (cf. 171); G. Kittel, *Theol. Wörterb. zum N.T.*, I, p. 216. W. Bauer remains hesitant (*Wörterbuch* 5, p. 1227), as does also the English adaptation of W. F. Arndt–F. W. Gingrich, *A Greek–English Lexicon of the New Testament and Other Early Christian Literature*, Cambridge–Chicago, 1957, p. 624.

prologues. The writer of an historical work takes pleasure in stressing the fact that he is not only indebted to others for information received, but that he was present at the events in person and played a part in them. Thus Luke would only be conforming to custom when, after having acknowledged his dependence in regard to the eyewitnesses, he is anxious to add that he also possesses a more immediate knowledge of the facts, at least of a part of them. The verb παρακολουθέω is in point of fact very appropriate for expressing the distinction between information received at second hand and that coming from the writer's personal presence at the events. Thus Josephus, in defining the duties of the historian, considers that 'he who undertakes to transmit to others a true account of the facts must first of all have an exact knowledge (ἀκριβῶς) of them himself, either from having followed the events (ἢ παρηκολουθηκότα) very closely, or from information obtained from those who have knowledge of them'.[40] In this context the verb is used currently in the perfect to show that at the time when he undertook his work the author was in possession of all the information we could expect from one who 'has followed matters closely'.[41]

Justified solely from the lexicographical point of view and from that of the literary genre to which the prologue belongs, this interpretation of παρηκολουθηκότι must also account for the adverb ἄνωθεν which defines the exact time from which Luke declares that he 'followed the events closely'. The *Jerusalem Bible* translates 'from the beginnings';[42] this is to set Luke in contradiction with himself when he distinguishes himself from those who were eyewitnesses from the beginning (v. 2) and to

---

[40] *Contra Apionem*, I, 10. 53. Another example often quoted is that of Demosthenes in his speech *De Corona*—the orator presents himself as a man who has 'followed the events from the beginning' (παρακολουθηκότα τοῖς πράγμασιν ἐξ ἀρχῆς), and he justifies his claim in speaking not of an investigation he has conducted, but of the fact that he alone remained at his post in the midst of the dangers and has not ceased to play a major part in the management of affairs (§§172f, pp. 284f).

[41] This explanation (*Expositor*, p. 408) contrasts with that of Lagrange ('The perfect indicates a prolonged investigation'—*Ev. selon saint Luc*, p. 5), and with that of Zahn (Luke's work was finished when he decided to write—*Das Evangelium des Lukas*. Komm. Zum N.T., III, Leipzig, 1913, p. 54).

[42] Osty insists—'From the beginnings: not only of the public ministry of Jesus, but of Jesus himself (like Matthew) and of his precursor John the Baptist' (*loc. cit.*).

attribute to him a presumption which it would be difficult to justify. ἄνωθεν, which means literally 'from on high', is used by Luke only in one other passage of his work in which, as in the prologue, it is contrasted with ἀπ' ἀρχῆς —'And my life indeed from my youth, which was from the beginning (ἀπ' ἀρχῆς) among my own nation in Jerusalem, all the Jews do know: Having known me from the beginning (ἄνωθεν) . . .' (Acts 26.4f). Paul is right to suppose that all the Jews are informed about the life he has led from his youth; but he is far from thinking that all know *him* from his childhood—it is sufficient that they have known him for a long time. Thus ἄνωθεν expresses less than ἀπ' ἀρχῆς[43] and the meaning which is applicable to Acts 26.5 fits perfectly Luke 1.3—the writer is stating that he has followed the events not from the beginning, but for a considerable time.[44] No more is necessary.

[43] Such is clearly the thought of Cadbury; however, in *Beginnings*, II (1922), pp. 502f, he speaks of these two expressions as being synonymous, and was followed in this explanation by Trocmé (*op. cit.*, p. 127). In his article in the *Expositor* in 1922 he wrote that ἄνωθεν designates 'that early time in his own life at which his touch with events began and from which it has continued' (p. 409), and denied that ἄνωθεν was necessarily the equivalent of ἀπ'ἀρχῆς—Luke simply meant that his familiarity with the events went back a long way, without claiming that it coincided with the beginning of his history. In *The Making of Luke-Acts* (1927), Cadbury stated—'ἄνωθεν carried back not from the ministry of John to Luke's birth stories, but from the time of writing back over a considerable period of the author's own association with the movement he is describing' (p. 347). The 1957 article is perfectly clear—'Luke does not claim knowledge of this kind (at first-hand) for all of his two books, but only for a late though substantial period. ἄνωθεν 'from a good while back', is quite different from ἀπ'ἀρχῆς in the preceding clause about the informants on whom the Gospel writers including Luke rely. A similar accurately discriminating use of the two words occurs in the successive clauses of Acts XXVI, 4f . . .' (*N.T. St.*, III, p. 130). J. H. Ropes took up Cadbury's interpretation again in *Journ. of Theol. St.*, XXV, p. 71.

[44] W. Bauer (*Wörterbuch*, col. 153) gives for Luke 1.3 the meaning 'from the beginning', for Acts 26.5 'from a long time past. In reality, the adverb does not indicate the point of departure; it only shows the direction—it is necessary 'to go back'. There is no reason for introducing the idea of beginning if it is not imposed by other factors. The interesting parallels pointed out by Bauer in favour of the meaning 'from a long time past' should be noted. Lagrange translates 'from a long time past' (*Luc*, p. 6), Loisy 'a long time back' (*Luc*, 74f). After having accepted the equivalence of ἄνωθεν and ἀπ' ἀρχῆς on the evidence of Cadbury, Trocmé turns the difficulty by explaining—'In Luke 1.2, ἀπ' ἀρχῆς applies to the ministry of the privileged witnesses; in Luke 1.3, ἄνωθεν is to be understood of the writer *ad Theophilum* and signifies that the latter has been *continually* kept informed, that he has *from the beginning* followed the events which have been happening under his eyes' (*op. cit.*, p. 127). In practice this is to return to the interpretation which corresponds to Cadbury's latest thought.

In his prologue Luke claims a direct knowledge of the events he recounts after following them for a long time past. This statement throws a considerable light on the presence of 'we' in the latter part of the work. Cadbury draws attention to the process by which, at the end of the we-passages, the writer is careful to dissociate Paul from his companions before continuing his narrative which now treats of Paul alone;[45] thus the 'we' is by no means inadvertent, it is quite deliberate. The prologue indicates its meaning—'A writer who declares that he has "followed the events" does not use "we" in speaking of certain episodes without intending to show that he was a witness to them.[46] The writer who uses "we" was the one who wrote the prologue to the work—the one to whom must be attributed not only a particular source, but the work as a whole.'[47]

[45] *N.T. St.*, III, pp. 129f. The final 'we' of the first we-passage occurs in 16.17—'This same (the possessed girl) following (us), *Paul and us*, cried out . . .' The final 'we' of the second we-passage occurs in 21.18–'The day following, Paul went in with *us* unto James.' The method used in the construction of these verses is quite clear. The writer might have been content with the pronoun: the possessed girl followed *us*; *we* went in unto James; he has preferred to separate Paul from the group of his companions, thus paving the way for the rest of the narrative which mentions Paul only. The case of the third 'we' passage is not quite so clear; the final 'we' occurs in 28.16—'And when we were come to Rome, Paul was suffered to dwell by himself, with a soldier that kept him.' The expression 'by himself' may mean that Paul was dispensed from having to be confined with other prisoners, or from the obligation of remaining with his keepers; in fact, however, it would also seem to imply that Paul was alone with the soldier who was guarding him, thus being separated from the group of his companions. In any case, this group does not appear again in the rest of the narrative; living 'by himself', Paul alone remains on the stage, as it were, and the statement of v. 16 paves the way for this new situation.

[46] E. Trocmé, *op. cit.*, p. 126, drawing the conclusion which emerges from Cadbury's explanations. See in the same sense what F. Stagg wrote in the introduction to his commentary, *The Book of Acts. The Early Struggle for an Unhindered Gospel* (Nashville, 1955)—'The author of Acts . . . plainly states that he was not a personal witness to much about which he wrote, but he does claim to have been a witness to and participant in some of the events. A writer so careful to acknowledge his sources (cf. Luke 1.1–4) would not have been so crude as to incorporate another's diary into his own work without even changing the narratives from first to third person. Whoever wrote "we" also wrote the book.'

[47] While accepting the fact that the work dedicated to Theophilus was composed by a companion of St Paul on his journey, Cadbury remains sceptical on the possibility of identifying this companion by name—'It is possible that in the second century it was really known that Luke had been the author, but probably the tradition would have come into existence quite as early and as definitely if it were not known' (*The Making of Luke-Acts*, p. 356). The traditional attribution to Luke would simply result from conjectures formed from the texts. In his review of our work, Cadbury regrets that we have not taken into consideration 'the possibility

A. D. Nock[48] long considered as impossible the attribution of Acts to the physician Luke, the companion of the Apostle; in 1953, however, he finally came to accept this view, expressing his argument with the exegesis of Cadbury and Ropes. Taking the forms of expression of ancient literature into account, the use of 'we' in certain narratives of Acts must be understood as an indication on the part of the narrator that he took part in the events. This indication links up with that of the prologue of the work, in which the author explicitly declares that he has been in personal contact with the Christian movement for a period which is already considerable. The hypothesis of an editorial rewriting being excluded for reasons of style, it would seem that no consideration is sufficient to justify us in rejecting the claim made by the author of the two books dedicated to Theophilus.[49]

Cadbury's explanations have not seemed convincing to all

---

that the traditional choice of Luke rests itself on early Christian interpretation of the "I" and "we" of Luke—Acts' (*Journ. of Bibl. Lit.*, 1961, LXXX, p. 79). He is right in thinking that it seems to us very difficult to assume so certain a talent for literature in a secondary personage, and that among Christians very close to the time when the work was composed—close enough for the third Gospel never to have had any other name than that to which this process of learned conjecture would have led.

[48] A. D. Nock in his review of M. Dibelius, *Aufsätze zur Apostelgeschichte* published in *Gnomon*, 1953, XXV, pp. 497–506. This long review (ten pages of closely printed text) forms an important contribution to the study of Acts. The passage which we sum up here is on pp. 502f.

[49] In his book published in 1959 (p. 126; cf. 129), F. C. Grant considers two explanations for the 'we'—the mechanical transcription of a 'we' source, or, the writer's unconscious appeal to his personal memories. The second hypothesis is given the preference, but the only argument brought forward is the analogy supplied by the *Histoire de Montréal* (1590–1672) written about 1673 by François Dollier de Casson (published in Montreal in 1868), who similarly uses the first person in speaking of events in which he took part. We have come across more significant parallels. In 1960, in the third edition of his work *Die Mitte der Zeit* (p. 7, n. 1), H. Conzelmann is no longer satisfied to recall that, in accordance with common opinion, the prologue to the third Gospel also refers to the narrative of Acts; he rejects this opinion, contrasting with it the general practice in regard to prologues in ancient literature—used in the first place in epidictic literature, it was only later that they came to be used in historical works, when history began to be written under the form of monographs. This consideration does not seem to us very enlightening. It can very well be granted that Luke's preface introduces a monograph, without its being necessary to conclude from this that this monograph must consist of a single book. An example will be more instructive than a long discussion—Flavius Josephus put at the beginning of his *Contra Apionem* (I, 1–5) a prologue which clearly concerns the whole work, Book II as well as Book I.

his readers.[50] This is particularly so in the case of Haenchen, who has set out his difficulties in a further study.[51] He considers that Cadbury's lexicographical arguments do not take sufficient account of the exact meaning that the terms used in the prologue to the Third Gospel acquire from their immediate context. In v. 1, Luke shows his knowledge of earlier attempts than his own to write a Gospel;[52] in v. 2 he places these attempts and his own in relation to the preaching of those who have been eyewitnesses from the beginning—the written narratives group and set in order the traditions whose origin and guarantee is from the eyewitnesses.[53] V. 3 defines the author's intention—he

[50] We would hesitate to refer to Cadbury's 'readers' as contradictors. However, among them we should note F. H. Colson, 'Notes on St Luke's Preface, suggested by reading the second volume of Foakes-Jackson and Kirsopp Lake's 'Beginnings of Christianity', *Journal of Theological Studies*, 1922–3, XXIV, pp. 300–9. This article (April 1923) shows no knowledge of the explanations given by Cadbury in the *Expositor* for December 1922. It drew a reply from J. H. Ropes in his note of October 1923. In repeating his explanation in *The Making of Luke-Acts* (1927), Cadbury cites another contradictor, A. T. Robertson, *Expository Times*, 1923–4, XXXV, pp. 319ff. His 1957 article, finally, answers the difficulties raised by N. B. Stonehouse, *The Witness of Luke to Christ*, Grand Rapids, 1951, pp. 35–40; this writer criticizes the interpretation of Cadbury and of Ropes, but without having taken the trouble to consult the articles in which they have set out the reasons which have guided them.

[51] Dr Haenchen has been so very kind as to let me see (July 1961) the manuscript of his article 'Das "Wir" in der Apostelgeschichte und das Itinerar', which is to appear in the *Zeitschr. für Theol. und Kirche* (the examination of the prologue of Luke occupies the final pages of this article); he has also kindly answered the questions I have put to him, thus enabling me to grasp his thought more precisely. I should like here to express deep gratitude to him.

[52] 'Forasmuch as many have taken in hand to set forth in order a narration of the things that have been accomplished among us.' If it is true that Luke possessed Gospel narratives and used them to compile his own account of the actions and words of Jesus, it is very unlikely that he had a similar source available for composing the Acts of the Apostles. From this point of view, the preface to the Gospel more directly concerns the first of the two books to Theophilus; but we do not think the statement is sufficient to allow us to exclude the second: according to the custom of the times, a preface placed at the beginning of a work is valid for the work as a whole, even if certain of its expressions apply only to a part (cf. Cadbury, *Beginnings*, II, pp. 489–92; *Expositor*, 1923, p. 414). Cadbury insists on the fact that it is a question of 'things accomplished among us', which is more applicable to the events related in the Acts (*Beginnings*, II, pp. 495f); to which Haenchen replies, not without reason, that it is a matter of events which have formed the subject of written narratives—this can scarcely apply to anything but to the attempts at a Gospel narrative. Thus it seems difficult to seek in such a narrative an indication relating to events in Acts and above all in the second part of Acts.

[53] 'As those have transmitted it to us, who, from the beginning have been eyewitnesses and ministers of the word.' What the eyewitnesses transmitted by their ministry of the word is to be found in the Gospel; Acts seek to show rather *how* they

is going to compose a narrative of the facts after having himself 'followed all things attentively for a long time'. Haenchen considers that with the adverb ἀκριβῶς the participle παρηκολουθηκότι cannot mean 'to follow the events personally by taking part in them'; we must understand 'to inform oneself carefully'.[54] It is certain, moreover, that the author does not want to, and, indeed, cannot say that he has personally followed 'everything' which is going to form the subject of his narrative; moreover, the expression ἄνωθεν is naturally understood as a synonym of ἀπ' ἀρχῆς, and it seems here to justify a narrative which starts

transmitted it. It is clear that Luke distinguishes himself from 'those who have been eyewitnesses from the beginning'. He also distinguishes from them all 'those who have undertaken to compose a narration of the events which have been accomplished among us'. Are we to conclude from this that he knew no attempt at a Gospel narrative attributable to an apostle? The question crops up in regard to Matthew: Luke clearly did not know the Gospel of Matthew as it has come down to us; but is it certain that he had not at his disposal one or other of those attempts at translations of the *logia* of which Papias said that they were written in Hebrew by Matthew? It seems to us that such an exclusion would force the meaning of the terms of the prologue; Cadbury considers that the antitheses there are less 'exclusive contrasts' than 'inclusive comparisons' (*Expositor*, p. 414); the remark is again valid for v. 3, where the author is seeking not so much to oppose his predecessors as to be in accord with them.

[54] It must be recognized that Cadbury's interpretation does not explain without difficulty the use of this adverb. It must also be admitted that his exegesis of the verb παρακολουθέω is open to argument. In his article in the *Expositor* (pp. 402f), he distinguishes six different meanings of this verb. We can put aside without hesitation 'to follow' as one follows someone (in the physical and the metaphysical sense), 'to follow' a rule by conforming to it, 'to follow' in the sense of 'to result from'. We are left with three—'to follow with attention and understanding' what is said or written (cf. *Beginnings*, II, p. 501), 'to follow personally' of events in the process of their development, finally 'to inform oneself', 'to make investigations'. Cadbury excludes this last meaning—there is no confirmation of it anywhere; he also puts aside without much explanation, 'to follow with attention and understanding' what is said or written; the meaning 'to follow (events) personally' is thus the only one left. The proof is perhaps faulty. When Demosthenes says that he has 'followed the events from the beginning', he is not only speaking of events in which he has taken part personally; some of them have taken place at a distance and he only knows them from the information he has received about them—and he has received such information because he has taken care to inform himself. It remains true, however, that Demosthenes has kept himself informed of events as they have occurred; the way in which he has 'followed' them presupposes that the events are contemporary. Luke, however, is in a different position; he clearly cannot say that he has followed 'all' (πᾶσιν) the events as they have developed—concerned with 'all things that Jesus began to do and to teach' (Acts 1.1) his first book only claims to be based on the 'traditions' (Luke 1.2) coming from eyewitnesses.

from the circumstances of the birth of Jesus.[55] Thus there is no
reason to look in this verse for guarantees supplied by the author
for narratives which will only occur in the second part of Acts;
Luke is thinking of the history of Jesus and is anxious to show
that he is qualified to write it.

[55] This explanation does not seem to us admissible. In the first place it must be
noted that, in the context of Luke, the word ἀρχή normally designates the Baptism,
the point of departure of the activity of Jesus (cf. Luke 3.23; 23.5; Acts 1.1, 22;
10.37; see U. Wilckens, *Zeitschr. für die neutestl. Wiss.*, 1958, LXIX, p. 232). It is
difficult to see how the term ἄνωθεν, much more vague, could go still farther back
into events. It would certainly be preferable to refer ἄνωθεν not to the events or to
the narrative, but to the time when the writer began to 'follow' the information
which reached him—he has 'followed' it 'for a long time past' and 'carefully'.

VII

THE ITINERARY

HERE AGAIN we are concerned with the narrative of Paul's journeys and with the source the writer used. Looking at the problem from the point of view of literary form, M. Dibelius defines this as an itinerary. A brief summary of his theory will be given, followed by the views of H. J. Cadbury, the trend of which is rather similar. The reactions to Dibelius's hypothesis among recent writers, both those who accept his views at least partially and those who think it necessary to modify the nature of the itinerary somewhat, will then be discussed. The critics who call in question the existence of this source will form the subject of the following chapter.

Dibelius's Hypothesis

The work of M. Dibelius, *Die Formgeschichte des Evangeliums*, published in 1919,[1] defined a method of approach to which at the same time it gave its name—*Formgeschichte* (Form-Criticism). Attention, however, was concentrated almost exclusively on the synoptic tradition; it was in order to get beyond the inextricable 'synoptic question'—a problem of sources—that people wanted to get back to the material which had been gradually elaborated in oral preaching before being given a fixed form in the Gospels. In 1923, in his article 'Stilkritisches zur Apostelgeschichte',[2]

[1] M. Dibelius, *Die Formgeschichte des Evangeliums*, Tübingen, 1919. A third edition, published with the help of G. Bornkamm and with the addition of an appendix by G. Iber, appeared in 1959. The hypothesis which will be discussed here is not, however, to be found in this particular book.

[2] M. Dibelius, 'Stilkritisches zur Apostelgeschichte', in *EYXAPIΣΘPION. Studien zur Religion und Literatur des Alten und Neuen Testaments Hermann Gunkel dargebracht*, vol. II (Forschungen zur Rel. und Lit. des A. und N.T., 36/2), Göttingen, 1923, pp. 27–49. This study has been reproduced in the series published by H.

Dibelius shows the possible application of the new method in the study of the Acts of the Apostles.[3] The situation was considerably different from that of the Gospels. The author was much less bound by an established tradition, since the doings of the apostles did not provide matter for preaching like those of Jesus. He must necessarily be more personal both in the choice of his materials and in their ordering and rewriting. He none the less must have used material which, for a good part at least, already existed; it had taken form and had developed in accordance with the laws of the literary genres to which it belonged. Dibelius sets out to distinguish the small literary units which have been incorporated in the narrative; he regroups them in accordance with their affinities and endeavours to define the genre on which they depend. This work was not to lead him to the discovery of continuous sources in which different passages have been combined in a continuous narrative prior to that of Acts; Dibelius is convinced, on the contrary, that sources of this kind never existed.[4] There is, however, one exception—the story of Paul's missionary journeys (13.4–14.28 and 15.36–21.16) is based on a written document which has supplied the framework and served as a guiding thread: 'the itinerary'.[5]

Greeven: M. Dibelius, *Aufsätze zur Apostelgeschichte* (Forschungen zur Rel. und Lit. des A. und N.T., 60), Göttingen, 1951, pp. 9–28. (The pagination is that of the *Aufsätze*.)

[3] Dibelius returned to the question in his survey 'Zur Formgeschichte des Neuen Testaments', *Theologische Rundschau*, 1931, N.F. III, pp. 209–42—see §IV, 'Das formgeschichtliche Problem der Apostelgeschichte', pp. 233–41 (not reproduced in the *Aufsätze*). He is there concerned with the analysis of small literary units, but does not dwell on the itinerary.

[4] No continuous source for the last chapters (from 21.17)—p. 14; or indeed for ch. 1 to 5, p. 15; or for ch. 6–12, although certain narratives of these chapters reproduce traditions already formed (6.8–8.3; 9.1–30; 10.1–11.18, excluding the discourses of ch. 7 and 10)—p. 16. The question of determining what depends on tradition and what belongs to the writer's own work should be given special investigation for each of the elements of the narrative—p. 17.

[5] The word occurs in J. Wellhausen, *Noten zur Apostelgeschichte* (Nachrichten von der Kgl. Gesellschaft der Wiss. zu Göttingen, Phil. hist., Kl., 1907), Göttingen 1907, pp. 1–21—cf. p. 21. Wellhausen was protesting against hypotheses which break up Acts into a series of sources which Luke merely had to juxtapose. It remains true, however, that Luke has used fragmentary sources, sometimes contenting himself with linking them together by means of very obvious joins; under-

The following is the way in which Dibelius imagines this 'itinerary'[6]—it was 'a report of halting-places on the journey, most probably containing brief information on the foundation of new communities and the success of the mission'.[7] The use of the 'we' plays no part in the determination of this source—first, because the we-sections are in no way different from sections written in the third person; secondly, because the 'we' may have been added or omitted by the compiler.[8] We must thus depend solely on literary factors. Dibelius stresses the uniform character of the information concerning the stages of the journey; if the editor had only local traditions at his disposal, it is possible to think that he would have lingered more over certain stages and passed over others in silence; reports like those devoted to Derbe,[9] Thessalonica,[10] Berea,[11] would doubtless have found no place in a work whose purpose was edification, if they had not been in some sort imposed on the writer by the source he was using. The use of this source is again shown

---

lying ch. 16–21 it is possible to recognize an itinerary, which has been re-edited and enriched with supplementary episodes. In 1914 Wellhausen indicated that this source was written in the first person and that the author of Acts only knew fragments of it (*Kritische Analyse der Apostelgeschichte*, p. 39).

[6] An excellent statement of Dibelius's hypothesis and of the arguments on which it is based can be found at the beginning of the article which G. Schille devoted to the refutation of this theory—'Die Fragwürdigkeit eines Itinerars der Paulusreisen', *Theol. Literaturzeitung*, 1959, LXXXIX, col. 165–74.

[7] *Aufsätze*, p. 12.

[8] In his article in 1939 in which, without knowing of Dibelius's study, S. E. Johnson embarked on the same work, the choice is given between two types of theory concerning the use of the 'we' in Acts—(1) the traditional explanation, according to which the book was written by some companion of Paul, who recounts in the 'we' sections events in which he has taken part; (2) if the author did not accompany Paul, his narrative is based on traditions or on a series of documents which have been worked over to such an extent that it is no longer possible to identify them. There would be an intermediate position, in accordance with which one of Paul's companions would have written a diary, the editor of the book afterwards contenting himself with incorporating it into his work as it was—this position is becoming increasingly difficult if not impossible ('A Proposed Form-Critical Treatment of Acts', *Anglican Theol. Rev.*, XXI, pp. 30f). The 'we' should find its explanation in the process of the book's composition; to want to account for it solely by its presence in a source is to have recourse to an expedient which explains nothing.

[9] Acts 14.21.

[10] Acts 17.1ff.

[11] Acts 17.10ff.

by the incoherences and lack of smoothness resulting from the addition of extraneous passages by the writer—14.8–18;[12] 16.25–40;[13] 20.7–12,[14] and the discourses. It is generally sufficient to exclude these sections to see the regular pattern of the itinerary come to light. In certain cases this pattern is no longer recognizable; Luke would naturally be suspected here of having abridged his source (thus for 16.6–6).[15] In his later works Dibelius often returned to his hypothesis and added new points to it.[16] In 1939,[17] he gave a more detailed definition of the 'itinerary'; it consisted of

> information about the stages of the journey, the hospitality received, the missionary activity and the success of the preaching, the foundation of new communities, the opposition and the departure, free or forced.[18] These reports have too little colour for us to be able to attach them to local traditions; by their brevity, their neutral attitude, their stereotyped character, they stand out markedly from the other elements of the narrative, whether anecdotes or speeches.[19]

[12] *Aufsätze*, pp. 13 and 25.
[13] Cf. p. 24–25. The itinerary must have mentioned the imprisonment of Paul and Silas without giving the motive, then at the time of their liberation mentioned Paul's claim demanding a complete rehabilitation.
[14] Cf. pp. 21–22.
[15] p. 12. Luke abridged in his desire to emphasize the initiative taken by the Holy Spirit, over and above all human intervention. In certain cases, such as 20.1–3, the indication of the stages of the journey may have been wanting in the source.
[16] On the question of the sources of Acts, there is nothing very new in the *Geschichte der urchristlichen Literatur* (Sammlung Göschen, 934 and 935), Berlin–Leipzig, 1926—see vol. II, pp. 100f. The only connected account which may have served as a source for the narratives of Acts is that used to recount the history of the Pauline missions—a kind of travel report, an enumeration of the halting-places in the journey and of foundations of churches, which constitutes the framework of the narrative, at least from ch. 13 to ch. 21. On another question, that of attributing the authorship of the two books to Theophilus, Dibelius in 1926 took up a position which he does not seem to have defended earlier—he was no longer satisfied to evade the problem, but pronounced clearly in favour of Luke, the physician and the companion of Paul (vol. I, p. 47; vol. II, p. 101). From this time, he has always maintained this point of view; we shall have occasion to refer to this again.
[17] M. Dibelius, 'Paulus auf dem Areopag' (*Sitzungsberichte der Heidelberger Akademie der Wiss., Phil. hist. Kl.*, 1938–9, fasc. 2), Heidelberg, 1939. A study reproduced in *Aufsätze*, pp. 29–70. His conclusions are summarized in the article 'Paulus in Athen.', *Forschungen und Fortschritte*, 1939, XV, pp. 210f = *Aufsätze*, pp. 71–75.
[18] *Aufsätze*, p. 64.
[19] In the Athens episode, vv. 17 and 34 of ch. 17 must come from the itinerary;

Taken together, they appear as so many fragments of a single source.

The itinerary hypothesis appears again, without change, in an article in 1941[20] and in what he wrote in 1944.[21] There is still the same definition of the content of the itinerary in an article in 1947,[22] in which the essential argument in favour of the existence of this itinerary is the fact that Luke notes halting-places which have no interest from the point of view of his narrative;[23] refusing to see in the 'we' an indication of this source, Dibelius shows himself inclined to attribute this 'we' to Luke's editing due to his desire to point out the fact that he shared in certain of Paul's journeys.[24] A further development is given in a subsequent study which formed the subject of an article in 1947:[25] Dibelius investigates the reason for the existence of a report of the various stages and thinks he has found

---

the mention of an Areopagite in v. 34 has perhaps provided the occasion for the discourse in the Areopagus and of the parts of the narrative linked with this. It is not, however, excluded that certain expressions of vv. 19 and 20 may also come from the itinerary. Cf. *Aufsätze*, pp. 69–71.

[20] M. Dibelius, 'The Text of Acts. An Urgent Critical Task', *Journal of Religion*, 1941, XXI, pp. 411–31. The original German version was published in the *Aufsätze*, pp. 76–83. The author stresses (pp. 77f) the discrepancies caused by the insertion of extraneous passages in the itinerary and shows the effort made by the copyists to conceal these discrepancies.

[21] 'Die Reden der Apostelgeschichte und die antike Geschichtsschreibung' (*Sitzungsberichte der Heidelberger Akad. der Wiss., Phil. hist. Kl.*, 1949/1). Heidelberg, 1949 (the statement had been made five years earlier). Again stated in *Aufsätze*, pp. 120–62. Dibelius considered that the use by Luke of an itinerary indicating the stages of Paul's journey was certain; he explains the reasons which led Luke to abridge his source in 16.6–10 (p. 128) and states that this source contained no discourses (p. 141, n. 1, and p. 151, n.).

[22] 'Die Apostelgeschichte als Geschichtsquelle', *Forschungen und Fortschritte*, 1947, XXI–XXIII, pp. 67–69 = *Aufsätze*, pp. 91–95.

[23] 'It must be admitted that, as a source for Paul's journeys, Luke had at his disposal a statement of the stages of the journey; in fact, he even indicates halting-places of no importance. In this itinerary there must also have been, according to all appearances, remarks as to their welcome, hospitality received, their activity and success' (p. 93).

[24] 'Under the influence of modern historical conceptions, it has been thought that the "we" represented the most primitive element of the whole account of the journey; it is possible, however, that it was only introduced by Luke's editing, desirous as he was of pointing out his own share in Paul's journeys' (*ibid.*).

[25] *Der erste christliche Historiker*, in Schriften der Universität Heidelberg, III, Aus der Arbeit der Universität, 1946–47, Heidelberg, 1948, pp. 112–25 = *Aufsätze*, pp. 108–19.

it in considerations of a practical order—if they were to make the same journey later, this would enable them to find their way again together with the sympathizers who had given them hospitality the first time.[26] The same explanation occurs in a study published in 1951.[27]

Dibelius constantly returns to the idea that his hypothesis is independent of the occurrence of the 'we' in certain passages which depend on the itinerary. This 'we' does not prove the existence of a source and, conversely, does not find sufficient explanation in the hypothesis which suggests that it refers back to a source. We should look for the explanation in the editing—whether the writer of the book retained it or introduced it in narratives which did not already contain it matters little; one thing is certain, that the 'we' is intentional and deliberate. Dibelius sees only one way of accounting for the procedure—the writer uses the first person plural to indicate his presence at the side of Paul. This explanation assumes that the third Gospel and Acts were composed by a companion of the Apostle. Dibelius accepts this assumption without hesitation. Since 1926[28] he has

---

[26] '(In ch. 13 to 21) Luke obviously has at his disposal a record of the journey's stages, such as were composed on the occasion of journeys of this kind, even if only for practical reasons—in order that when the journey was repeated it would be possible to find the same route and the same hospitality. That such a source has been used is clear from the fact that Luke even mentions stages of the journey which are of no importance, about which in actual fact he had nothing to recount . . . (cf. 20.13–14)' (p. 110). Farther on (pp. 113f) Dibelius returns to the reasons which urged Luke to abridge the itinerary in 16.6–10.

[27] Dibelius died on 11th November 1947. The study to which we refer was published in the *Aufsätze*, pp. 163–74, under the title—'Die Apostelgeschichte im Rahmen der urchristlichen Literaturgeschichte'. The itinerary is discussed in pp. 167–70. Dibelius observed in the first place that Luke's way of proceeding would be incomprehensible if, mentioning as he does stages of the journey without any importance, he did not do this in dependence on a source—cf. 14.25; 16.11; 17.1; 18.22; 20.13–14; 21.16. He goes on to point out that it is not possible to attribute to this source the discourses which have been added to it by the editor (13.16–41; 14.15–17; 17.22–31; 20.10–35); the same applies to the stories which must have circulated as isolated pieces of information (13.8–12; 14.8–18; 16.25–34; 19.14–16). When account is taken of Luke's editing the source stands out clearly as an itinerary, a record of stages of the journey, which was to serve to find the route and the houses where they had been given hospitality, again. Dibelius again refers to the itinerary in his work *Paulus*, which was finished and published by W. G. Kümmel (Sammlung Göschen 1160), Berlin, 1951, p. 12.

[28] *Geschichte der urchristlichen Literatur*, I, pp. 45–47; II, p. 101—Dibelius used the same explanation in 1941 (*Aufsätze*), pp. 79–81; in 1947 he emphasized that his positions on this point had not changed for twenty years (*ibid.*, p. 85, n. 2), and

not ceased to repeat that the traditional attribution of the work
to Luke, the physician (of Antioch?) and companion of Paul,
deserves to be taken seriously. To justify this assertion, he draws
evidence from the prologue to the Gospel: by placing this
passage at the head of his work, the writer makes literary claims
that are not contradicted by the rest of his narrative, especially
in Acts; by inserting in the prologue a dedication to someone
who occupies an official position, the writer also shows his
desire, in accordance with the custom of the time, to see the
fruit of his labours published. A work published in these circumstances should bear the name of its author. Since any substitution of names is most unlikely in the present instance, the
ecclesiastical tradition which attributes the work to Luke must
have found its origin in the title that the work possessed from
the beginning, from the time of its publication, that is, from the
time when it was sent to the 'most excellent Theophilus'. The
exact terms of this title have not been preserved—we could, for
instance, suppose it to be—'Acts of Jesus, by Luke (of Antioch)'.
The essential thing is to realize that the name of Luke could not
fail to be mentioned, from the beginning, in the title which
preceded the prologue.

Dibelius knew quite well that this attribution raised difficulties. The narratives which Acts devotes to Paul do not give
us the exact picture of the life and thought of the Apostle that
we should have the right to expect from a man who had lived
in his company for a long time: Dibelius thrust aside this
objection which sought to define *a priori* the line of conduct
expected of a companion of Paul. From the historical point of
view, it is considered improbable that a companion of Paul
should have been able to write what Acts says of the Council of

---

repeated the explanations he had already given (*ibid.*, pp. 92 and 96); what he
wrote in 1944 and his 1948 article revert to the question with new details, especially
as far as the original title of the work is concerned (*ibid.*, pp. 126–8 and 118–19; see
also p. 108). The same theory occurs again in his posthumous publications (*ibid.*,
p. 163; *Paulus*, p. 12)—The consideration to which Dibelius attached so much
importance is not really new; Harnack, for instance, had already drawn attention
to it in 1907 (*Luke the Physician*, p. 2), and Zahn, the same year, denied that it had
any value (*Einleitung in das N.T.*, II, p. 365). It was given a good deal of pro-
minence in B. H. Streeter, *The Four Gospels* (1924), pp. 558–60.

Jerusalem, an account which it is difficult to reconcile with what the Apostle himself says about it: Dibelius's answer was[29] (1) the conception that Luke and his contemporaries formed of history was not that of a reporter; (2) Luke had not necessarily to ask for precise details from Paul at a time when he had not yet formed the intention of writing his work; (3) Luke attached less importance to detailed accuracy than to calling attention to the movement of history[30] such as he conceived it. From the theological point of view, it is submitted that a companion of the Apostle could not have credited him with the views which are developed in the discourse in the Areopagus: Dibelius's reply[31] was that this, too, is erroneous, for in writing this discourse, Luke was thinking primarily and above all of his readers and of the practical needs of catechesis in the circles for which he was writing his work; he had no obligation to reproduce literally and in a servile way the exact thought of the Apostle of the Gentiles.

Whatever may be the value of some of Dibelius's arguments, it seems certain that the hypothesis which attributes to Luke the authorship of Acts supplies the simplest and most natural explanation of the use of the 'we' in certain places of the narrative. Dibelius was right in thinking that nothing is gained by linking up this 'we' with a source; whether the author retained it from elsewhere or introduced it into his text, he must have had precise reasons for preferring the first person in the incidents where he uses it. Among such reasons, the most obvious is the desire to emphasize his participation in the events recounted.

Cadbury's Theories

Independently of Dibelius, but, like him, following the line of research deriving from Norden, H. J. Cadbury, in 1927[32], also referred to an 'itinerary' in connection with the account of

---

[29] *Aufsätze*, p. 88, n. 3.

[30] Cf. *ibid.*, p. 113.

[31] The two studies of 1939—*Aufsätze*, pp. 29–70 and 71–75 (see in particular the conclusions—pp. 70 and 75).

[32] H. J. Cadbury, *The Making of Luke-Acts*, New York, 1927, 2nd ed., London, 1958. Dibelius's name does not appear in the *Index*. On the other hand, Dibelius never referred to Cadbury in his theories concerning the itinerary.

Paul's journeys. This narrative raises different problems, such as that of knowing whether certain longer incidents inserted in its pattern form part of the original framework or not, or that of explaining the presence of the 'we' in certain sections of the itinerary but not throughout. By all the evidence this material is not a mere collection of episodes, but a connected geographical pattern, suggesting a crystallization of the information made at an early period and really with a biographical (autobiographical?) intention. It offers the advantage of supplying the editor with a sequence of events and a plan already drawn up. A work of this kind finds its parallels in contemporary literature, whether serious or of the imagination. There is a whole series of them, from the round voyage of an admiral or the military advance of a general down to the *True History* of Lucian and the novels of other Gullivers of ancient times. The style of a travel diary occasionally serves as an editorial framework in which are inserted episodes, isolated incidents, somewhat like the string on which the beads of a necklace are threaded—such an instance is the march of the Israelites in the desert or the narrative of the journey of Jesus in Luke. The itinerary of Acts, which is as discontinuous as it well can be, is in any case of a different genre from that of any other material.[33] This genre is that of the travel narratives which we find in Greek literature. It has its common features, such as the story of a storm and a shipwreck on a desert island;[34] it has its peculiarities of style, such as the use of the first person.[35]

Cadbury does not venture further than this. He contents himself with defining the literary genre on which the narratives of Paul's journeys, which form the framework of the second part of Acts, depend; what he says of the primitive 'crystallization' of the itinerary could lead us to deduce the existence of a source in the usual sense of the word, but Cadbury does not draw this conclusion.[36] His comparison with the journey of Jesus in the

---

[33] *The Making*, pp. 6of.
[34] Cf. *ibid.*, pp. 135 and 144.
[35] pp. 144f and 156f.
[36] Cadbury recalls the hypothesis, p. 230; after saying that the introduction of the 'we' into the places where there is question of an embarkation can be very

third Gospel, a journey which simply provides a literary framework for a whole series of isolated incidents, makes us think
rather of an editorial process. The 'we', a characteristic feature
of travel narratives, can, moreover, be attributed to the writer
of the work and is not explained by appealing to a source.[37] In
speaking of an 'itinerary', like Dibelius, Cadbury merely intends
to define a literary 'form', without pronouncing as to the
existence of a source made use of by Luke.

The Problem of the 'We'

Among the writers who, in varying degrees, have followed in the
wake of Dibelius, a general tendency is shown which more or
less consciously seeks a compromise between the hypothesis of
'the itinerary' and that of a we-source. E. Haenchen has shown
a fairly energetic reaction which emphatically puts the stress on
the editorial character of the 'we'.

In the commentary he published in 1939, O. Bauernfeind[38]
agreed to call the source that underlay the travel narratives of
the second part of Acts an 'itinerary', but from the idea he
formed of this source, he remained closer to Norden than to
Dibelius. The presence of the 'we' is the surest indication of the
use of a source; this does not mean that the editor has not sometimes introduced the 'we' in passages which do not depend on
the source in question; it does not mean, either, that the source
from which the 'we' derives was wholly written in the first
person. These reservations do not prevent the 'we' from appear-

---

naturally explained by the fact that the writer of the book was actually with Paul
at those times, he seeks another explanation for the case in which the use of a source
is admitted: 'if he was embodying a written diary'. It is clear that, without wishing
to reject this explanation outright, Cadbury is not favourable to it. On p. 333 he
points out that the last part of Acts contains fewer Semitisms than the rest of the
work, that it stresses Paul's innocence, that it uses a 'we' which might be autobiographical—all this 'may reveal the free hand of the final editor writing without
extraneous influence in a style and with a purpose congenial to himself'. On
p. 337 he writes prudently: 'If Luke is his own source for the we-passages . . .',
expressing under the form of a hesitation an opinion which might well be his.

   [37] See above, pp. 101ff.
   [38] O. Bauernfeind, *Die Apostelgeschichte* (Theol. Handkomm. zum N.T., V),
Leipzig, 1939, pp. 7-9.

ing as the most characteristic feature of the itinerary used by the editor. Written in the first person, at least partially, it presented itself as the narrative of one of Paul's travelling companions and it must in point of fact have come, there is no reason to question the fact, from a companion of the Apostle. He was at his side on the occasion of the journeys recounted in the 'we' style in ch. 16.20–21 and 27–28. It is not possible to define exactly what the writing of the book owes to the itinerary, the editor having rewritten his source, of which he has, however, preserved the 'we'. While recognizing that the itinerary may well have contained narratives in the third person, Bauernfeind cannot see how to determine concretely what Acts could owe to the source outside the 'we' passages. In practice we are thus more or less back at the we-source. Its author, Luke, it seems, must be distinguished from the writer of Acts;[39] the latter, in fact, can scarcely have lived in Paul's company, for (1) it is clear that he is ill informed on Paul's journeys to Jerusalem (11.30; 12.25); (2) he writes that on the road to Damascus Paul saw a 'light' (9.3), whereas Paul declares that he saw the Lord in person; (3) he refuses Paul the title of 'apostle' which he regarded as so important. These explanations, even taken together, do not seem to us to form any advance on those of Dibelius.

W. G. Kümmel, in 1942,[40] considered that the research carried out by L. Cerfaux, J. Jeremias and W. Grundmann had shown the fruitlessness of the efforts made with a view to determining the presence of continuous written sources in the first part of Acts; for the second part, the conclusions of Dibelius have retained their full value—the only information used by the editor was a narrative of Paul's journeys which must have existed in a written form. This source supplied the 'we' which characterizes certain passages of the book; the use of the document, however, was not limited to these passages, for the we-passages are not distinguishable from their context either by style or by subject-matter. It is scarcely possible to fix the

[39] *Ibid.*, pp. 11f.
[40] W. G. Kümmel, 'Das Urchristentum', *Theol. Rundschau*, 1942, XIV, pp. 171f.

exact limits of the narratives which come from the source; it is, however, possible to recognize fairly easily different passages which have come from elsewhere and been inserted in the pattern of the travel narrative. Kümmel differs from Dibelius on a vital point—he makes of the presence of the 'we' in Acts an indication of the use of a source. Dibelius absolutely refused to draw an argument in favour of a source from this 'we', judging that, whether maintained or added, this 'we' was used deliberately by Luke. The lack of agreement came from the fact that Kümmel did not think it possible to attribute the writing of Acts to Luke, the companion of the Apostle.

W. Michaelis, in 1946,[41] considered that the sole determinable source which Luke had at his disposal for the writing of Acts was the we-narrative used in the second part of the book. The sections written in the first person contain so many details of times and places that we cannot think they were composed without the help of a travel diary. Luke, the writer of the work, thus used notes he had taken at the time of the events. The extension of these notes does not necessarily coincide with that of the we-passages; Luke would not take over all that his journal contained and the journal could well have included information on events in which the author had not taken part. The use of the first person was intended to make us understand that he recounts certain events as an eyewitness.

In his commentary on Acts, published for the first time in 1938, A. Wikenhauser[42] rejects the idea of written sources for the second half of Acts—Luke wrote the we-passages from his personal memories; for the rest he had at his disposal information which he was able to get from eyewitnesses without difficulty. In the *Einleitung*[43] which Wikenhauser published in 1953, his position has somewhat changed. He again asserts that in the writing of the we-passages Luke writes as an eyewitness;

[41] W. Michaelis, *Einleitung in das Neue Testament. Die Entstehung, Sammlung und Uberlieferung der Schriften des Neuen Testaments*, Berne, 1946, pp. 124f.

[42] A. Wikenhauser, *Die Apostelgeschichte* (Regensburger N.T., 5), Ratisbon, 1938. We have used the 3rd edition (1956, pp. 11f) which maintains the same position.

[43] *Einleitung in das Neue Testament*, Fribourg in Br., 1953, pp. 232–4. On the point which concerns us here, there is no change in the 2nd ed., 1961, pp. 232–4.

but he makes a distinction—'For these sections, Luke is clearly using personal written notes—a kind of diary—especially for the narrative of the journeys he made in the company of Paul.' The accuracy of the information contained in these passages—an accuracy unparalleled in the other narratives—is thus explained. In proposing this new theory Wikenhauser seems to be willing to make a concession to the hypothesis of Dibelius, the success of which he recognizes;[44] in fact, however, the manner in which he presents the use of Luke's diary tends to reduce the latter to the rôle of a we-source.[45]

A. Metzinger (1949)[46] considered that the extreme accuracy of the details concerning persons, places and times should lead us to think that the we-sections, especially the last two, which recount Paul's journeys to Jerusalem and Rome, are based on a diary in which Luke kept his notes at the time when he was a companion of the Apostle.

Reverting, in 1959, to the question of the source of Acts, L. Cerfaux recalls the opinions of Dibelius and of Kümmel, who 'have denied all possibility of tracking down other written sources than the we-sections', form-criticism thus scoring a fresh victory.[47] Cerfaux seems to find this victory satisfactory, for he later writes on the subject of these we-sections—'They are fragments of a travel-diary of one of Paul's companions. It is clear, however, that passages juxtaposed with these sections may come from the same author, who would merely recount the events objectively.[48] Moreover, people willingly put on the same foot-

---

[44] Cf. by the same author the article 'Apostelgeschichte' in the *Lexicon für Theologie und Kirche*, 2nd ed., vol. I (1957), col. 743–7 (see 745f)—he states that a certain unanimity has been reached on the idea that a written report was used in the account of Paul's journeys, and that the we-sections would be based on this report. While declaring Dibelius's explanations to be preferable to many others, Wikenhauser considers that they call for certain reservations.

[45] G. Ricciotti might have been quoted here; the way in which he envisages the use of the travel diary has led us to rank him among the supporters of the *Wirquelle* (see above, pp. 91f).

[46] H. Höpfl–B. Gut, *Introductio specialis in Novum Testamentum* (Introductionis in sacros utriusque Testamenti libros compendium, III), 5th ed. by A. Metzinger, Naples–Rome, 1949, p. 274.

[47] L. Cerfaux, *Les Actes des Apôtres* in *Introduction a la Bible*, vol. II, Tournai, 1959, p. 349.

[48] 'Objective' in the sense that the author writes in the third person. Cerfaux

ing as this travel diary the itinerary of Paul's journeys, from 13.4.[49]

E. Haenchen has not always professed the same opinion on the subject of the hypothesis of the itinerary as formulated by Dibelius. At first he came forward as a convinced supporter. Such was his attitude in an article published in 1955.[50] He explained that to recount the Pauline missions, the writer of Acts had at his disposal a report on Paul's missionary journeys which came from Paul's own circle. On this point it was necessary to hold to the theory of Dibelius, the demonstration of which could be completed. Since the author of Acts rewrote this source both for stylistic and theological reasons, it was not possible to determine the extent of it except approximately, by basing ourselves on the lack of harmony occasioned by the insertion of material foreign to this source. Discrepancy of this kind can be found in ch. 27—contrary to the opinion of Dibelius,[51] the account of the storm and shipwreck must go back to a source which recounted Paul's journey to Rome; it would be normal to attribute this source to one of Paul's companions. Haenchen has not pronounced on the question of ascertaining whether the source used for the writing of ch. 27–28 is to be identified with the itinerary which recounted Paul's missionary journeys. However this may be, the editor has rewritten the source or sources from which he derived his information as to the Apostle's journeys. To them he owes the use of the 'we', but he has introduced it in passages from another source. It can be conjectured that 'Luke the physician' is the author of the

---

puts the name of P. Feine in brackets—cf. *Einleitung in das Neue Testament*, 8th ed. (re-edited by J. Behm), Leipzig, 1936, pp. 84–86 (the 'we' fragments come from personal notes made by the author of the work).

[49] Art. cit., p. 350. Cerfaux agrees with Dibelius in making the itinerary begin at ch. 13, 4, in supposing that the first and third persons alternated in it and in attributing the compiling of Acts to Luke.

[50] E. Haenchen, 'Tradition und Komposition in der Apostelgeschichte', *Zeitschrift für Theologie und Kirche*, 1955, Bk. II, pp. 205–25—see pp. 220–2.

[51] Taking his inspiration from J. Wellhausen (*Kritische Analyse der Apostelgeschichte*, p. 54), Dibelius saw in the story of the tempest the imitation of a 'secular' narrative (cf. *Aufsätze*, pp. 14, 117, 173f, 180); the mention of Paul would only come as an addition. Haenchen shows the difficulties to which the cutting up to which people want to submit this narrative gives rise.

itinerary, but no decisive proof can be given of this; it is in any case impossible to attribute the writing of Acts to a companion of Paul.[52]

Not much later, Haenchen adopted the same position in the first edition of his voluminous commentary on Acts (1956)[53]—the writer had at his disposal an itinerary of Paul's journeys; he did not content himself with reproducing this, but inserted other traditions and passages of his own invention; the incident in Athens, in particular, must have had a few brief indications from this source as its starting-point.[54] As regards the extent of the itinerary, Haenchen disagrees with Dibelius, who had already made the essence of ch. 13 and 14 derive from it; he considers that the information supplied by these two chapters has not the detailed accuracy of the data attributable to the itinerary;[55] he thus rejects the argument drawn from a so-called discrepancy between 14.6–7 and 14.8.[56] Dibelius does not extend the influence of the itinerary beyond 21.16; Haenchen, on the contrary, thinks that 21.15–26 depends on it;[57] the narrative of ch. 27–28 is also based on a travel diary coming from a com-

---

[52] In his 1955 article, Haenchen gives no explanation as to the reasons for this impossibility. Some indications will be found in the commentary we are going to quote (pp. 102–5). Two considerations stand in the way of making the writer of Acts a collaborator of Paul—the fact that he refuses Paul the apostolic dignity and the conception he forms of Christianity as a prolongation of Judaism, whereas Paul establishes an absolute opposition between the religion of the Law and that of faith. Haenchen has taken up the question again with further developments in his 1959 re-edition (pp. 99–103)—the author of Acts is in opposition to Paul on three points—(1) the legitimacy of the mission to the Gentiles is not based on the same theology; (2) the relationship between Judaism and Christianity is not conceived in the same way; (3) the picture of Paul does not correspond to the reality—Acts makes him a wonder-worker and a powerful orator, but refuses him the title of Apostle. We must admit that these large distinctions impress us very little; the thought of Paul seems to us much more complex than the rigid system to which people are trying to confine it and that of Luke has shades of meaning which do not fit in satisfactorily with the framework which people seek to impose upon it.

[53] *Die Apostelgeschichte* (Krit.-exeg. Komm. über das N.T., III, 10th ed.), Göttingen, 1956. See p. 96 of introduction (and p. 33, summary of Dibelius).

[54] Cf. pp. 101 and 473.

[55] Cf. pp. 350f and 385–7 (on this point Haenchen is in agreement with Bauernfeind—p. 385).

[56] Haenchen supports Kirsopp Lake's interpretation (*Beginnings,* IV, p. 167)—vv. 6–7 indicate the missionaries' sphere of action, whereas from v. 8 onwards the narrative of particular incidents which have happened in the course of the evangelization is given.

[57] Cf. pp. 547–9.

panion of Paul,[58] but it is not certain that this document is identical with that used in ch. 16–21.[59]

The commentary supplies some more recent explanations on the subject of the use of the 'we'.[60] It is not sufficient to show that the information in we-narratives must come, at least partially, from an itinerary to be able to conclude from this that that itinerary was written in the first person—the 'we' may very well come from the editor. Moreover, what is the significance of this 'we'? We have become too easily used to the idea that it indicates the presence of Luke alongside Paul; it is time we disposed of this 'historicist' interpretation and accounted for the 'we' by basing ourselves on the literary point of view. The first 'we' occurs in 16.10. At that moment, Paul was travelling in the company of Silas and Timothy. On seeing the narrative move to the first person, the reader of ancient times spontaneously understood that one of the three persons concerned, Paul, Silas or Timothy, was addressing him; since Paul was excluded by the context, the narrator could not be other than Silas or Timothy. The reader in New Testament times did not worry overmuch about identifying this narrator; he was content to realize that he was dealing with the narrative of an eyewitness, or, more simply, that the 'we' was a mere technique of style intended to give him the impression of a closer contact with the facts. It was the reader himself who, perhaps unconsciously, saw himself introduced into the little group of missionaries to experience with them the events they have lived through, and to associate himself with the response they were making to divine revelation (vv. 6–7). In a certain way the use of the 'we' plays a corresponding rôle to that of the audience who, at the end of the account of a miracle, acclaim the divine intervention. We must, then, take this 'we' for what it is—a technique of style whose aim is to make the narrative more forceful.

Such exegesis of the 'we' can hardly be said to be satisfactory. Haenchen speaks with a good deal of assurance of the reactions

---

[58] Cf. pp. 643–4.
[59] Cf. p. 652.
[60] pp. 433–6. These theories should be compared with those of H. Windisch, mentioned above, p. 87.

of the New Testament reader; but it may well be asked if this reader ever existed other than in Haenchen's imagination. Numerous travel narratives written in the first person have been cited by Norden, Dibelius, Cadbury, Nock; the impression we get from them is that their writers intend to pass in their readers' eyes as eyewitnesses of the events they recount.[61] To judge of the way in which a reader of New Testament times would naturally understand the presence of the 'we' in Acts, we should certainly be on surer ground if we relied on Irenaeus's[62] interpretation rather than on Haenchen's subtle considerations. Haenchen's explanations are purely theoretical and do not seem capable of standing comparison with the ancient evidence.[63]

[61] A. D. Nock, who displays a very extensive knowledge of ancient texts which employ the 'we' style, expressly remarks that outside the literature of imagination, clearly fictitious, only a single case could be quoted in which perhaps the stressed use of the 'we' could be open to argument (*Gnomon*, 1953, p. 503). Nock speaks the language of facts, Haenchen that of imagination. F. Dornseiff sees in the 'we' a literary device and he stresses this idea with insistence; he none the less thinks that this 'we' has a meaning and that, unless there is clear proof of the contrary, it is preferable to admit that the narratives written in the first person really emanate from an eyewitness (*Zeitschr. für die neutestl. Wiss.*, 1936, pp. 137f).

[62] *Adv. Haer.*, III, 14, 1. Ireneaus draws argument from the 'we' to prove that the author of Acts (he knows from other sources that it is Luke) has been and presents himself expressly as a travelling companion of Paul. C . Haenchen, *Apostelgeschichte*, pp. 7f.

[63] The case of John 21.24, which might be thought of in this context, is quite different. We have just emphasized that Haenchen's explanation is arbitrary; placing ourselves on the author's own ground, we should have to add that his hypothesis cannot fail to raise the question— or what reason did the writer of Acts use the procedure in certain sections rather than in certain others? If he wanted to associate his reader with the narrative, should he not do so in a more constant manner, or at least on particularly important occasions? The journey from Troas to Philippi and the foundation of the church in Philippi do not appear as particularly striking events in the plan of the book. To speak in this connection of the starting-point of the evangelization of Europe or of the Greek world is to place ourselves at the point of view of a modern; Acts only speaks of the evangelization of Macedonia. The evangelization of Achaia (Corinth) and of Asia (Ephesus) occupy a much larger place in Paul's apostolic ministry, and it is clear that, in the perspective of Acts, Paul's stay in Athens constitutes one of the culminating points of the narrative. Rather than the journey from Troas to Philippi, is it not that from Berea to Athens that merited the honour of a narrative in the first person? Is it not the preaching of Paul before the philosophers and Areopagites of Athens which should have received the distinction of the 'we', rather than his teaching in the presence of the few women who constitute his audience at Philippi (16.13)? At another highlight of the book, Paul's discourse before King Agrippa (ch. 26), the 'we' comes in just too late (27.1)! We should have to believe that the writer was at one and the same time skilful enough to have recourse to a refined technique of style and too clumsy to use it to good purpose. Is this really easier than to attribute to the 'we'

Haenchen returns to the question of the 'we' in his 1961[64] article. His view has not altered, but his explanations are more detailed. In regard to ch. 16 he writes—'The "we" is to give the reader the assurance that he is learning things at first hand; better, that he is himself personally taking part in the events with the eyewitness who is speaking.' In regard to ch. 20–21, he writes—'Thanks to the "we", Luke can make the reader share personally in Paul's fateful journey to Jerusalem.' Thus the procedure was to give more life to the narrative. Its significance, however, was not confined to that—it was at the same time to make the reader understand that the writer of Acts had first-hand information at his disposal; it conferred on the narratives the historical guarantee which attaches to the account of an eyewitness. The question then arises of ascertaining why Luke did not use the 'we' more, and why he did so at one particular moment rather than another.[65] Haenchen explains that in ch. 16 the decisive importance of the circumstances would seem to demand some additional guarantee—Paul is leaving Asia Minor to enter upon a new field of missionary work, that of Macedonia and Greece;[66] it is from an eyewitness that we learn the circumstances which have given rise to this initiative.[67] On the travel narratives of ch. 20–21 and 27–28, the

---

the significance of a testimony, the writer thereby attesting his presence at the events he recounts, even if they are not particularly remarkable?

[64] We must refer again to the article, 'Das "wir" in der Apostelgeschichte und das Itinerar', the manuscript of which Dr Haenchen has very kindly allowed us to consult; it will appear in 1961 or 1962 in the *Zeitschr. für Theol. und Kirche.*

[65] In examining this point, Haenchen endeavours to answer the question we have put forward in note 63.

[66] Rather than 'Europe'. But we expressed ourselves badly in note 63 in saying that to speak of Europe in regard to Acts 16 was 'to place oneself at the point of view of a modern'. Haenchen rightly points out that this geographical distribution was known to the ancient world. Our intention was simply to emphasize that the division Asia-Europe does not correspond to Luke's point of view—he only speaks of 'Asia' in the most restricted sense, in which the word is applied to the region of which Ephesus is the centre, and he never mentions Europe. We should like to add that Antioch or Ephesus are as 'Greek' as Philippi or Thessalonica.

[67] Luke wants to stress the divine origin of this initiative, which, on this count, should be compared to that of Peter granting baptism to the first pagan admitted to the Church (Acts 10.1–11.18). The importance of the Caesarea episode is shown by the length of the narrative devoted to it; the importance of the decision taken at Troas justifies and explains the first appearance of the 'we'.

purpose of the 'we' is essentially to give the reader the impression of immediate contact with the life of the Apostle. Luke, however, does not constantly maintain the use of the 'we'. It is because he wants to write the history of Paul and centre his narrative on Paul's actions and discourses; it was fitting that the 'we' should be effaced to leave Paul alone on the stage in the accomplishment of his apostolic mission.[68]

These new observations will enable us to form a clearer idea of the hypothesis advocated by Haenchen. It seems to us, however, that they leave the essential difficulty untouched—is it really in this way that a reader of New Testament times would interpret the 'we' of these narratives?[69] Would it not be natural that he should rather see in them an indication from the writer of his personal participation in the events? Could Luke ignore this spontaneous interpretation that would be given to his technique of style?[70]

In the introduction to his commentary to the third Gospel

---

[68] It is thanks to the discretion he shows in the use of the 'we' that Luke avoids transforming the history of Paul into a novel about Paul. In making this remark Haenchen seems to admit that the use of the 'we' in Acts belongs, in his opinion, to the literary genre of the novel.

[69] What are referred to are narratives which, in the author's intention, should give the impression of belonging to the historical genre, not that of the novel.

[70] Haenchen wants to confine himself to the data of the text. Acts does not mention Luke. If we set aside tradition (of which Irenaeus is the first witness), it is not normal to think of Luke when we meet the first 'we' in ch. 16. Realizing that what he has before him is the narrative of a companion of the Apostle's journey, the reader naturally thinks of one of those whose name he has come across—Silas or Timothy. In recognizing the narrative of this direct witness, he does not conclude from it that the witness himself wrote the narrative—the narrator is not necessarily the author; it is the first, not the second, whom the reader should be able to identify. The procedure would be ineffective if it were a question of a person not mentioned. This interpretation does not seem to us wholly convincing. If the author of the work does not name himself, that does not mean that he supposes that his readers are unaware of his identity; it is inconceivable that the first readers of the fourth Gospel should have been incapable, in the thought even of the author, of putting a name to the beloved 'disciple' whose actual name is not mentioned. The explicit attribution of the third Gospel to Luke is certainly made well before Irenaeus; it must go back to the time when the Gospels were provided with a title. It is dangerous to ignore this factor. The distinction between narrator and author seems to us even more difficult to admit, for want of being able to appeal to analogous examples in ancient historiography; we have pointed out above why it would naturally lead to identifying the narrator, not with a secondary character, but with the main character, Paul—an explanation which Haenchen is certainly not prepared to accept.

(1961), W. Grundmann[71] considers three explanations of the 'we'—it might come from a source used by the author; it is, however, preferable to see in it a technique of style by which the writer is either presenting himself as a witness of the events which he is relating in the first person, or else uses to give more colour to his narrative. The last hypothesis, that of Haenchen, is rejected as improbable; Grundmann supports the second—the author of Acts indicates that he is an occasional companion of the Apostle.[72]

In a study on Acts published in 1957,[73] Haenchen summarized the ideas of Dibelius, giving the impression that he was adopting them—the only continuous source used in Acts was the itinerary, which supplied information as to the route followed by Paul and the hospitality received by him in the course of his journeys. It was in 1959 only that Haenchen gave up this itinerary; we shall refer later to the position he then adopted.

More Recent Theories Concerning the Itinerary

In agreement with Dibelius in principle, two writers, however, represented each in a rather different way the source which underlay the narrative of Paul's journeys; the idea they formed of it is expressed in new terms—A. Kragerud referred to a missionary report, E. Trocmé to a 'diary'.

In 1955 A. Kragerud[74] considered that the hypothesis of the itinerary merited a new investigation, since the suggestions of Dibelius would not all stand up to criticism. A detailed literary analysis of the section of the missionary journeys (13.4–21.16) led him to think that the basic document was not an 'itinerary' but a 'missionary report'—the account that the missionaries

---

[71] W. W. Grundmann, *Das Evangelium nach Lukas* (Theol. Handkomm. zum N.T., 3), Berlin, 1961, p. 34.

[72] Cf. pp. 35 and 39.

[73] 'Apostelgeschichte', in *Die Religion in Geschichte und Gegenwart*, 3rd ed., fasc. I (1957), col. 501–7—cf. 504.

[74] A. Kragerud, 'Itinerariet i Apostlenes Gjerninger', *Norsk Teol. Tidsskr.*, 1955, LVI, pp. 249–72. Despite our efforts, it has not been possible for us to see a copy of this work; the summary we give of it is dependent on that of G. Münderlein, in the *Internationale Zeitschriftenschau für Bibelwissenschaft und Grenzgebiete*, 1955–6, IV, p. 79.

presented on their return to justify themselves and as a means of edification for the community which had sent them. This double purpose would explain the 'historical' and at the same time 'edifying' nature of the narrative, its positive facts and its anecdotes of miraculous events. The identification of the literary form enables us to dispense with the work of dissection which would claim to separate the purely objective itinerary from the 'legendary' elements which had slipped into it later.

E. Trocmé in 1957[75] presented an hypothesis which linked up with that of Dibelius,[76] but he developed it by adding details which gave it a somewhat novel appearance. He began by showing that the narrative of ch. 16–28 can hardly be considered as an original composition, based solely on personal memories. We notice indeed—(1) that certain passages interrupt the course of a narrative into which they have been clumsily inserted;[77] (2) that several passages depend on a popular tradition rather than on the memories of an eyewitness;[78] (3) that the narrative is encumbered with superfluous remarks pointless for the general plan of the work or for the biography of Paul—a mention of halting-places where nothing occurred.[79] The compiling of the second half of Acts would thus seem to be based on a document; in particular for ch. 16–21, the great chronological and geographical accuracy of the narrative must come from an account of Paul's journeys made by one of his companions. This account cannot be limited to the we-passages alone, for too close a relationship exists between these passages and others written in the third person;[80] the 'we' moreover is to be explained by reference to the writer's literary procedure rather than by reference to his documents.[81]

---

[75] E. Trocmé, Le 'Livre des Actes' et l'Histoire, Paris, 1957, pp. 128–38.

[76] See in particular p. 135, n. 1, where, in connection with what he says about the 'diary', the author points out 'It is the hypothesis which M. Dibelius supports. . . .'

[77] Cf. 17.22–31; 22.1–21; 27.21–26.

[78] Cf. 16.25–34; 19.14–16; 20.7–12.

[79] Cf. 16.11; 20.13–14.15; 21.1.

[80] Cf. 16.11–15 with 17.1–9.

[81] Cf. pp. 123–8—following Cadbury, Trocmé shows that, by the use of the 'we', the author sets himself up as an eyewitness of the events he recounts.

How is the source relating Paul's journeys to be described?
We must begin by removing everything which cannot justifiably
claim to belong to it; we are then left with a rather dry series of
narratives stripped both of all edifying and all literary character.
Clearly a text of this kind did not lend itself to publication—it
was impossible to see in it a ὑπόμνημα, 'memoirs' which could
have had an independent existence. It is difficult to conceive
of the existence of a report on Paul's missionary activities.[82] The
best solution would be to think

> of simple travel notes, a kind of personal 'diary', in which one
> of the missionaries of the little group led by Paul would have
> inscribed, with a practical aim and through regard for good
> order, a few remarks on the sayings and doings of each
> important day's work. The mention of halting-places or per-
> sons without interest for Paul's biography would thus be
> explained satisfactorily—notes taken as the events occurred
> do not permit of the selection which the biographer or
> historian would effect later. The dry objectivity of many of
> the indications on Paul's journeys would be less surprising,
> since the 'diarist' would never have thought of showing his
> to anyone at all. The existence of the document even does not
> raise the problems evoked in connection with the ὑπόμνημα[83]—
> what more natural for a traveller than to take notes, especially
> if he considered himself invested with an important mission?
> Even without envisaging a written report, he wants an aide-
> mémoire which will enable him to recall his memories in an
> orderly fashion when he returns. . . . We believe the writer
> ad Theophilum used notes of this kind, which would include the
> indication of the stages, of the duration of the halts,[84] of the
> most notable persons who offered hospitality,[85] of the success

[82] Trocmé considers this hypothesis and rejects it without knowing of Kragerud's
article which we have just referred to.

[83] The existence of this document raises a further problem—'We possess no
document of this kind from ancient times' (p. 135). Trocmé sets himself to solve the
difficulty by showing that 'diaries' must have existed even if they have not been
preserved. This difficulty simply results from insufficient information—A. D. Nock
instances several examples of 'diaries' which have been preserved or attested, in his
review of Dibelius (Gnomon, 1953, XXV, pp. 497–506; cf. p. 500).

[84] Acts 17.2; 18.11; 19.10; 20.3, 6; 21.4, 7, 10.

[85] Acts 16.14–15; 17.5–6; 18.3, 7; 19.9; 21.8, 16.

of the preaching if there had been any, sometimes of the principal converts or adversaries,[86] and of the missions entrusted to Paul's collaborators.[87]

One final question remains, that of the author of the 'diary'. He must be sought among the members of Paul's group, and since the writer to Theophilus is one of them, it is of him we think primarily; it would be quite natural that he should have composed his work basing it on his own notes. This attribution, however, raises difficulties. They result from the fact that the information originating from the 'diary' does not coincide with the we-sections, that is to say with the periods during which the writer accompanied Paul: (1) between 16.17 and 20.5, representing a lapse of time of at least five years, there is not a single 'we' indicating the presence of Luke; now the 'diary' was continued in this interval. (2) Moreover, as Dibelius has shown, the 'itinerary' already formed the basis of ch. 13–14, where several passages present all the characteristic features of the 'diary'. (3) On the other hand, the account of the shipwreck (ch. 27), although written in the first person, does not seem to derive from the travel diary; the writer has here introduced a passage of his own invention.[88] It follows from these remarks that the 'diary' contained information on Paul's journeys from his departure for Cyprus (13.4) until his arrival in Rome (ch. 28), whereas Luke, on his own evidence, was only at Paul's side at certain moments. But if the writing of a diary covering the whole period of Acts 13–28 cannot be attributed to him, no other of the Apostle's companions was so constantly at his side to be able to keep a diary so complete.

---

[86] Acts 16.14; 17.34; 18.2, 8, 24–28.

[87] Acts 16.1–3 perhaps; 17.14; 18.5, 18; 19.22; 20.4, 14—The passage taken from Trocmé's book will be found on p. 135.

[88] pp. 137f. Acts 27.1–8 and 28.7–16 would come from the 'diary', whereas 27.13–44 'has all the appearances of a literary composition of the author *ad Theophilum*. . . . The "we" of 27.1–8 and 28.7–16 proves that he was present. But there is nothing to prevent his having given a conventional description, in a romantic style, imitated from some fashionable writer, of the events of these days of the storm. The hypothesis of the textual reproduction of an earlier narrative is not unavoidable, for the references to Paul in vv. 9–11, 21–26 and 33–38, if they are a little clumsy, do not necessarily form an addition.'

The solution consists in admitting either that the diary was from the hand of Paul himself, or that the Apostle was accustomed to have a travel diary kept by one of his companions in the name of the group. The 'secretary' thus appointed would have changed with the years, but Paul, to whom it served as an *aide-mémoire*, would have continued the document. It is not impossible that in this case the writer *ad Theophilum* occupied this function at certain periods. It could even be suggested that he did so during the last period of Paul's life and preserved the diary after the Apostle's death or after his own separation from him.[89]

It would seem that Trocmé has allowed himself to be drawn too far. His conjectures as to the conditions in which the 'diary' was compiled perhaps start from an hypothesis which he accepts unconsciously after having explicitly rejected it; nothing authorizes us to think that the information on which the narrative of Paul's journeys is based was written in the first person or was written in a continuous form. Thus it is not necessary to attribute the diary to one or several persons recounting events in which they have taken part personally. As to the supposition which credits Paul with the preoccupation of having an *aide-mémoire* at his disposal, there can be differing opinions on its probability; it is, in any case, not sufficiently warranted to constitute a sure foundation, and any explanation which has to appeal to it will thereby necessarily be weakened. Except in so far as the extension of the source to ch. 28 is concerned, the details by which Trocmé's 'diary' differs from Dibelius's 'itinerary' would seem to be of only slight interest; the hypothesis of the 'diary' deserves attention chiefly on the points in which it corroborates and completes that of the 'itinerary'.

[89] p. 138. Trocmé's hypothesis has been repeated, with sufficient discretion, in a commentary intended for the public at large—J. P. Benoit, *Combats d'apôtres pour une humanité 'nouvelle'. Traduction et commentaire du livre des Actes des Apôtres*, Paris, 1957—see pp. 12 and 234.

VIII

THE FRAGMENTATION OF THE ITINERARY

THE HYPOTHESES which account for the composition of the second part of Acts by the use of a source look for their support to observations made on the text. The evidence which holds our attention is not always the same: literary criticism is sensitive to the lack of harmony which occurs from time to time in the course of the narrative, to clumsy or artificial transitions, to differences of style and vocabulary, etc.; form-criticism is more concerned with the processes characteristic of a particular literary genre which in themselves enable us to form an idea of the documents of which the writer of the book made use. We can discuss the accuracy of these observations, disagree as to the significance that should be attached to them, introduce new observations which tend towards a better solution; but not to take them into account can never be a good method. This, however, is what too often happens. Many writers begin by establishing, with the help of external and internal criteria, that Acts was written by Luke the physician, travelling companion of Paul; after which the question of the sources used in the narrative of the Apostle's travels seems to them purposeless: it was sufficient for Luke to appeal to what he remembered, he had no need of sources, therefore he did not use any. We do not claim that the conclusions of these writers are wrong, but their way of procedure is too much open to question for it to be particularly useful to dwell on their theories. Whether Paul's travels were written by Luke or by someone else, the problem of the sources of these narratives arises and it must be dealt with on the basis of the texts themselves. It is therefore not necessary for us to discuss all the literature devoted to Acts, as this would only complicate our study, to little purpose.

The observations with which Dibelius thought he could establish that the second part of Acts made full use of the information of an itinerary have been challenged by a few writers. In the first place some attention will be given to what A. D. Nock has said on this point; we shall then indicate the reasons which led Haenchen to abandon the hypothesis to which he first gave his support, then an examination will be made of the study which G. Schille devoted to the refutation of Dibelius's theory. We shall end by a few references to works which might justify a fresh investigation of this hypothesis.

The Reservations of Nock

The study which A. D. Nock devoted to the *Aufsätze* of Dibelius[1] makes reservations which, for the question with which we are concerned, raises two main points. He first of all challenges the value of the argument by which Dibelius convinces himself that Acts was composed by Luke. The dedication to Theophilus, confirmed by the literary care of which the work gives proof, indicates that the writer intended his work for publication; now, a work of this kind cannot appear without an indication as to its author; given in the title, which has now disappeared, this indication once existed, which explains the tradition which attributes the work to Luke. A debatable argument, replies Nock. The dedication merely signifies that the author has put the finishing touch to his work and that he wants it to be made public;[2] it does not necessarily presuppose mention of the author's name: other works with a dedication omit it, as, for instance, the *Letter to Diognetus*.[3] In fact, Nock agrees with

[1] In *Gnomon*, 1953, XXV, pp. 497–506.
[2] pp. 501f. On the relative implications of a dedication, see H. J. Cadbury, *The Making of Luke-Acts*, pp. 201–4; H. I. Marrou, 'La technique de l'édition à l'époque patristique', *Vigiliae Christianae*, 1949, III, pp. 208–24; id., *A. Diognète* Sources chrétiennes), Paris, 1951, p. 92.
[3] Modern scholarship has gone to a great deal of trouble to put a name to this work; Marrou gives a list of the names that have been put forward—there are no less than nineteen (*A Diognète*, pp. 242f). Taking up a theory of J. R. Harmer and P. Battifol, he inclines in favour of Pantaenus (pp. 266f), followed in this by F. M.

Dibelius in attributing Acts to Luke, but he does so by reason of another argument, the one by which Cadbury accounts for the use of the 'we' by appealing to the claims set out by the author in his prologue.[4]

Another hesitation expressed by Nock is the question whether the itinerary put forward by Dibelius really constitutes a single source.[5] We can just as easily think of several documents, relating to different periods; in particular, we can very easily imagine the existence of a diary concerning the last journey to Jerusalem. This fragmentary explanation would have the advantage of avoiding the difficulty of having to account for omissions in the hypothesis according to which Luke had a complete document at his disposal—why should he suppress certain passages when he reproduces others so carefully? The considerations of Dibelius which tend to make us think of the reproduction of a document are not all, moreover, beyond criticism. It is quite true that Luke enumerates halting-places on the journey that are without interest for the over-all plan of his narrative and which make no contribution to the aim of edification he set before himself—for instance, the statement of 20.13–14; but these passages can have a literary significance, that of providing a pause, giving the reader a little relaxation from the tenseness of the narrative. The aim of these remarks, Nock prudently concludes, is not to call in question Dibelius's conclusions on the kind of documentation which Luke had at his disposal in his narrative of Paul's journeys, for this series of documents belongs to a well-attested literary type,[6] that of the *ephemerides*, dated personal records, and in particular the diaries, which are travel journals; what can be questioned in Dibelius's hypothesis is the perhaps over-precise picture he has formed for himself of the itinerary used by Luke.

Braun, *Jean le théologien et son Evangile dans l'Eglise ancienne* (Etudes Bibliques), Paris, 1959, p. 71. The *Letter to Diognetus* is not the only one of its kind; the four books of rhetoric *Ad Herennium* may be mentioned and in the New Testament canon the small treatise, without an author's name, entitled πρὸς Ἑβραίους.

[4] See above, pp. 101ff.
[5] *Art. cit.*, pp. 499f.
[6] The references supplied by Nock, p. 500, supplement Dibelius's indications.

Haenchen's Change of Opinion

In the new edition of his commentary published in 1959, E. Haenchen[7] has endeavoured to take account of recent publications. After meeting the theory of the Antioch source restored to honour by Bultmann, he was led by Trocmé's work to submit the hypothesis of the itinerary to a new investigation—an investigation directly aiming at the form under which the hypothesis is presented in Trocmé, which is reasonable; the result, however, is to call in question the theories of Dibelius, in relation to which those of Trocmé only constitute a variant.

The supposed source would have taken the form of a personal diary; this explains the use of the first person which occurs over and over again in the narratives of Acts. The diary would contain brief indications on each day's events—hence the dry, precise items of information often referring to halting-places on the journey where nothing happened and which are of no interest for the purpose pursued by the author in composing his work. Haenchen begins by pointing out that this hypothesis rests on an extremely narrow basis: the two characteristic features of the diary—the use of the 'we' and the enumeration of halting-places—are only found together in a few verses (16.11–12; 20.5–6, 13–16; 21.1–9, 15–16). He then goes on to refute the interpretation that the hypothesis in question claims to give of these two characteristic features:

(1) The intervention of a source is not necessary for the use of the 'we'. Dibelius has shown this—it can be explained as a borrowing from a source equally well or better than as an editorial feature. In Acts 16.16–17[8] it has been introduced into an independent anecdote which cannot depend on an itinerary; it has again been inserted in 27.1 and 27.6 to adapt the passage

---

[7] E. Haenchen, *Die Apostelgeschichte* (Meyer's Kommentar III, 12th ed.), Göttingen, 1959, pp. 72–78 (for the point under consideration, 76–78).

[8] Dibelius shows himself much more prudent in making the complementary fragment begin not at v. 16 but at v. 25 (cf. *Aufsätze*, pp. 26–28, 168, etc.), and is prepared to show some hesitation on the question of the relationship existing between the story of the miraculous deliverance and that of the cure preceding it, and on that of the source on which the narrative of the cure would depend (p. 168, n. 3). The story of the possessed girl serves as an introduction to a scene of judgement which links up with that in Corinth (18.12ff).

to the narrative of Paul's journeys and give it the appearance of a narrative made by a companion of the Apostle. In short, the 'we' is a simple stylistic device and depends only on the editor.[9]

(2) Is the travel diary necessary to account for the book's information on the details of Paul's journeyings? Haenchen does not think so. He points out that if some of the less important events are, in fact, highly detailed, others are tiresomely lacking in precision and vague; the hypothesis of the diary does not explain this aspect of the data. The preoccupations because of which, according to Trocmé, Paul felt the need of a diary as an *aide-mémoire* are defined in a purely arbitrary manner and are highly improbable. Finally, convinced that, contrary to what Dibelius and Trocmé think, Acts cannot have been composed by a companion of Paul,[10] Haenchen does not see how the

---

[9] On this 'stylistic device' the 1959 edition (pp. 428–31) repeats the explanations of the 1956 edition, on which we have already dwelt at some length (pp. 194f).

[10] We said above (p. 127, n. 52) that this refusal is essentially founded on considerations not of a literary, but of a theological order—the ideas of Luke are not those we have a right to expect from a disciple of the Apostle. We are very little impressed by this reasoning. It should be pointed out that besides the paragraph devoted to setting Luke in opposition to Paul (pp. 99–103), Haenchen devotes one page of his study on the sources of Acts (pp. 79f) to an exegesis which had already been developed by O. Linton, 'The Third Aspect. A Neglected Point of View. A Study in Gal. i–ii and Acts ix and xv', in *Studia Theologica*, 1949 (published in 1950), III, pp. 79–95. Acts would be dependent on traditions which Paul had already combated. In Gal. 1.15–20, Paul refutes a calumny according to which he went up to Jerusalem immediately after his conversion and there received the Gospel transmitted to him by the Twelve; Acts recounts that Paul went to Jerusalem immediately after his conversion and insists on his close link with the apostolic community. In Gal. 5.11 Paul rejects the mistake of certain Judaizers who imagined that he preached circumcision; Acts recounts that Paul wanted to circumcise Timothy, to avoid difficulties with the Jews. Such antitheses seem to us very superficial. Haenchen stresses Gal. 1, 19—on the occasion of his first stay in Jerusalem Paul saw no apostle apart from Peter (and James, the brother of the Lord); but he leaves aside the detail of v. 18—Paul went to Jerusalem precisely 'to see Peter', ἱστορῆσαι Κηφᾶν, or, as G. D. Kilpatrick translates, 'to inform himself from Peter' (*Galatians*, 1.18 ἱστορῆσαι Κηφᾶν in *New Testament Essays. Studies in Memory of T. W. Manson*, Manchester, 1959, pp. 144–9). Clearly it is most regrettable that it should be Paul himself and not Luke who expresses himself in such an 'un-Pauline' way. By the side of this, the short cut by which Luke makes Paul go to Jerusalem without passing through Arabia seems truly indulgent. Paul is obliged to flee from Damascus, where he is no longer safe and quite naturally goes to Jerusalem, without there being any question of intending to make contact with Peter. In the case of Timothy Haenchen emphasizes the precision of Acts in saying that Paul circumcised him 'because of the Jews who were in those places' (16.3); but he omits the explanation —'for they all knew that his father was a Gentile'. Paul will not allow that a Gentile should be circumcised; but he does not ask the Jews to renounce circumcision, contrary to what his adversaries assert against him (Luke himself says so—

author entered into possession of a document coming from the immediate entourage of the Apostle.

Haenchen is not content merely to thrust aside a theory that does not satisfy him; he sets out his way of conceiving the method of working followed by the author when, planning his book, perhaps about the year 75, he obtained the necessary information. Three ways lay open to him: (1) he could set out and pay visits to the principal churches founded by Paul—Philippi, Corinth, Ephesus and Jerusalem; Haenchen does not insist, doubtless considering, not without reason, that this procedure would be improbable. (2) The author could again, without troubling himself personally, apply to Christians who frequented these different churches and ask them to give him information on what people could remember of a period that was not so very remote. (3) Finally, there was the post—it was sufficient to write to the churches to obtain all the documentation they had at their disposal. As a result of an inquiry conducted in these conditions, the author would have found himself in possession of varied information which was inserted in the framework of his travel narratives. He arranged its insertion as he could, sometimes interrupting one narrative to make room for another.[11] For certain facts of long standing, such as the events of the first missionary journey, he must have had to content himself with rather vague reminiscences. For Paul's last journey to Jerusalem, he perhaps had at his disposal the travel diary of some person from Philippi who, in the capacity of delegate of the community,[12] would have accompanied the Apostle; 'Luke' would have reproduced this document, fortunately introducing

---

Acts 21.21); being the son of a Jewish mother, Timothy is legally a Jew and should have been circumcised. The problem which arises in connection with him has nothing to do with the principle that Paul defends with so much force in the epistle to the Galatians—the Gentiles should not submit to circumcision. All these contradictions which people claim to establish between Luke and Paul falsify the thought of both.

[11] Hence the impression that certain passages give of having been inserted in a pre-existing framework—14.8–20; 18.18–21; 20.16–21.1 and the interpolations of ch. 27.

[12] Charged with handing over the gifts which were intended for the community in Jerusalem.

only a few revisions. The story of the sea-voyage to Rome depends not on a diary (which would not have survived the shipwreck) but on narratives made from personal memories. The greater part of the material taken over in Acts seems to have reached the author under the form of traditions which were not yet fixed; it is by his work that they passed to the literary stage. There were also items already in written form; the author may have taken his inspiration from them, editing them in his own way, or he may equally well have transcribed them almost without change,[13] in the form in which they reached him (journal of Philippi).

What are we to think of these explanations? To begin with, we grant to Haenchen willingly enough that the hypothesis of a source is not necessary to explain the presence of the 'we' in Acts and that it does not supply a sufficient explanation for this peculiarity—it is at the editorial level, not at that of the sources, that account must be taken of the use of the first person. This first concession prevents us from making a second—from the moment the 'we' ceases to be a criterion indicating the use of a source, there is no reason to separate from the we-passages the they-passages which are similar to them and contribute to the enlargement of the basis of a hypothesis as to their origin. The merit of Dibelius's theory is precisely that it supplies an explanation which seeks to account for these passages as a whole. Telling, perhaps, as regards certain observations made by Trocmé, Haenchen's objections are much less forceful if we place ourselves at the point of view adopted by Dibelius, quite apart from the difference of opinion which sets Haenchen at variance with the latter on the question of the authorship of the book.

Rather than appeal to a source which would account for the accuracy with which Acts recounts the itineraries of the Apostle, Haenchen imagines different methods of information whose probability seems rather debatable. We do not, moreover, think that they are sufficient to explain the data such as

[13] In saying this, would Haenchen be thinking of the use of the 'we'? He does not say so in so many words.

they are presented to us. There are two observations we wish to make.

(1) The investigation which Luke is credited with must have put him in possession of different local traditions preserved in the individual churches. A certain number of narratives do, in fact, show traits which enable us to link them with traditions of this kind. There is, however, the remainder—all the details on the halting-places of the journey, the length of the stages, etc. It is difficult to see how these elements, which constitute the framework of the book, could depend on local traditions. The character of this information leads us to suppose that it has quite a different origin.

(2) Haenchen accepts the idea of a travel diary in the case of the journey from Philippi to Jerusalem (ch. 20–21). It must, however, be admitted that the information concerning this particular journey is not of a different type from that we possess on the others. Information of this nature does not perhaps so much reveal the sources from which it derives as the personality of the author who is interested in such details. It is not accidental that the same turn of mind is shown throughout the whole book and earlier in the third Gospel[14]—we have only to think of the literary artifice which joins together the majority of the episodes proper to Luke by incorporating them in a journey of Jesus going from Galilee to Jerusalem. The fact that this is so forces us to face the problem of ascertaining whether it may be taken for granted that Luke owes this information which so well expresses his personal interests to reports at second hand. For this we should have to admit that his informants had exactly the same special interests as he had, or else that they supplied him with such a large mass of information that he had nothing more to do than to choose the details in which he was most interested. Both explanations raise many difficulties, and we should really ask ourselves if it would not be much simpler to assume that the author depended only on his own information. Haenchen does not reject this idea, since he is

[14] Of the indications supplied by the Gospel on the personality of Luke, Haenchen does not seem to make as much use as we might reasonably expect.

ready to impose on the writer of Acts a journey which would repeat, at least in part, the journeys of Paul. Rather than demand such efforts from him, would it not be preferable to allow him to travel in Paul's company? We do not wish to dwell further on this for the moment; we shall return to the question after having set out the ideas of Schille.[15]

Haenchen has again taken up the question of the itinerary in an article which is to appear shortly.[16] After replacing Dibelius's hypothesis in its historical context, and emphasizing its merits and its weaknesses, he embarks on a detailed analysis of the travel narratives, in order to characterize the kind of information which underlies them. For the first missionary journey (ch. 13–14), the precise and concrete information is reduced to very little—Luke knows that Paul has preached at Cyprus and that he has met with great difficulties 'at Antioch, at Iconium, at Lystra' (2 Tim. 3.11);[17] he has a few anecdotes— the episode of Sergius Paulus, the cure of a crippled man and the stoning at Lystra. All the rest is only padding. It is useless to appeal to an itinerary for these two chapters. The narrative of the second missionary journey (15.36–18.22) bears the mark of Luke everywhere—both of his style and of his special interests; he is certainly not contenting himself with transcribing a source. Haenchen, however, accepts the idea of a written source; it must have contained, not an itinerary, but the reminiscences of a companion of Paul—Haenchen would willingly identify the author with Timothy.[18] Luke edited this document (17.6; 18.18–21), abridged it (16.12) and added to it passages coming

---

[15] Haenchen was able to consult Schille's article before going to press; he indicates his point of view in a short *Nachtrag* (pp. 14*–15*). Schille seems to have shown him that the arguments of Dibelius in favour of the use of an itinerary cannot be considered valid. Schille, however, clearly goes too far in attributing to the literary genius of Luke all that Dibelius explained by the hypothesis of the itinerary, and Haenchen shows a certain embarrassment in the presence of the unlooked for help given to him by so compromising an ally.

[16] G. Schille, 'Die Fragwürdigkeit eines Itinerars der Paulusreisen', *Theol. Literaturzeitung*, 1959, LXXXIV, col. 165–74.

[17] See the article we have already mentioned in connection with the interpretation of the prologue of Luke and of the use of the 'we' in the second part of Acts—'Das "Wir" im der Apostelgeschichte und das Itinerar'.

[18] Haenchen does not think it possible to question the reality of this first missionary journey, as certain writers do.

from elsewhere (such as the story of the possessed girl of Philippi); clearly we must leave him full responsibility for different reports describing the preaching of Paul, and that for the discourse in Athens. Prepared for by the rewriting of 18.18–21, the narrative of the third journey (18.23–21.17) is centred on Ephesus. On the foundation of the Church in Ephesus, Luke is in possession of a few traditions—very little concrete information, much too little for us to be able to form an exact idea of the conditions in which Paul exercised his ministry. Then comes the journey that was to bring Paul and his companions to Jerusalem; Luke indicates that it was a matter of taking to the Holy City the amount produced by a collection.[19] This narrative presupposes the use of a written source, which Luke, moreover, treats very freely; it is possible to think that this document comes from the narrator whose information was used in the narrative of the second journey. There is no reason to see in it an itinerary in the way in which Dibelius conceives it. There remains the journey to Rome (ch. 27–28). Strongly marked with Luke's imprint, it must be based on the memories of a companion of Paul;[20] Luke's version is inspired both by literary concerns and the desire to glorify the Apostle.

This new study of Haenchen gives a simpler picture of the way in which the author of the Acts of the Apostles procured the necessary documents to carry out his project. It must not, however, be forgotten that this impression of simplification to a certain extent comes from the fact that Haenchen is only concerned with a part of the information, that there has been an attempt to link up with the itinerary; discussing the theory of the itinerary, he had not to concern himself with sections such as, for instance, the episode of the seizure of the apostles at Philippi. For the itinerary Haenchen substitutes a document, or

[19] The fact that Acts mentions Timothy and speaks of him in the third person would not be sufficient to put aside his name (as Conzelmann again says). From the moment the writer of Acts uses the 'we' deliberately, attaching to it a very precise meaning, the presence of the first or third person in the narrative is of no significance so far as the use of a source is concerned.

[20] In coming to the allusion of 24.17, the reader of Acts cannot but remember 21.24–26; it is only by comparison with Paul's epistles that the allusion becomes patient of an entirely different meaning.

two documents, coming from a companion of Paul and supplying the substance of the information contained in ch. 16–21.
The identification of this companion with Timothy is purely
conjectural; the way in which Luke rewrites his sources removes
all possibility of discovering in his narrative the traces of a style
and of interests which would not be his.

The Theories of Schille

The article which G. Schille has recently devoted to Dibelius[21]
is divided into three parts—he first of all sets out the ideas of
Dibelius on the itinerary which is supposed to have served as a
source for the writing of ch. 13–21 of Acts; he then makes a
critical examination of the arguments on which he bases his
hypothesis; finally he makes certain observations which aim to
show that the composition of Acts cannot be explained from the
hypothesis in question. There is no need for us to dwell on the
first part, since we have already given our own résumé of
Dibelius's explanations. It will be sufficient to indicate the trend
of the other two parts.

Dibelius's Arguments

Leaving secondary considerations aside[22] the arguments that
would justify us in concluding that an itinerary was used may be
reduced to three.

(1) Dibelius finds first of all that the narrative of ch. 13–21
is often interrupted by added passages introduced from elsewhere; the clearly extraneous character of these passages would
lead us to conclude that the narrative, the normal sequence of
which they break, was continuous. The insertion of the Lystra
episode (14.8–20) has obliged the editor to mention the mis-

---

[21] Hence perhaps the imperfects of ch. 27, whereas we should expect aorists.
Haenchen does not seek to identify Luke's informant here; it might be remembered
that Timothy was in Rome with Paul when the latter was writing to Philemon
(v. 1) and to the Colossians (1.1), but there were also others—Aristarchus, Mark,
Jesus Justus, Epaphras, Luke, and Demas.

[22] That, for instance, which states that the information devoted to Thessalonica
and Berea is colourless; or again what Dibelius writes on the subject of Acts 16.6ff,
and 20.1—3. Schille considers that there is no difficulty in attributing these
passages to the editor, independently of any source.

sionaries' arrival at Derbe twice (14.6–20b); the interpolation is clear, as Schille recognizes, but according to him it simply proves the existence of a piece of information which could equally well refer to the evangelization of Lycaonia as to Paul's missionary journeys as a whole. Dibelius has discovered another interpolation in the narratives referring to Philippi—the episode of the earthquake and the miraculous setting free of the missionaries (16.25–34) constitutes a superfluous passage of which the immediate context (cf. vv. 35–40) takes no account; Schille readily agrees that vv. 25–34 constitute an independent tradition,[23] but he holds that the context (vv. 20f and 35ff) should be attributed not to a source but to the editor, whose personal interests it reflects.[24] The interpolation of vv. 25–34 proves nothing as to the existence of an itinerary. The discourse in Antioch of Pisidia (13.16–31) would form a further interpolation which would be revealed by the doublet of vv. 42 ('as they went out') and 43 ('when the synagogue was broken up')—the itinerary must have passed immediately from v. 14 to v. 43; the doublet is only apparent, argued Schille—of himself Luke could quite well have mentioned in succession the request addressed to the missionaries as they came out of the synagogue and the fact that several followed Paul and Barnabas as they left the gathering. The same applies to the Athens episode: the frame-

[23] Taking up again a theory that he had already proposed earlier ('Die Topographie des Markus — evangeliums, ihre Hintergründe und ihre Einordnung', *Zeitschr. der Deutschen Palästina-Vereins*, 1957, LXXIII, pp. 133–66—cf. p. 144), Schille considers that the literary genre of the 'legends' concerning the foundations of communities justifies him in considering the cure of the witch (Acts, 16.16ff) as a secondary development of the miraculous liberation (16.25ff). We have seen that Dibelius makes an independent narrative of vv. 25–34, but that he does not dare to pronounce on the question of deciding whether vv. 16–24 were in the itinerary or not. Schille is on too good a track to stop; vv. 13–15, the story of Lydia's conversion, which Dibelius attached to the itinerary without any hesitation, become in his eyes an independent tradition inserted in a context on which they do not depend; perhaps originally what was in question was a tradition of Thyatira (since Lydia was a seller of the city of Thyatira) relating to Paul's visit to that town (Luke has passed it over in silence). We shall refer later to this surprising stream of theories.

[24] vv. 20f, on the theme of the accusations levelled against the Christians; Luke presents them according to the order of the brief discourse. vv. 35ff give the reply to these accusations, made concrete by the step of the Roman magistrates who recognize that the accused are in the right. The framework is thus assured by a simple literary fiction, intended to give a new significance to the traditional narrative which it introduces and concludes. In all this there is no room for an itinerary.

work in which the discourse has been inserted is explained much more satisfactorily by Luke's literary composition than by having recourse to the data of an itinerary.[25] The presence of passages which seem to have been added afterwards thus does not favour Dibelius's hypothesis.

(2) Dibelius again puts forward as an argument the uniform manner in which the halting-places during the journey are treated. It is clear, replies Schille, that the remark does not apply to certain halting-places richly provided for, such as Corinth or Ephesus; but, even if we make the desired exceptions, it is too summary. In fact, the reports given in Acts of the towns evangelized can be reduced to three different types: (a) In certain cases, Luke gives a lively and colourful description in which the local tradition, when there is one,[26] is only a pretext for development; this is the case, notably, for the reports devoted to Athens, Caesarea, Antioch in Pisidia, Sebaste[27] and Ephesus. (b) In other cases he contents himself with reproducing

[25] Without stopping over 17.17, Schille concentrates his line of argument on 17.34—the conversion of Denys the Areopagite, of Damaris and a few others. This is, in fact, the verse which Dibelius most easily attaches to his itinerary. Schille thinks that it is rather a simple literary corollary composed by Luke on the basis of information the equivalent of which is found in the episode of Corinth, Acts 18.8— the conversion of Crispus and of many others. He adds that in the case of 18.8 Luke shows himself to be ill informed. His text could lead us to suppose that Crispus was the first convert in Corinth, whereas, according to I Cor. 16.15, this honour must fall to Stephanas; since the information of Acts 18.8 is defective, it is possible to think that the parallel of 17.34 likewise only represents a tradition that has already been badly blurred. Schille's remarks are completely unfounded. Acts 18.8 does not say that Crispus is the first convert in Corinth, but names him as being the most notable—'Crispus, the ruler of the synagogue, believed in the Lord with all his house. And many of the Corinthians hearing (Paul) believed and were baptized'. Paul expresses himself in the same way in I Cor. 1.14—'I give thanks that I baptized none of you but Crispus and Caius'; he adds in v. 16—'And I baptized also the household of Stephanus'. Thus Paul himself mentions Crispus in the first place in mentioning the converts in Corinth on whom he has conferred baptism. Can the author of Acts be blamed for not being better informed than Paul? The information in Acts 18.8 is thus excellent, and it can be considered that that of 17.34 is so, too— this independently of any hypothesis as to the origin of the information.

[26] The reports devoted to 'Sebaste', Caesarea and Ephesus would make use of information borrowed from tradition; those which relate to Antioch in Pisidia and to Athens would have no traditional foundation: the editor only draws on his imagination.

[27] Sebaste is not mentioned in Acts. Schille has 'the city of Samaria', mentioned in 8.5, in mind. H. H. Wendt identifies this with Sebaste, a pagan Greek city built on the site of the former Samaria; this conjecture has been very much questioned and is doubtless questionable.

a stereotyped pattern whose genre is linked with that of the 'summaries'; this is the case for Sebaste, Thessalonica, Berea, Corinth and Ephesus[28]—reports which Dibelius attributes to the itinerary. (*c*) Sometimes a few words are made to suffice, a verse at most—information given in the raw state, the author being careful to avoid a too frequent repetition of the pattern (*b*) —reports on Salamis, Derbe and Pergamum.[29] He concludes that this classification shows that it is misleading to speak of a uniform treatment of the missionary halting-places of the Apostle and to draw an argument from them in favour of the use of a source.

(3) Dibelius finally claims to have discovered a difference of style between the travel narratives contained in ch. 13–21 and what we find in the rest of the book. Schille considers this a fanciful distinction. Taking into account divergencies which come from the nature of the events recounted, the way of presenting matters in ch. 22–28 corresponds fairly closely to that of ch. 13–21; the halting-places on the captivity journey are indicated with as much detail as those on the missionary journeys. If we admit that Luke wrote freely in the last chapters, there is no reason to suppose anything different for the central part of the book. In ch. 1–7 it is clear that we should not expect to find reports of halting-places, since everything takes place at Jerusalem;[30] nor should we so expect in ch. 8–12, since if certain changes of place do come into the picture, the subject does not allow a continuous journey to be made of it. It is a happy chance and no more than that if a richer tradition concerning Peter has made it possible to introduce the pattern of a journey to assure the link between the episodes of ch. 9–11.[31]

Such are the criticisms which Schille puts forward against

---

[28] Certain names occur twice; it may be supposed that it is not for the same narratives. In any case for this second list Schille gives references: Acts 8.5–8; 17.1–13; 18.4–11; 19.8–20.

[29] Acts 13.5; 14.21, 25.

[30] It is curious that Schille does not seek to take advantage of the discourse of Stephen, which does not fail to present certain points of contact with the pattern of an itinerary (topographical and above all chronological details).

[31] 9.32–11.2.

Dibelius. Haenchen considers them conclusive.[32] This is not the place for a thorough examination of them, but it does not seem out of place to call attention to one or two points. (1) It is clear that the presence of episodes which seem to be superimposed on narratives whose normal sequence they interrupt, at times somewhat clumsily, does not constitute a proof that the basic narratives belong to a single source; it simply tends to make us think that the writer had written documents at his disposal. (2) We should readily grant that it is not possible to isolate the writing of ch. 13–21 of Acts, although in these chapters the narrative style is different from that of the other chapters of the book. (3) On the second point, the main argument of the system, Schille's refutation leaves more to be desired. It does not allow the argument it is attacking its full strength. Dibelius stresses insistently the mention of halting-places on journeys about which Luke has nothing to recount;[33] Schille's reply only concerns itself with reports about the founding of communities, leaving until later the question of halting-places as such.[34] By proceeding in this way, he isolates the elements of an argument which draws its force from the combination of a variety of evidence; a procedure which is easy, but which takes away from the reply a good part of its effectiveness.

Dibelius's hypothesis

After having shown the weakness of the arguments put forward by Dibelius, Schille indicates the reasons why he thinks the hypothesis of the use of an itinerary unacceptable. He makes four points.

[32] See above, p. 145, n. 15.
[33] See above, p. 118, n. 26 and 27.
[34] Cf. the third point of the last part (col. 173f). Schille there divides the halting-places of the journey into two groups: (*a*) Those that mention cities which possess a Christian community; in citing them, Luke endeavours to give the impression of a vast diffusion of Christianity. (*b*) Mere points of call on which Luke possesses no information and which he mentions solely to give a more concrete appearance to his reconstructions of the journeys. Everything is explained by literary methods without the need to appeal to a source. Schille shows himself very generous towards Luke's power of imagination; it is very doubtful whether, if the exegetes were forced to choose, they would incline to a theory which attributes so much to the discretion of Luke, rather than towards an explanation presupposing the use of a source.

(1) In his epistles Paul often makes brief allusions to his apostolic activities. From I Cor. 15.3 we learn that Paul went to Ephesus immediately after leaving Corinth;[35] from I Cor. 16.19, that he did not linger at Ephesus but hastened to found communities throughout the region.[36] Rom. 15.19 mentions Illyria.[37] The second epistle to the Corinthians enables us to visualize an intense missionary activity extending from Macedonia to Achaia, Illyria and Asia, all of it almost at the same time, so that it is difficult to fix a chronological order.[38] Paul is always on the move, passing rapidly from one town to another without ever stopping. What a contrast when we return to the narrative of Acts. Here everything is simple and clear. The Church first of all establishes herself in Jerusalem; the persecution gives full scope to the first missionary endeavours and to the establishment

[35] This is at any rate what Schille thinks he can see. Paul reminds the Corinthians of what he announced to them 'at the very first', ἐν πρώτοις. The expression would indicate that no long time had elapsed since Paul set forth this teaching in Corinth; now when he wrote that, he was at Ephesus. There is clearly some confusion.

[36] Paul transmits the greetings of the 'Churches of Asia'. Schille concludes that, having left Corinth shortly before, Paul has already founded communities in several cities. It would be possible to point out that a letter written by Paul to one of these communities has been preserved for us; it informs us that the Christian church of Colossae was founded by Epaphras (Col. 1.7), and that the latter had extended his activity to Laodicea and to Hierapolis (4.12–13). The remainder is only imagination.

[37] In Rom. 15.19, Paul draws attention to the ministry he has accomplished 'from Jerusalem, round about as far as unto Illyricum'. If we blame Acts for saying nothing of the evangelization of Illyricum, the same complaint could be made as regards Jerusalem—it attributes no missionary activity to Paul in the Holy City. This omission, however, seems justified, for it corresponds to what Paul writes elsewhere, notably in the epistle to the Galatians. When in Rom. 15.19 Paul gives Jerusalem as the starting-point of his ministry, we must not, perhaps, press his statement too far; similarly, also, no doubt, when he cites Illyricum as the extreme limit of his apostolate. Has he not travelled over all Macedonia (cf. Acts 20.2)? Macedonia borders on Illyricum—Paul has thus been to the frontiers of Illyricum. The movement of his phrase does not demand greater accuracy. This would be even truer if, according to a recent note by A. S. Geyser, it is necessary to see in the formula of the Epistle to the Romans an allusion to that which defines the sphere of action of the apostles—from Jerusalem to the ends of the earth ('Un essai d'explication de Rom. XV, 19', *New Test. St.*, 1959–60, VI, pp. 156–9). It would be for a theological reason rather than for reasons of historical accuracy that Paul was anxious to mention, on the one hand, Jerusalem, on the other the extreme limits to which he has penetrated. Luke could not then be blamed for having said nothing about a ministry of Paul in Illyricum.

[38] It turns out from I Thessalonians that Paul arrived in Achaia after having visited in turn Philippi, Thessalonica and Athens; as if by chance, Acts follows the same order.

of Christianity in Antioch. The information concerning Paul's activity is grouped into four main geographical sections— Cyprus, Pisidia and Lycaonia (Acts 13–14), Macedonia and Achaia (ch. 16–18), Ephesus and Asia (ch. 19–20), return to Jerusalem and trial (ch. 21ff). These sections are purely artificial, without foundation in historical reality; the journeys whose purpose is to establish a link between these sections are simply a literary fiction.[39] The hypothesis of an itinerary is completely useless.

(2) The writer has made many mistakes in the geographical distribution of the information he possessed. He places the conversion of Lydia, the seller of purple of Thyatira (Acts 16.13–15), at Philippi, whereas this episode has nothing to do with the town of Philippi; it is perhaps a question of a tradition coming from Thyatira.[40] The references to Thessalonica (17.5–9), and the disturbance made by the goldsmiths at Ephesus

[39] It is indeed necessary to summarize what Schille explains in detail. We have not, however, omitted the arguments, as there are none! The author is content merely to make assertions.

[40] To show that 16.13–15 does not depend on the context in which Luke has placed it, Schille brings forward two arguments: (1) Lydia is touched by Paul's words (v. 15): this cannot have taken place in Philippi, for there Paul was in the company of Silas and v. 15 makes mention of Paul alone. (2) v. 13 refers to a river which flowed near the town—the detail can with difficulty be applied to Philippi where the Gangites is over a mile from the town; it is more applicable to Thyatira, where the Lykos flows only a little over half a mile from the town and where, since that is still too much for a sabbath day's journey, a tributary of the Lykos passes through the town itself. Is there any purpose in discussing considerations of this kind? The first has clearly no value at all. The second shows that the writer is very badly informed as to the topography of Philippi and on the problems it sets for the exegesis. The difficulty does not consist in finding a place which agrees with the narrative of Acts; it consists in choosing between two places—as soon as the Western Gate is passed through, the scanty watercourse coming from the 'small springs' which gave the town its first name, Crenides, is found; if we continue on our way following on the Via Egnatia, over a mile farther on, a few steps from the Gangites, we find the remains of the monumental arch which may possibly represent the official 'Gate' of the colony of Philippi and which, in this case, would at the same time mark the limit of the free space. If we know that the route allowed to the Jews on the sabbath day was calculated from the outer limits of a town and that it was lawful for them to walk at their pleasure within these limits, we cannot see why the Jews of Philippi should not have been able to go as far as the Gangites. However this may be, it is not excluded that their place of prayer may have been found on the margin of the Crenides, although the Gangites hypothesis fits in better with the rest of the narrative (cf. v. 16). It should be noted that by detaching Lydia's conversion from the Philippi episode, Schille ignores the reference to this same lady in v. 40.

(19.24–40) derive from anecdotes which, originally, had nothing to do with Paul; the latter is only mentioned in them by skilful editing.[41] It is altogether unlikely that Paul's preaching brought difficulties upon him; for that he would have to have remained for a certain time in the same town, which the apostolic rule of the *Didache* 11.4–6[42] forbade him to do. The episodes which Acts assign to Paphos (13.6, 9–12) and Troas (20.7–12) are no more credible.[43] The many errors in the locating of events show that the author had not at his disposal the detailed information that an itinerary would have given him.

(3) It is possible that in certain cases Luke was acquainted with a genuine tradition concerning the halting-places of some missionary journey; the presumption is favourable as regards the evangelization of Pisidia and Lycaonia,[44] or that of Macedonia followed by a stay in Athens and in Corinth.[45] Luke could

[41] The argument is that these episodes mention other names, Jason in Thessalonica, Sosthenes in Corinth, Caius and Aristarchos in Ephesus; the precise significance of these names does not appear in the actual narratives, Paul having become the hero of incidents which originally concerned these persons.

[42] This passage of the *Didache* clearly plays an important rôle in the picture that Schille gives of Paul's missionary activity; it is in the light of this that he tries to interpret the epistles and claims to reject *en bloc* the manner in which Acts presents the facts. He does not ask himself whether it is legitimate to appeal to this text as evidence of a practice which would have been imposed upon Paul, or whether it was in keeping with the latter's character docilely to accept a rule of this kind.

[43] For Paphos, the same argument holds as for the Philippi episode—it is Paul who addresses the magician (13.9f); this cannot have happened at Paphos, since there Paul was in the company of Barnabas and not alone. It is true that Luke mentions Barnabas in vv. 7f, but, explains Schille, this is by an editorial addition. As far as Troas is concerned, tradition must have fixed the episode in a town of the province of Asia (cf. with 19.22). The fact that there is a question of a night of vigil during which the Eucharist is celebrated indicates that originally it was the paschal vigil that was referred to. We can realize this from Acts 12.12 (which would presuppose that Paul must have been judged on the very day of the feast!).

[44] The succession of the names of the towns visited by the missionaries and then revisited in reverse order on their return (ch. 13–14) is not pure invention on the part of the writer of Acts. It is striking to see that the first town on the list is Antioch in Pisidia, which also marks the most distant point in relation to Antioch in Syria. It is to explain this particular detail that Luke has recourse to a journey via Cyprus and Perga; the procedure is betrayed by the fact that he has nothing to say on the long journey which separates Perga from the real starting-point of the mission, Antioch in Pisidia. It would thus depend on an independent tradition relating to Pisidia and Lycaonia; he ensures the link between Antioch in Syria and Antioch in Pisidia by a fictitious journey.

[45] The order followed is confirmed by I Thessalonians—perhaps Luke was acquainted with this epistle? But, between Thessalonica and Athens, he adds Berea; this is perhaps because, knowing the name of a certain Sopatros of Berea

equally well have been acquainted with traditions worthy of credence concerning the apostolic origin of different communities—Corinth, Ephesus, Caesarea, Philippi, Tyre, Ptolemais, Sidon, Paphos, Troas and Puteoli. In order to compose the account of a journey, it was sufficient to link these different foundations together and to be ready to insert intermediate stages intended to increase the credibility and the concrete character of the reconstruction. If mistakes sometimes occur, as in the case of Perga, to account for which an enormous detour, certainly without historical foundation, would be necessary,[46] it must be admitted that, on the whole, the success is excellent.[47] Its merit is due not to the information the editor had at his disposal, but to his literary skill; there is no need to appeal to an itinerary to account for what is only a method of composition.[48]

(4) The compilation of a record of halting-places with a view to an eventual repetition of the same journeys is utterly unlikely in the case of Paul. (a) As Dibelius conceives it, this itinerary would not have been of great help to him in finding his way again. (b) Paul left behind him nuclei of communities with which he was well acquainted; he had no need of notes to find them again. (c) Further, he was expecting the parousia—the

---

among the companions of Paul (Acts 20.4), he has concluded that Paul must have evangelized Berea; in any case, he possesses no information about this evangelization.

[46] The same thing may be presumed for the halting-place of Salamis (13.5); it is only mentioned for the sake of introducing a transition between Antioch and Paphos, Paphos being the only place in Cyprus about which Luke possesses information.

[47] Schille cites as an example the mention of Apollonia, introduced to provide a halting-place midway between Philippi and Thessalonica, but without any details as to its evangelization, since Luke possessed no information on this subject. Is it necessary to point out that the text (17.1) mentions two halting-places, Amphipolis and Apollonia? It is clear that the detail of the texts has little interest for Schille, who is wholly concerned with putting forward his own version of the events.

[48] The record of the halting-places in 20.13–15 is a simple stylistic technique intended to help to throw into relief the journey of Paul, who is going towards the trials which await him in Jerusalem. Another literary process leading to the same end is the mention of three visits of Paul to Christian communities (Tyre 21.3f; Ptolemais 21.7; Caesarea 21.8ff) where on two different occasions an effort is made to retain him. This is likewise a simple literary device, the way in which Luke prepares a journey by saying that Paul sent his companions on before him—19.22; 20.5 and 20.13; the same thing again for the halt at Miletus (20.16ff), a welcome pause in the middle of a journey that was hurried.

idea of composing a journal with a view to journeys whose eventuality he could not foresee, would not occur to him. (d) There is no reason to speak of travels properly so-called, or, consequently, of the repetition of the same journey, in the case of an itinerant missionary, always on the road, stopping nowhere according to the apostolic rule of the Didache;[49] the way in which Luke presents matters reflects the missionary conditions of a later period far removed from the Apostolic age. (e) In speaking of an itinerary Dibelius supposes that this was a kind of literary genre which really existed; not knowing any similar example,[50] Schille calls in question the existence of the literary genre to which the itinerary could belong.

We have deliberately dwelt somewhat at length on Schille's theories; the most devastating treatment that can be meted out to them is, in point of fact, to examine them closely. They show much imagination and little critical sense; to discuss them would be of no great advantage. Haenchen[51] has already pointed out the mistake made in applying to Paul the rule laid down by the Didache at a later period and in relation to a completely different situation;[52] the missionary rule of apostolic times must be sought in the Gospel phrase prescribing that preachers were not to pass from house to house, but to remain in the same house during the whole of their stay in one town (Mark 6.10 and parallels)—such a prescription clearly presupposes a stay that is prolonged. It is, moreover, clear that a Christian community is not founded in a day. If it is true that the hypothesis of the itinerary is not inevitable, adds Haenchen, there is no reason to fall back on a hypothesis which claims to explain everything by speaking of the facility with which Luke could compose a narrative and give it the appearance of history.

[49] *Did*. II, 4–6. See above p. 146, n. 2. The persons whom Luke presents as companions of the Apostle must have been in reality collaborators arriving after him in the communities he founded; their task was to complete the work, to 'water' what Paul had just planted (I Cor. 3.6).

[50] Schille draws attention, to reject it, to the parallel that could be sought for in the *Pilgrimage of Etherea*. He seems to be very badly informed!

[51] *Die Apostelgeschichte* (1959), pp. 14*–15*.

[52] By limiting the stay of itinerant apostles to one day, two at most, the *Didache* seems to want to avoid any endangering, by their prolonged presence, of the authority of the bishops charged with the government of the communities.

In conclusion we can say that Schille's article is useful in that it reminds us that the hypothesis of the itinerary is only an hypothesis and that in some of its aspects it is fragile and rests on suppositions that are not well founded. Schille's article thus constitutes a salutary warning—he shows in a concrete way the danger there can be in thrusting aside the data of Acts in order to create out of nothing an imaginary reconstruction of the facts; in such an attitude there is a risk of coming into conflict not only with critical sense, but with simple common sense.[53]

The Characteristics of Luke

Criticism of the hypothesis of the itinerary is not yet very far advanced. For the appreciation of this hypothesis, the studies which discuss and point out its difficulties and propose restatements are not the only ones available; other writers, without having such a theory in mind and even without knowing of it, contribute suggestions which should open up research in another direction. It is quite impossible to review here all the literature that has been devoted to Luke, the third Gospel and Acts, in order to select from it suggestions useful for the interpretation of the narrative of Paul's journeys; a few examples must suffice. They will emphasize, by enlarging upon it, a remark that has already been made in opposition to Dibelius, that from the literary point of view it is arbitrary to separate the travel narratives of ch. 13–21 of Acts from those of ch. 27–28;[54] Schille[55] goes further, considering that the manner of recounting Paul's travels does not essentially differ from that which recounts the journeys of Peter. It would be possible to go as far as to ask ourselves whether the traits by means of which Dibelius defines the itinerary used by Luke would not characterize the work as a whole, and whether the main interests they reflect do

[53] By the way in which it takes pleasure not in completing or dovetailing the information in Acts and that of the epistles, but in setting the two in opposition, Schille's method is not without analogy with that used by Vielhauer and Haenchen to set the thought of Luke in contradiction with that of Paul. Such methods are too arbitrary to spring from healthy criticism.

[54] The remark will be found in particular in O. Bauernfeind, E. Haenchen, E. Trocmé, and G. Schille—cf. what has been said of these writers.

[55] See above, p. 139ff.

not coincide exactly with those of the writer to Theophilus. If
this way of looking at the matter were to prove correct, it would
be necessary to admit that the passages attributed to the
itinerary reveal a personality which does not differ from that of
the author.

(1) The exegetes have not failed to be struck by the importance Luke gives to geographical considerations in the
general arrangement of his work; it is a geographical pattern
that governs the general plan of the Gospel as much as it does
that of Acts.[56] The procedure is particularly apparent in the
central part of the Gospel, where the materials are grouped
together under the pattern of a journey taking Jesus from
Galilee to Jerusalem (Luke 9.51–19.38).[57] Norden[58] had already
pointed out that by the very form of the travel narrative, this
section of the Gospel links up with that part of Acts which

---

[56] For a summary of this question and bibliographical details, see our article
'Le Salut des Gentils et la signification théologique du Livre des Actes' in *New
Testament Studies*, 1959–60, VI, pp. 132–5: cf. pp. 134f. For the third Gospel,
H. Conzelmann, *Die Mitte der Zeit. Studien zur Theologie des Lukas* (Beiträge zur
historischen Theologie, 17), 3rd ed., Tübingen, 1960, pp. 12–86, should primarily
be consulted; for Acts, see Ph. H. Menoud, 'Le plan des Actes des Apôtres,' *New
Testament Studies*, 1957–8, I, pp. 44–51.

[57] Solemn introduction to the journey in 9.51; sending of precursors (9.52, then
again 10.1); numerous references: they are on the way (9.56–57—note the addition
in relation to Matthew 8.19; 10.38; 14.25), they go up to Jerusalem (13.22, 33;
17.11; 18.31), they draw near to Jericho (18.35—according to Mark 10.46 they go
out of it), they enter it (19.1). During the journey up to Jerusalem Jesus walks in
front (19.28—this is not mentioned in Mark); as they approach, each stage is carefully noted—they first of all approach Bethphage and Bethany (19.29—Mark 11.1
already mentions Jerusalem), Jesus continues to advance (19.36—against Mark
11.8), he approaches the descent (19.37—particular to Luke), he catches sight of
the city (19.41—particular to Luke), and finally he enters the Temple (19.45:
Mark 11.11). After taking so much care in describing the journey, Luke cannot
resign himself to letting Jesus go out of Jerusalem; he shows him teaching in the
Temple (19.47, changing Mark; 20.1 an addition) and omits the going away
(Mark 13.1) which precedes the eschatological discourse, so much so that in Luke
this discourse seems to have been pronounced in the Temple (21.5); it is, moreover,
followed by a passage insisting on the fact that Jesus teaches in the Temple (21.37–
38). Clearly he must leave it for the night, but he does not go farther than the
Mount of Olives, and Luke is careful not to mention a visit to Bethany (Mark 14.3–
9). After the Passion and the Resurrection, it is in Jerusalem, not in Galilee, that
Jesus shows himself to his disciples (see the revision of Luke 24.6 in relation to
Mark 16.7), and he enjoins upon them not to leave the city (Acts 1.4).—On all this,
see the remarks of Père Léon-Dufour in *Introduction à la Bible* (A. Robert–A.
Feuillet), vol. II, Tournai, 1959, pp. 238–40, and those, more developed, of H.
Conzelmann, *op. cit.*, pp. 53–71.

[58] Ed. Norden, *Agnostos Theos*, p. 327, n. 1.

depends on the literary genre of the *Memoirs*; according to him such an agreement cannot be the result of chance. In point of fact, he made no use of this observation and it has since not been of great weight in the discussion on the travel diary. If exegetes are to be found who think that the journey in the Gospel is based upon a particular source,[59] the majority have not hesitated to recognize that the presentation of the episodes within the framework of a journey is the result of a simple editorial device;[60] there is no need to go back to the state in which Luke found his documents. The narrative of Paul's journeys is of quite a different nature in that it presupposes very extensive information; it is not only made up of editorial additions. But the centre of interest to which it corresponds is very similar to that which led the author to adopt the form of travel narrative in the Gospel, and we may wonder whether the resemblance could not be explained quite simply by the fact that the writer of the Gospel is to be identified with the narrator of Paul's journeys.

(2) To this first observation, still very general, a second must be added—the taste of the writer to Theophilus for geographical details, at least when they fit in with the course of his narrative.[61] He likes to locate the towns he mentions. Here are a few examples, taken from a list drawn up by Cadbury[62]—'a city of

[59] It is clear that this section is based on documents, perhaps even on a single source; the argument bears solely on the point of knowing whether the materials were already organized in accordance with the pattern of a journey (or of several journeys). There are not many who think it possible to maintain this opinion nowadays; it may be found in L. Girard, *L'Evangile des Voyages de Jésus, ou La Section 9.51–18.14 de saint Luc*, Paris, 1951. This writer considers that the supposed source recounted three journeys (9.51; 13.22; 17.11) and suspects a 'rationalist tendency' among those who 'see in the allusions to the journeys of Jesus only a *fictitious framework*' (p. 56; see p. 57, n. 1, references to writers whose orthodoxy is above suspicion). On this work, see the remarks of P. Benoit, *Revue Biblique*, 1953, LX, pp. 446–8.

[60] The study of Père Léon-Dufour (*loc. cit.*) brings out this point excellently.

[61] Luke does not hesitate to omit the indications which would upset the geographical arrangement. He does not recount the journey of Jesus into the country with the return through Decapolis (Mark 7.24–31); he omits to mention Decapolis in the episode of the possessed man of Gerasa (Mark 5.21; cf. Luke 8.39) and Caesarea Philippi in the incident of Peter's confession (Mark 8.27; cf. Luke 9.18). We have already noted that after his entry into Jerusalem, Jesus does not again return to Bethany (Mark 14.3–9; more or less equivalent episode in Luke 7.36–50, without the indication of place). We have likewise drawn attention to the suppression of the appearances of Jesus in Galilee.

[62] H. J. Cadbury, *The Making of Luke-Acts*, p. 241.

Galilee called Nazareth' (Luke 1.26),[63] 'Capharnaum, a city of Galilee' (4.31), 'the country of the Gerasenes, which is over against Galilee' (8.26), 'a town which was sixty furlongs from Jerusalem named Emmaus' (24.13), 'the mount called Olivet which is nigh Jerusalem, within a Sabbath day's journey' (Acts 1.12), 'Perga in Pamphylia' (13.13), 'Lystra and Derbe cities of Lycaonia' (14.6), 'Philippi, which is the chief city of part of Macedonia, a colony' (16.12), 'Tarsus in Cilicia . . . no mean city' (21.39; 22.3), 'Lystia which is in Lycia' (27.5), 'a place called Good Havens, not far from the city of Thalassa' (27.8), etc.[64] It is difficult to think that these small touches[65] come from different sources, going back to several different authors; they betray a mind which another series of features, likewise distributed throughout the whole work, enables Cadbury[66] to characterize as that of a townsman, interested in towns and in their special characteristics. The question is whether there is any conclusion to be drawn from these observations in the interpretation of the reports on the stages of Paul's journey. Dibelius considered that all these geographical names did not contribute to the purpose of edification pursued by the writer and that he would not have mentioned them had they not been imposed upon him by his source. It is quite true that Luke wants to edify his readers; but this desire in no way prevents him from punctuating his whole narrative from the beginning with geographical observations; if these observations have no interest for readers preoccupied with defining what they consider edifying and what seems to them to be not so, they are none the less of interest to him, Luke, by reason of his personal turn of mind. This turn of mind is a clearly attested fact; is it not

[63] Cf. the reference in 4.16—'Nazareth, where he had been brought up'.

[64] Cadbury points out, in contrast, the absence of any indication for Syracuse, Rhegium, Puteoli, and in particular Forum Appii and Three-Taverns; details concerning these last two places would seem to be desirable if the work was intended for readers who had no reason to know the surroundings of Rome.

[65] Details slightly different, but prompted by the same type of mind in Luke 3.3, where the evangelist is careful to indicate the place where John the Baptist was exercising his ministry—'all the country about the Jordan'. In Mark this information does not come until later and then only in an indirect manner—the people come to get baptized in the Jordan (1.5). Cf. H. Conzelmann, *op. cit.*, pp. 12–13.

[66] *The Making of Luke-Acts*, pp. 245–9.

the obvious thing, therefore, to appeal to this distinctive note of the author, rather than to invoke a source the author of which would have presented exactly the same peculiarity?[67]

(3) There is another kind of detail, to which Harnack has drawn attention[68] and which Cadbury has analysed minutely:[69] Luke notes the addresses of the people in his narrative, the place where they live, the house which receives them and where they lodge. Dibelius has objected that, according to the rules of logic, an author who writes with a view to edification ought not to dwell on such details. So much the worse for logic, as we cannot escape the fact that Luke does dwell on them. And information of this kind is scattered throughout his narrative.

Such details are particularly frequent in the latter part of Acts—we learn that at Philippi Paul lodged with Lydia (16.14f),[70] in Thessalonica with Jason (17.5-7), in Corinth with Aquila and Priscilla,[71] while he preferred for preaching the house of Justus, adjacent to the synagogue (18.3, 7). In Ephesus he preached in the room of Tyrannus (19.9); in Caesarea, he dwelt with Philip the evangelist (21.8) and at the next halting-place he was welcomed by Manson (21.16);[72] in Malta the shipwrecked men were hospitably received by the natives (28.2) and Publius gave them hospitality for three days (28.7); in Rome Paul had his own dwelling (22.16, 23, 30).[73] It is in the

---

[67] The halting-places on the journey are several times mentioned in series; in this connection we may note Luke's taste for lists of names—cf. Luke 3.1-2, 23-38; 8.1-3; Acts 1.13-14; 6.5; 13.1; 20.4.

[68] A. Harnack, *Die Apostelgeschichte* (1908), p. 95, n. 1.

[69] H. J. Cadbury, 'Lexical Notes on Luke—Acts, III. Luke's Interest in Lodging', *Journal of Bibl. Lit.*, 1926, XLV, pp. 305-22; *The Making of Luke—Acts*, pp. 249-54.

[70] vv. 13-15 comprise about ten lines, the sole purpose of which is to explain the circumstances which have brought Paul to take his lodging with this lady. Note also in v. 34 the hospitality of the goaler.

[71] Seven lines are devoted to this couple (18.2-3) who have given Paul hospitality.

[72] There is no other reason for the verse than to indicate the name of the man who received Paul into his house.

[73] It is generally understood that Paul hired his lodging. Cadbury is doubtful whether this is the meaning of the text. Acts 28.23 would mean that numerous Jews came to Paul's reception; in 28.30 μίσθωμα does not mean the money that Paul paid over to the owner of his lodging, but that which he earned by his work—he lived 'at his own expense'.

first part of the book that we find the most precise indications—
in Damascus Paul lodges in the street called Strait, in the
house of a certain Judas (9.11); in Joppa Peter lives with Simon,
a tanner, whose house is by the sea (10.6). Other details are left
less definite—in Jerusalem, the house of Mary, mother of Mark
(12.12), the upper room where the Eleven meet (1.13).[74]

In the Gospel it is not Matthew but Luke who has taken the
trouble to note that in Bethlehem the parents of Jesus did not
find room in the inn and that the child was born in a stable
(Luke 2.7),[75] a circumstance which will permit the shepherds to
discover the new-born babe (v. 12).[76] It is Luke, too, who has
collected the parables of hospitality—the importunate friend
(11.5–8), the unjust steward (16.4–9), Dives and Lazarus
(16.19–31), the Good Samaritan who takes the injured man to
the inn (10.33–35). It is in Luke, too, that we see Jesus
receiving hospitality—that of Simon (7.36ff), of Martha and
Mary (10.38–42), of a leader of the Pharisees (14.1) and of
Zacchaeus (19.5ff).[77] Two significant passages—(1) in the
incident of the possessed man of the Gerasenes, Luke is the only
one to mention that the unfortunate man did not live in a house
(8.27);[78] (2) when the disciples intervene and ask Jesus to send
the people away so that they may go and buy something to eat
(Mark 6.36), Luke is anxious to add: 'and to find a lodging'
(9.12).

Cadbury[79] has pointed out in this connection that we come
across the same turn of mind everywhere, that which was to
urge the author to point out the names of the halting-places of

---

[74] Cf. 9.37, 39; 20.8.

[75] The word φάτνη can mean 'manger' or 'fold for cattle'. Cadbury considers
that in the context of Luke the second meaning should be preferred—Luke is
interested in the fact that the child had no roof to shelter him, he was out in the
open.

[76] 'The address' of Mary at Nazareth (Luke 1.26f) is no less precise than those
of the itinerary.

[77] See again Luke's very special insistence (10.5–9) on the duties imposed by
hospitality; the description of the welcome the father reserves for his prodigal son
(15.22–32); the promise of Jesus to his disciples that they will take their places at
his table (22.30).

[78] 'He had his dwelling in the tombs' (Mark 5.3); 'neither did he *abide in a house,*
but in the sepulchres' (Luke 8.27).

[79] *Journ. of Bibl. Lit.,* 1926, p. 308, n. 1.

each day and even the names of the persons the memory of whom was linked with such places. For doing this there was no utilitarian reason;[80] it is equally pointless to appeal to a source which someone else edited—all these traits reveal the attentive curiosity of a very individual mind, precisely that of the man who wrote the work to Theophilus.

The remarks we have just made, almost all of them taken from Cadbury, tend to show that the features by which Dibelius characterizes the itinerary are precisely those which are found throughout the work as a whole and correspond to an original aspect of the writer's personality. It is true that we have not drawn attention to all the characteristics by means of which Dibelius defines the content of his itinerary. At least, those to which Cadbury has called attention are the most specific—the report of the halting-places and information as to the hospitality received. The others seem to have only a secondary importance and there is no doubt at all that the demonstration would continue without difficulty, so far as they are concerned; when he notes the success obtained by Paul's preaching or the conflicts it provoked, Luke reverts to one of the points which had particularly attracted his attention in the Gospel and in the first part of Acts, and which, moreover, touches on the deep significance of the history he is retracing. Moreover, how are we to think that a source would be necessary to persuade Luke to speak of the departure of the missionaries when they have finished their work in a town?

It is more important to define precisely the exact significance we attach to the remarks which we have thought fit to recall in regard to the hypothesis of the itinerary; they are of such a kind as to make us reject the idea that the writer to Theophilus used a source composed by another writer. The linguistic arguments, drawn from vocabulary and style, cannot go as far as that, for an author can very well make use of information from a source, at the same time expressing it in his own language. The considerations we have evoked, however, do not only concern the

---

[80] Not more so in the case of the 'address' of Lydia in Philippi than in that of the 'address' of Mary at Nazareth or of Jesus at Bethlehem.

formulation of the narratives, they touch on their very substance; they call in question the author's psychology, his turn of
mind which leads him to take an interest in such and such an
aspect of things, rather than in another. From this point of view,
the kind of information which has come down to us in the
narratives of Paul's journeys bears to a high degree the mark of
the characteristic personality of the writer to Theophilus.
According to our way of thinking, it must be concluded from
this that he does not owe this information to a written source
which someone else supplied him with.

These remarks, however, do not justify us in concluding that
there has been no source whatever. It remains very possible
that, to compose his work, the author had at his disposal notes
which he himself had written earlier. Several remarks seem to
favour this explanation. In the first place the presence of a large
mass of detailed and very varied information;[81] this would seem
to presuppose the use of a series of documents. Then the
particularities of editorial work which is not at all homogeneous,
which gives the impression of combining different sections without arriving at a completely continuous narrative—the author
seems to be working on texts which he manipulates more or less
successfully.[82] It is not clear, indeed, how it is possible to give a
precise shape to this documentation; the difficulty comes from
the fact that the text not only does not betray the intervention of
several different hands—this is understandable if the editing
has unified the style—but it does not even allow us to suspect,
beneath the documentation, the presence of a mind different

[81] As far as the persons are concerned, Harnack (*Die Apostelgeschichte*, pp. 101–8)
divides them into four groups, not including those whose names are borrowed from
the Bible or mentioned by others (Pilate, etc.); there are actors of first, second and
third importance, then those who may be called mere spectators; for the latter
group only he counts about seventy persons, almost always referred to by name.
See also, H. J. Cadbury, *The Book of Acts in History*, pp. 7f.

[82] This kind of remark calls for a certain caution. To appeal to the intervention
of a source or to the combination of several sources could become a convenient
procedure for explaining all the discrepancies of the editing. We should only have
recourse to this expedient when it can be used to good purpose. Luke is an uneven
writer; he is so both in vocabulary and style and also in the ordering of his materials
and the composition of his text. We must not attribute to the influence of his sources
certain instances of a lack of homogeneity which can very well come from his way
of writing.

from that of the author.[83] To compose his narrative of Paul's journeys, had Luke scattered notes, an itinerary, or a travel diary at his disposal? We should perhaps not trouble ourselves too much if we cannot answer this question with certainty, for the moment we become aware that Luke is using his own notes, we shall find there the kind of information in which he takes an interest which characterizes his individual way of seeing things.

[83] B. H. Streeter based his argument on this fundamental unity to attribute to the same writer, Luke, in the first place the composition of the documentary sources, the Proto-Luke and the 'travel-document' of Acts, then, after several years' interval, the composition of the work to Theophilus which would incorporate these partial studies in a wider whole, joining to it information drawn from other sources, notably the Gospel of Mark (*The Four Gospels*, 9th ed., London, 1956, pp. 218–22).

CONCLUSION

Now that we have come to the end of this inquiry, we can look back over the distance we have travelled and try to assess the results of so many pieces of research carried out in such different ways. Rather than giving a dry catalogue summarizing summaries, we shall simply give a few general impressions.

(1) The predominant impression is certainly very negative. Despite the most careful and detailed research, it has not been possible to define any of the sources used by the author of Acts in a way which will meet with widespread agreement among the critics. We do indeed find certain exegetes who will give their assent to such and such an hypothesis, that of the 'Antioch source' or that of the 'itinerary'; no theory has managed to impose itself by its probability and in virtue of the indications given by the texts.

(2) To this predominant impression is added another, no longer negative but positive. All these efforts are not lost. They have stressed the special features of the book's composition and these special features justify us in thinking that the author did not write it at one sitting. We find traces of rewriting, cases of juxtaposition, even of insertion of different materials one in the other. There are so many indications which set us on the track of pre-existing sources. We seize a link, which is very clear; we try to follow the source from which it comes and, almost immediately, it becomes lost and disappears, whereas other links present themselves, just as clear and just as disappointing. This can be explained by the literary work of the author: he is not satisfied with transcribing his sources, he rewrites the text by putting the imprint of his vocabulary and his style everywhere. Perhaps it would be necessary to go even further, taking account of the fact that, as a whole, the materials used in Acts reveal, at the same time as the author's main interests, his very

individual turn of mind. The information is not only reported in his own style, in its very substance it generally reflects his personality. Everything is done as if Luke were at the origin not only of the edited version, but even of the sources on which this version is based. The remarks with which we ended the last chapter of our study link up with those of Père Benoit to which attention was drawn at the end of the first part; Père Benoit, to account for the facts, suggests the hypothesis of a version in stages—the composition of the Book of Acts would be directly based not on sources coming from another author, but on Luke's own notes.

(3) In research on the sources of Acts, the we-sections have occupied an important place. Many exegetes have thought they could consider this 'we' as evidence of a source. Its presence in the text would be the result simply of the overliteral transcription of a travel diary the author had at his disposal. We consider that the realization of the fact that the 'we' should find its explanation on the editorial level, not on that of the documents which served to compose the work is an important step forward accomplished by recent research. As to knowing whether the author retained the 'we' from an earlier document or introduced it into narratives which did not already contain it, the question is of relatively little importance; what is essential is to realize that he uses the first person plural deliberately. Comparison with ancient texts which present the same peculiarity makes the significance of the procedure clear—the author wishes it to be understood that he has personally taken part in the events he is recounting. In the case of Acts, this interpretation is confirmed by examination of the prologue of the work to Theophilus where precisely the author lays claim to have been present at a part of the events to which he is devoting his narratives. Accepted by certain first-class critics, this explanation is rejected by others, who seem little concerned to justify their rejection by literary arguments.

(4) The way in which the problem of the 'we' arises leads us to conclude by a remark on method. The interpretation of this 'we' necessarily raises the question of the identity of the

writer to Theophilus, or, more accurately, the question of ascertaining whether this writer is a travelling companion of the apostle Paul. To answer this question different ways of approach suggest themselves. Some exegetes are more influenced by the historical argument supplied by the evidence of ancient tradition ascribing Acts to Luke the physician, Paul's collaborator. Others are more struck by the fact that Acts gives a picture of Paul's life and teaching appreciably different from that they think they can discover in the epistles; it seems to them that this difference cannot be reconciled with the attribution of the work to Luke. The use of the 'we' makes it possible to approach the question from another angle, that of the literary processes and their significance. It would be desirable for research to keep to the literary plane, and that considerations of another order should not interfere with those inspired by a strictly literary discipline. Confusion of methods cannot produce good results. However little we try not to establish a theory conceived *a priori*[1] but to account for all the data of a problem, it is vital to examine each of the data in its own perspective, determining its significance in the context of all the considerations capable of elucidating the problem. The stand adopted in our study has led us to stress the literary significance of the 'we' and its repercussions on the question of the author of Acts; this approach is not the only one to which we should give our attention, but it certainly deserves to be taken seriously.

[1] An example of *a priori* arguing which has nothing in common with sound criticism is the use of epithets by which one describes one's contradictors, e.g. 'rationalist' or 'conservative'. We hope that M. Kümmel, who describes our findings on Acts as 'strictly conservative' will forgive us (*streng konservative Einstellung — Theol. Rundschau*, 1954, p. 195). M. Kümmel has devoted a good deal of study to the exegetes of the nineteenth century, a period when Biblical science first reacted against the traditional conformism. The situations are greatly changed today. The traditional conformism has not disappeared; but another conformism has come into being, an academic conformism, rooted in a reaction against tradition. It is no more critical than the old conformism was. The maturity of age will no more be confused with the revolts of adolescence than with the naïve docility of childhood. There is nothing surprising in the fact that, once it has arrived at maturity, exegetical scholarship should return to certain traditional positions. A traditional affirmation is not necessarily erroneous. At the level of critical thought, the reasons which make one opinion preferable to another are more important than the fact of knowing whether this opinion has been put forward by ecclesiastical or academic authorities.

INDEXES

INDEX OF AUTHORS

(An asterisk * indicates a bibliographical reference)

INDEX OF BIBLICAL REFERENCES

(References to chapters are placed before references to verses)

Old Testament

New Testament